# Cold War Europe
# 1945–89

*A political history*

23.

# Cold War Europe 1945–89

*A political history*

## John W. Young

Edward Arnold
A division of Hodder & Stoughton
LONDON NEW YORK MELBOURNE AUCKLAND

© 1991 John W. Young

First published in Great Britain 1991
Reprinted 1992

Distributed in the USA by Routledge, Chapman and Hall, Inc.
29 West 35th Street, New York, NY 10001

*British Library Cataloguing in Publication Data*

Young, John W.
   Cold War Europe 1945–89 : a political history
   1. Copy to follow
   I. Title
   Copy to follow

ISBN 0-340-55142-9
       0-340-55324-3 pbk

Typeset in 10/11pt Plantin by
Hewer Text Composition Services, Edinburgh
Printed and bound in Great Britain for Edward Arnold, a division of
Hodder and Stoughton Limited, Mill Road, Dunton Green,
Sevenoaks, Kent TN13 2YA by Clays Ltd, St Ives plc.

*For Julie and Linda*

# Contents

# List of Abbreviations

| | |
|---|---|
| BHE | West German refugees' Party |
| CAP | Common Agricultural Policy |
| CDU | German Christian Democratic Union |
| CGT | French confederation of trades unions |
| COMECON | Council for Mutual Economic Aid |
| COMINFORM | Communist Information Bureau |
| CSCE | Conference on Security & Co-operation in Europe |
| DC | Italian Christian Democrats |
| EAM | Greek National Liberation Front |
| EC | European Community |
| ECU | European Currency Unit |
| EDC | European Defence Community |
| EEC | European Economic Community |
| EFTA | European Free Trade Association |
| EMU | European Economic and Monetary Union |
| ERM | EC Exchange Rate Mechanism |
| ETA | Basque separatist movement |
| FDP | German Free Democratic Party |
| FLN | Algerian National Liberation Front |
| GDP | Gross Domestic Product |
| GNP | Gross National Product |
| ICBM | Inter-Continental Ballistic Missile |
| IMF | International Monetary Fund |
| INF | Intermediate-range Nuclear Forces |
| INI | Spanish National Industrial Institute |
| IRI | Italian Institute for Industrial Reconstruction |
| MBFR | Mutual Balanced Force Reduction |
| MFA | Portuguese Armed Forces Movement |
| MPLA | Popular Movement for the Liberation of Angola |
| MRP | French Popular Republican Movement (Christian Democrats) |
| NATO | North Atlantic Treaty Organisation |
| OEEC | Organisation for European Economic Co-operation |

## List of Abbreviations

| | |
|---|---|
| PASOK | Greek Socialist Party |
| PS | French Socialist Party |
| RPF | Rally of the French People (Gaullists under Fourth Republic) |
| RPR | Rally for the Republic (Gaullists after 1976) |
| SALT | Strategic Arms Limitation Treaty |
| SPD | German Social Democratic Party |
| START | Strategic Arms Reduction Talks |
| UCD | Spanish Christian Centre Union |
| UDF | Union for French Democracy (Centrists) |
| UN | United Nations |
| WEU | Western European Union |

# Acknowledgements

I am particularly grateful to Dr John Stevenson, with whom I worked at Sheffield University, for first suggesting that I write a general history of post-war Europe, and to Christopher Wheeler at Edward Arnold, for encouraging the project. The study makes no pretence to being a work of original research. It draws on the author's knowledge of British and French politics and international history, but relies heavily on the published works of others, which are mentioned in the bibliography. Numerous friends and colleagues also discussed different issues with me and have had an impact on the book, but I would particularly like to thank Dr Michael Burleigh, Dr John Kent and Dr David Stevenson of the London School of Economics, Dr Philip Taylor of Leeds University, Dr Judy Batt of Leicester University and two of my postgraduate students, Klaus Larres and Evanthis Hatzivassiliou. The manuscript was typed up by Janet Smith, Mary McCormick and Lindy Brownbridge and the text was read over by Brigette Vale. Despite my great debt to all these individuals the final product is my own and I am responsible for any flaws which remain in it.

John W. Young
2 September 1990

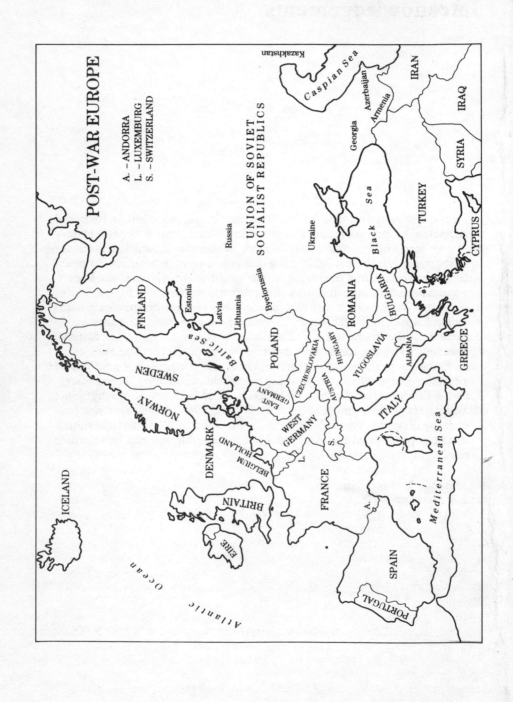

POST-WAR EUROPE

A. – ANDORRA
L. – LUXEMBURG
S. – SWITZERLAND

UNION OF SOVIET
SOCIALIST REPUBLICS

# Introduction

This book is intended as a general introduction to the political history of Europe from the end of the Second World War to the collapse of the post-war Communist regimes in the East. The latter development will have a major impact on the whole Continent, even if it does not initially have a great impact on internal developments in the Western democracies. When the book was first conceived there was no valid end-date to 'post-war' history, but the events of 1989 supplied one, allowing a rounded treatment of a distinct era, an era characterised by US–Soviet tension, the division of Europe between Communist and capitalist systems and, at the centre, the existence of two Germanies. It is impossible, in a short, single work to deal with every important subject in over 40 years of history, and so the book directs itself primarily at the major European states – the Soviet Union, West Germany, France and Britain – and at four other important developments – the rise and decline of Cold War tensions, Western European unity, the triumph of liberal democracy in Southern Europe (including the fifth major state, Italy) and the failure of Communism in the East. The approach inevitably means some overlap between chapters, but this is kept to a minimum. It also means that there is no detailed coverage of the smaller West European democracies, including the Scandinavian and Benelux states as well as Eire, Austria and Switzerland. This does not mean that their history is insignificant, merely that pressures of space made such exclusions inevitable.

What follows in the introduction is a brief review of major developments, especially in Western Europe, in the period 1945–89. This is particularly important in providing a reference point for comparisons between the main Western European democracies, West Germany, France, Italy and Britain.

In May 1945, at the end of the greatest war in history, much of Europe lay devastated. Tens of millions of people had died, millions more were injured and there was a massive refugee problem. Food and fuel were in short supply, communications were broken, whole cities lay ruined, industry was geared to the needs of war. The discovery of Nazi death camps stunned even those hardened by six years of conflict. Inevitably the early post-war years became ones of reconstruction, as European states not only sought to rebuild their economies but also, in many cases, created new political institutions to replace those which had failed the test of war. Most of continental Europe had fallen under authoritarian rule before 1939 and those who now had new constitutions included the two aggressor states, Germany and Italy. This period of reconstruction was also marked by a new international order in Europe, with the United States and the Soviet Union emerging as the principal powers on the continent, thanks to the decline of the other great powers and the defeat of Fascism.

The 'Cold War', which developed between these two powers, divided the continent. Arguably an East–West division of Europe was not new: comparisons were made at the time to the division of the continent between Roman and 'barbarian' influences in the ancient past; the River Elbe in Germany had long served as a dividing-line between areas subjected to serfdom and the freer social systems of the West. Nevertheless, the 'iron curtain' which split the continent after 1945 was unprecedented in effect on all levels – ideological, military, economic, social and cultural. In the East the Soviet Union asserted its dominance, Communist policies were enforced by a police-state, and rigid methods of central planning were used to create heavy industries under state ownership. In the West the US provided economic aid and led a military alliance (NATO), liberal democracy was generally fostered, and capitalist measures were used to achieve growth. In Western Europe, following the inter-war depression and the trials of war, there were hopes of creating a fairer society through social democratic reforms and until 1947 the coalition governments in France and Italy even included Communists. Social security provisions were extended, trades unions rights respected, key industries were nationalised and Keynesian economic methods (successfully tested in the war) were used to achieve full employment through greater state intervention in the economy. Yet, by 1952, the predominant forces in government in West Germany, France, Italy and Britain were Conservatives or Christian Democrats, strongly anti-Communist and claiming to protect individual rights, whilst maintaining social welfare.

By about 1952 post-war reconstruction was largely achieved, the Korean War (1950–3) stimulated economic growth and the subsequent decade proved to be one of growing confidence, despite the ever-present danger of nuclear war. In the USSR and Eastern Europe, following the death of Stalin in 1953, the use of state terror was eased and the production of consumer goods was expanded. In the West meanwhile, governments were able to achieve political stability and overcome social problems thanks to sustained economic growth, although exactly why such formidable growth rates were achieved is still debated.

The 1950s and 1960s were years of population growth, greater urbanisation and the production of consumer goods such as vacuum cleaners, refrigerators, washing machines and televisions. Such products soon came within the reach of working-class, as well as middle-class, incomes. Energy sources, including Middle Eastern oil, seemed cheap and inexhaustible, and the workforce in manufacturing industry was expanded by absorbing workers from the land. An important development in Western Europe was the growth of the 'tertiary sector' of employment, those working in distribution and other services. (In Italy between 1954 and 1980, the proportion of the workforce employed in agriculture and fisheries fell from 43 per cent to just 14 per cent, the increase in manufacturing industry was from 30 per cent to 38 per cent and those employed in distribution and services mushroomed from 27 per cent to 48 per cent). Western Europe benefited from trade with the larger US market, from the lowering of Western trade barriers under the General Agreement on Tariffs and Trade (GATT) and from the energetic commitment of most governments to growth.

Economic growth enabled Western European countries to provide higher wages, better welfare payments, more paid holidays, a shorter working week, improved health and education – all of which helped to secure social peace and consolidated the 'post-war settlement' (or, as it is sometimes called in Britain, the 'political consensus'). The post-war settlement differed in each country but usually included opposition to Soviet Communism, participation in the world economy, the acceptance (in many countries) of the US alliance, the extension of social reform, a commitment to full employment and recognition of workers' rights. In contrast to the inter-war years, democratic governments were able to provide economic improvements, liberal political rights, reasonable co-operation between capital and labour, stable constitutions and peace abroad. The economic successes helped to compensate Europeans for the loss of their colonial empires and for Superpower dominance, whilst also ensuring the success of the Western European unity movement.

The idea of a stable post-war settlement in the 1950s and early 1960s should not be exaggerated. Important political elements, the French and Italian Communists, for example, were excluded from the political consensus after 1947. There were strong critics of the Cold War, the American alliance and nuclear weapons in the West European Socialist parties. The 'settlement' was very different from country to country; in Italy the Christian Democrats effectively created an anti-Communist state; in Sweden a model social democracy thrived; in France the Fourth Republic failed to provide suitable political institutions for such a dynamic society and was replaced in 1958. Not all social groups gained: those on fixed pensions lost out because of inflation, small shopkeepers could not compete with the new 'chain stores', unskilled workers often lacked trades unions to protect them. Not all the politicians were pleased either: some right-wingers were already disenchanted with the idea of state intervention and economic planning because of the threat these supposedly represented to individualism and healthy competition. Certain regions, especially rural areas such as southern Italy, were left behind by the advances. Some states also seemed more successful than others. West Germany for example, the pariah of 1945, witnessed a remarkable recovery under Konrad Adenauer in 1949–63 whilst Britain, in many ways a model for the new Europe – as the first industrial nation, the 'mother of parliaments' and a pioneer of the 'welfare state' – was beset by self-doubt and unable to match continental growth rates. Nevertheless, the overall stability of Western Europe was remarkable compared to earlier periods. Major political parties now sought to appeal to all classes, regions and religions in their countries. (Again, this was to imitate the 'Anglo-Saxon' example: past continental practice had been for parties to represent sectional interests, leading to unstable government). By about 1960 even ideological differences between the Socialist and Conservative parties appeared to lose their significance, hence the talk of a 'Grand Coalition' between the two main parties in Germany, of a Christian Democratic 'opening to the left' in Italy and of 'Butskellism' in Britain. For many of those who had lived through the Depression and the war, Western Europe seemed a promised land.

Increasingly after about 1965, however, the post-war settlement was threatened. By the very nature of pluralist democracies there were strong pressure groups and interests which lay beyond the control of government. This was seen as a source of strength compared to the rigid, one-party states of Eastern Europe. But in the 1960s new forms of protest arose in the West, the failings of 'consensus politics' were exposed and the democracies became troubled. The continuation of the Cold War, the doctrine of 'Mutual Assured Destruction' and moral doubts about US policy in the Vietnam War (1965–73) led to greater questioning of Western foreign policy and a readiness to tolerate Soviet policy in the East. In domestic politics the 'New Left' condemned inequalities of wealth, the existence of 'poverty traps', the power of elite groups, and authoritarianism and corruption in government. Such criticism were already evident in the early 1960s but by about 1965 protest was taken up by the growing 'youth movement'. Middle-class students were more educated and better off than ever before, and seemed to gain much from these years of growth, but they had been raised without the experience of war, they questioned the values of their parents and found the new world morally confusing: religious observance had declined, but science and consumerism were no substitute for spiritual belief. In the search for a 'cause' the youth of the mid-1960s rejected both traditional Marxism and capitalism as a model, experimented with new kinds of art, personal behaviour and politics, and was not prepared to accept old injustices.

1968 proved an explosive year, marked by student demonstrations in America and Japan (and Czechoslovakia) as well as Western Europe, with the worst disruption coming in Paris in May. The students proved to be a disunited minority and could not be said to have achieved much directly, except for some University reform. 'Permissive' legislation to extend individual choice on divorce, abortion and other issues, was already on the way in some states. However, students involved in 1968 had an important role in developing the political movements of the 1970s and 1980s, including demands for equality for women, ecological concern, the campaigns for nuclear disarmament and greater social reforms which affected European Socialist parties in the early 1980s, and, at the extreme (for those unprepared to play a role in 'the system') left-wing, political terrorism. In the long-term the real significance of 1968 was that the student discontent became fused with serious and long-lasting working-class discontent. Workers, resentful of overtime demands, of repetitive factory work, of poor housing and of low social mobility, were no longer satisfied with the promise of a job and social welfare in times of need. Economic growth had bred higher expectations. Young, unskilled workers, who shared the moral confusion of the students, and who were unprotected by trades unions were particuarly likely to take 'lightning' strike action. In the late 1960s inflation – itself a result of expansion, wage increases and state spending – added to the pressures on the working classes.

The 1968 unrest in France had united both students and young workers. In 1969, Italy saw a 'hot autumn' of strikes which marked the final demise of the country's 'economic miracle'. Even Sweden saw a wave of unofficial strikes in 1969–70. Everywhere the strikes achieved better wages, greater workers' rights and improved working conditions but these concessions also added to industrial costs, reduced growth and contributed to the 'inflation spiral'. In Western Europe in the early 1970s all the old certainties seemed to disappear. In 1971 the US government, no longer the towering economic giant of 1945, tried to cope with its own problems by ending the Bretton Woods system, whereby currencies were 'fixed' in value against the dollar: Western commerce then had to adjust to 'floating' exchange rates and suffered in the process. Population growth was slower after 1970. The extension of the European Community to Britain, Eire and Denmark failed to bring a new boom. Much worse came after October 1973 when a Middle East war led to a quadrupling of oil prices. Inflation received another boost and trade deficits were instantly created as the age of cheap energy came to an end. Much of Western Europe now experienced 'stagflation' as low growth combined with inflation. Escape seemed impossible. Higher interest rates harmed businesses without cutting inflation, whilst government attempts to 'reflate' the economy made inflation still worse. Again, not everyone suffered to the same extent. West Germany and Austria had a better 'social partnership' between employers and workers than other countries, making it easier to keep wage demands down, to restrict inflation and to maintain high employment. But in the mid-1970s the continent as a whole was in the political doldrums. 1974 saw the death of France's President Pompidou, the resignation of West Germany's Chancellor Brandt and electoral defeat for Britain's premier Heath (as well as the fall of US President Nixon). Western societies were said to have become 'ungovernable', and Communist parties now hoped to exploit the situation by posing as moderate 'Eurocommunists'. The fall of right-wing regimes in Greece, Spain and Portugal merely added to the state of confusion. Meanwhile, the USSR seemed more confident than ever, with an active policy in the Third World and an apparently impenetrable position in Eastern Europe.

In 1979–80, following the overthrow of the Shah of Iran, oil prices rose again, this time by 250 per cent. The Western economies now plunged into a deep depression. Inflation remained a problem, businesses collapsed and unemployment (already growing since 1970) leapt to over 10 per cent in Britain, France and Italy, and over 20 per cent in Spain. Traditional industries, for example, coal mining and steel production (the past indices of a nation's strength), were in decline anyway, undercut by cheaper production in Brazil, India and other developing states. Chemicals, cars and electrical goods were still in demand but the new expanding fields for the 1980s were in computers, robotics and communication technology, where Europe was challenged by the ever-growing might of Japan and other 'Pacific Rim' lands, including California, Taiwan and South Korea. Yet, new industries also provided the opportunity for a revival of growth, and Western European societies proved their resilience by recovering from the depression after 1981. Actually, even in the difficult years of the 1970s, there were many grounds for confidence about European democracy: time and again elections showed most people's preference for political moderation; reforms in such areas as sexual and racial equality (even if they did not work a revolution) answered discontent; terrorist outrages, like the murder of Aldo Moro in Italy, alienated most people; and new democracies were successfully established in Southern Europe. Some countries even coped relatively easily with the post-1979 depression. Norway's small population was shielded from unemployment by North Sea oil earnings, and Sweden and Austria also managed to hold unemployment down. In general, however, the depression was to prove the final demise of the post-war world of Keynesian economics and state intervention, and led to a new political-economic approach, shaped by the Right.

In the 1970s even conservative governments stuck to Keynesian methods of economic management, maintained high government spending and tried, somehow, to shore up the post-war settlement. By about 1980, however, there was a search for new answers to political and economic problems. Some left-wingers wanted to increase state control of the economy, shorten working hours (to reduce unemployment) and raise welfare payments (to boost demand), but when such policies were attempted in France in 1981–3 they ended in disaster. On the Right, meanwhile, it was argued that full employment had become impossible, that social spending was taking too much national wealth, that high taxes were crippling personal initiative and that nationalised industries were an inefficient investment. The Thatcher government in Britain became the foremost exponent of spending cuts, 'privatisation' and economic policies designed to reduce inflation rather than to maintain full employment. The state was in retreat, Socialism had lost its appeal and in some countries, notably Spain and Italy, Socialist parties themselves proved ready to introduce reforms associated with the new 'market liberalism'. At the same time there was natural recovery from the depths of the depression in 1981, oil prices lessened in real terms and the US economy became an expanding market again under Ronald Reagan. Growth was restored and new 'spending sprees' began on video recorders, microwave ovens and home computers. Most Western Europeans seemed ready to put their trust again in a mixture of consumerism and traditional morality. The late 1980s saw growing moral concern over drug abuse, the Aids virus and environmental pollution.

In 1989, the collapse of the Communist regimes in Eastern Europe seemed to provide the ultimate vindication of Western liberalism. The Soviet Union, crippled by planning deficiencies, overburdened by defence spending and unable to motivate its people, could not match the capitalist challenge in the long term. Eastern European peoples threw off an alien political system, won new democratic rights and multi-party elections and committed themselves to Western policies of market economics. Following the collapse too of authoritarian right-wing regimes in the 1970s, a new European-wide 'consensus' appeared possible as democratic values triumphed everywhere, the Cold War ended and the continent began to function as a whole once more. Despite four decades of division, Europe had come a long way from the death and devastation of 1945. The continent included the five largest economies in the world after America and Japan – the USSR,* West Germany, France, Italy and Britain. In terms of GNP *per head* the Scandinavian and Benelux countries, Austria, Switzerland, West Germany and France were among the wealthiest in the world, with Italy and Britain lagging a little behind. The European Community, although it included the poorest Western European nations (Spain, Greece and, poorest of all, Portugal), had undergone a resurgence in the mid-1980s and was a formidable economic force, the world's largest trading bloc and consumer market, with a GNP almost as large as America's. Despite considerable national differences, Western European countries had become remarkably similar since the war – committed to world trade and growth; tolerant of different political beliefs, religions and cultures; with less people living in rural areas but more industrial workers, managers and professional groups living in towns, and with smaller families than before. In Western Europe the difficulties which had beset governments and society since the 1950s were often the problems of plenty: how to create and share wealth, how to avoid the ill-effects of industrial expansion on health and the environment, how to fill people's leisure time. Europeans may have lost their colonies, lived under the shadow of the bomb and become the victims of oil price increases, but they had also lived largely in peace, were far wealthier than Third World states and between 1948 and 1989 had seen very few violent changes of government.

Events at the end of 1989 did not guarantee an easy future. Political reform in Eastern Europe had come swiftly but economic changes would be much more difficult to achieve and serious discontent was possible. Many were fearful of a new, reunited Germany. Talk of 'the triumph of

---

* Soviet statistics are difficult to compare to Western GNPs but in 1987 the USSR was still reckoned to be the world's third largest economy.

liberalism' did not provide people with a detailed idea of what the future held, partly because liberalism itself allowed for diversity. Communist regimes may have collapsed in the East, but they had long seemed bankrupt anyway and in Western Europe the problems of the 1970s were not far in the past. Western governments in the late 1980s were accused of becoming more authoritarian, secretive and intolerant under the influence of the New Right. Their ability to deal with environmental problems was in doubt. Some hoped that 1989, far from bringing the triumph of market economics, would result in a 'third way' between capitalism and Marxist-socialism, similar to the ideals many had held immediately after the war. In Western Europe, after all, many social reforms had survived the 1980s, whilst in Eastern Europe some of the new political parties wanted to avoid major inequalities of wealth once capitalism was introduced. Market liberalism, then, was not unchallenged as a political force and the new era would undoubtedly breed its own intense political debate, albeit in a very different atmosphere to that of the Cold War.

# 1
# Cold War and Détente

## The East–West breakdown, 1945–9

The alliance of America, Russia and Britain, the 'Big Three' powers who defeated Hitler, was born of dire necessity in 1941. Britain by then had been at war with Germany for two years, but the Soviet Union was only drawn into the conflict in June by a sudden German invasion, whilst the US entered the war in December after the Japanese attack on Pearl Harbor. In the inter-war years relations between the Western powers and Moscow had often been strained: America did not open diplomatic relations with the Bolshevik regime until 1933. In 1939–41 furthermore, the Soviet dictator, Josef Stalin, had been in a pact with Hitler, which allowed Russia to annex the Baltic states (Lithuania, Latvia and Estonia) and much of Poland. To an extent East–West distrust continued throughout the war. Stalin particularly resented the Anglo–American failure to open a 'Second Front' in western Europe before June 1944, suspecting this was a deliberate attempt to bleed Russia white as she fought the bulk of the German army. The shared struggle against Nazism did however hold the Big Three together until victory was achieved, and there were high hopes of maintaining the alliance into peacetime. America's President, Franklin Roosevelt, hoped that peace could be built under a new United Nations (UN) organisation. Roosevelt and British premier Winston Churchill, had vaguely proposed such a body in August 1941, when they issued the 'Atlantic Charter', a propagandistic document which also promised the restoration of independence to conquered peoples, territorial changes by consent and freer trade after the war. It was hoped the UN would commit all states to the ideal of 'collective security', where international problems would be settled by conciliation and arbitration rather than the traditional methods of balance of power, alliances and war. The US, by far the world's wealthiest and most powerful state, also hoped for a stable, expanding world economy where freer trade would prevent a return to the depression and unemployment which had led to militant nationalism in the 1930s. In 1944, at the Bretton Woods conference, plans were laid for a new commercial and financial system with the formation of an International

Monetary Fund (IMF) to deal with monetary problems and a World Bank to help with economic development. In April 1945, on the political side, the UN Charter was drawn up in a conference at San Francisco attended by all Allied States.

Even before San Francisco the Big Three were divided in their vision of post-war Europe. Stalin, as a Communist, did not accept the American definition of 'democracy' nor could he welcome a global security and commercial system defined according to Western values. Concerned with Soviet security he wished to retain the territorial gains made under his pact with Hitler. In 1944, when the liberation of Europe began in earnest, it was clear that Stalin might use his military predominance in eastern Europe to create pro-Soviet regimes there. Arguments raged, in particular, over the future of Poland, the first major state which the Red Army entered. Poland was strategically placed between Russia and Germany, and for centuries had been a bone of contention between them. Britain and France had gone to war over Poland when it was invaded by Hitler in 1939, there were numerous Polish-Americans concerned about its future, and a Polish 'government-in-exile' already existed in London. Yet in July 1944 the Red Army installed a group of Moscow-trained Communists in the town of Lublin to administer the country. The Russians were ruthlessly determined to end any Polish attempts to achieve independence, failing for example to assist the Warsaw Rising of Poles against the Germans.* In February 1945 Stalin, Roosevelt and Churchill met face-to-face at Yalta in the Crimea, and Poland was the most important subject. Yalta was condemned by many afterwards as marking a Western betrayal of eastern Europe, as grave as Munich in 1938: Roosevelt, in his eagerness to secure world peace, was duped, it was said, by Stalin. However, there was no formal document at Yalta which divided Europe up into 'spheres of influence'. That division already existed on grounds of harsh military logic. The Red Army had won control of eastern Europe by force of arms in early 1945 and only force of arms could drive them out. Yet no one in the West could seriously contemplate a war with Russia at this time. Instead a cosmetic 'Declaration on Liberated Europe' was issued at Yalta, restating the Atlantic Charter principles of independence and sovereignty, but with no means to enforce these high-sounding ideals. On Poland, an arrangement was made whereby the Communists would form a joint administration with elements of the London government-in-exile, but this did not prevent the country's long-term domination by Moscow.

In April 1945, a few months after Yalta, the world was stunned by news of Roosevelt's death. The new President, the inexperienced but determined Harry Truman, seemed at first to take a tougher line with the Soviets. On 23 April he told Russia's foreign minister, Vyacheslav Molotov, in no uncertain terms, that Russia must fulfil its agreements with America in full in future. In July–August there was a more co-operative atmosphere at the Potsdam conference, where the Big Three agreed on

* For a fuller discussion, see p 200.

principles for the post-war control of Germany, including its disarmament. But US confidence in dealing with Russia was bolstered soon afterwards by the use of the atomic bomb to defeat Japan, and in the two years following a breakdown in East–West relations occurred which, with the decline of Britain to secondary status, left Europe divided between American and Soviet spheres of influence. The Continent, though devastated by war, was still of enormous significance, a centre of technologically-advanced industrial production, with a large population and it exerted colonial control over much of Africa and Asia. But with the decline of France, Italy and Germany from great power status it had become a power vacuum. The process by which this vacuum was filled in 1945–7 can best be surveyed by looking at four geographical areas: eastern Europe, Germany, the Near East and western Europe.

At Yalta both Roosevelt and Churchill were willing to concede that Russia should have 'friendly' neighbours in eastern Europe. June 1941 was the second devastating German invasion of Russia in recent times and it was understandable that Moscow wished to create a buffer zone between itself and Germany. But whereas Roosevelt and Churchill hoped that 'friendly' policies could be guaranteed through liberal-democratic regimes, Stalin, with bitter memories of Western policy in eastern Europe between the wars, was willing to trust himself only to Communist-led governments. A gradual process began in countries liberated by the Red Army, which eventually resulted in governments across eastern Europe using police-state methods and carrying out Soviet-style economic reforms, the very antithesis of liberal democracy. The pace of change differed from country to country: Poland, Romania and Bulgaria were effectively Soviet puppets by 1946, but Hungary was only brought under Moscow's control in mid-1947 and a coalition government survived in Czechoslovakia until February 1948. (The final tightening of control seems to have been a *response* to Western actions.) Stalin's general motives in absorbing eastern Europe have, however, provoked great debate. Was he merely an opportunist who, having conquered these states during the war decided to exploit the situation to Russia's advantage, or did he have some more grandiose scheme in mind? If he had an overall plan were his motives defensive or offensive – with eastern Europe a launching pad for further expansion? These issues were hotly debated but in February 1946 George Kennan, a US diplomat in Moscow, wrote an analysis of Soviet policy which had a major impact on thinking in Washington. Kennan saw the USSR as an expansionist state both because of its crusading Marxist ideology and because of the traditional Russian suspicion of outsiders. The ideological basis of Kremlin policy seemed confirmed at this time by Stalin, who declared in a speech in February 1946 that the Second World War had vindicated the Soviet system of government. In March 1946 at Fulton, Missouri, Winston Churchill declared that an 'iron curtain' had fallen across Europe and he wanted an Anglo–American alliance to be made to halt the Soviets. The speech gravely offended Stalin. There was still little the West could do to free eastern Europe and peace treaties were made with Romania, Bulgaria and Hungary (all former allies of Hitler) in February 1947 which effectively left them at Stalin's mercy. But events in the region had offended the West's democratic sensibilities and aroused fears of greater Soviet ambitions.

Germany, the principal ex-enemy state, lying at the heart of Europe, presented complex problems in 1945, not least because it was placed under joint occupation by the Big Three and France who were joined together in an Allied Control Council. The French were granted an occupation zone mainly thanks to Britain. The British believed France would be vital to the control of Germany in the future, especially because American troops were expected to leave Europe in 1947. France's leader, General de Gaulle, had his own aims in Germany however and ironically France, rather than Russia, became responsible for the early failure of the joint Allied administration. De Gaulle, determined to weaken Germany after three invasions of France in living memory (1870, 1914 and 1940), wanted to destroy all signs of a centralised German government and vetoed moves by the Allied Control Council to treat the country as a whole. As a result the military occupation zones became four distinct political entities, where each power pursued policies which reflected its own values, with the 'Sovietisation' of the economy in the East, the fostering of capitalism in the US zone and the encouragement of social democratic reforms in the British zone. Meanwhile, other important East–West differences arose. The Soviets, ravaged by Germany during the war, hoped for large-scale reparations payments from the defeated enemy, to pay for their own reconstruction. In America and Britain however, there were fears that such a policy would cripple Germany; America and Britain would then be forced to provide aid to keep Germans alive, and the health of the European economy in general would suffer. In May 1946 the governor of the US zone, General Lucius Clay, ended reparations removals from his zone and so antagonised the Soviets. Moscow was also offended by the refusal of the Anglo–Americans to give her a share in controlling the German industrial heartland, the Ruhr, which lay in the British zone. It was probably through exasperation with the lack of Anglo–American concessions that, in a speech in July 1946, Molotov appealed for support from the German people themselves. Playing down Russia's reparations demands, he offered to create a centralised, united Germany as an independent force on the world stage. The US responded in September when the Secretary of State, James Byrnes, speaking in Stuttgart, also offered new hope for Germany, on the basis of a federal, liberal government and economic resuscitation. Just as important, he said that US troops would now remain in Europe until peace was assured. Meanwhile the British, partly owing to financial difficulties, had agreed to unite their zone with that of the Americans. Thus by March 1947, when the foreign ministers of the occupation powers met in Moscow to discuss a German peace treaty, the Anglo–Americans and Russia were already far apart in their German policies. Both sides indeed seemed to be pleading for German support against the other.

As the Moscow conference opened, US–Soviet tension was also reflected in a major statement by Truman which had its roots in events in the

Near East, traditionally an area of Anglo–Soviet rivalry. In March 1946 strong diplomatic pressure had been exerted by America and Britain to force Soviet troops out of Iran, which they had helped to occupy during the war. There were also Western fears in 1946 that the Soviets would force Turkey, a wartime neutral, to concede territory and navigation rights through the Dardanelles. The gravest problems, however, were in Greece where British troops had restored a Royalist government in 1944 and become embroiled in a civil war with a Communist guerrilla movement. In early 1947 the British, financially drained, and facing complicated imperial problems in India and Palestine, told Washington that they could no longer provide their traditional assistance to the Greek and Turkish governments. The State Department believed that the US must either take on Britain's role as protector of Near Eastern states from Russia, or witness a major advance for Communism. As a result Truman went before Congress on 12 March and asked that US money be provided for these two states. In justifying this decision Truman depicted events in the Near East as a struggle between freedom and totalitarianism, and stated that 'we must assist free peoples to work out their own destinies in their own way'. This 'Truman Doctrine' may have been intended primarily to 'scare' Congress into giving the required money. Greece was far from being a model democracy and there was no evidence of large-scale Soviet support for the Greek Communists. But certain elements in Washington had become convinced that a Communist cancer was spreading through the international system and that it must be met by an American policy of 'containment'. This idea was developed further a few months later in the 'Marshall Plan', a highly significant US commitment to European affairs.

Just as Moscow supported the creation of Communist regimes in eastern Europe after 1944, so the Anglo–Americans had fostered liberal-democracy in areas they liberated. This was so despite America's traditional policy of 'isolationism' and its strong aversion to involvement in European affairs. The Anglo–Americans succeeded in restoring democracy in Belgium, Holland, Norway, Denmark and elsewhere but the strategically vital states of France and Italy both had large Communist parties who shared power in coalition governments, and all countries faced the daunting task of economic reconstruction after the war. In early 1947 a bitterly cold winter damaged industrial output and trade, and although the economic impact was only short-term the psychological blow to popular morale seemed significant. The failure to resolve Germany's future added to Europe's economic problems and it seemed that Communists in France and Italy might exploit the consequent social discontent in order to seize power. In May the Communists were expelled from the French and Italian governments, but they remained a potential menace. Thus the new US Secretary of State, George Marshall, came forward on 5 June 1947 with the Marshall Plan, to help pay for a comprehensive recovery plan which would set Europe on its economic feet.

The Marshall Plan was supposedly open to *all* Europeans and in late

June Molotov came to Paris to discuss it with the British and French foreign ministers, Ernest Bevin and Georges Bidault. But Russia's ability to accept capitalist economic aid was always in doubt and Molotov walked out of the Paris talks on 2 July, complaining tht the Marshall Plan would lead to Germany's industrial revival and infringe the economic independence of European States, which would become US puppets. The Soviets were already concerned at America's creation of a world-wide network of military bases, her possession of the atomic bomb and her economic strength. What specifically seems to have worried the Russians most about the Marshall Plan was the temptation it represented for eastern European states. What was presented in America as a bid to resolve Europe's economic problems was seen in Moscow as an attempt, using US dollars, to subvert the Soviet hold on eastern Europe, Russia's hard-won prize in the war. In response the Kremlin tightened its grip in the East still further. Thus Stalin prevented Poland and Czechoslovakia from attending the conference of 16 European nations,* which met in Paris between July and September, and drew up a joint economic recovery programme to be financed by America. Then, in late September, Eastern bloc Communists together with French and Italian party representatives, were called by Moscow to a meeting in Poland. Here they were presented with a new interpretation of world events from the Kremlin which saw the world as divided into 'two camps' and called on Communists everywhere to resist US 'imperialism'. An Information Bureau, the Cominform, was established which Western observers saw as the re-creation of the old Communist International, designed to foster Marxist revolution. Shortly afterwards Communists encouraged a series of strikes in France and Italy which were evidently designed to sabotage the Marshall Plan.

The completion of the West European scheme for economic recovery and the formation by the East Europeans of the Cominform in September 1947, meant that the Continent had been severed in two. The failure of more talks, in London in December, on a German peace treaty meant that the line of division between the two blocs ran right through the centre of the defeated enemy of 1945. It was in the wake of the London conference on Germany that the Americans, British and French initiated a number of policies designed to resolve the future of Western Europe without Soviet interference. These policies also served to institutionalise the Cold War. Of special importance was the decision to unite the Europeans and Americans in a security pact. The West's military experts did not, at this time, expect a Soviet invasion of Western Europe. The USSR's economy still needed to recover from the war and Stalin could rely on local Communist parties to try to subvert French and Italian democracy from within. But the Red Army was larger than Western forces in Europe, war *could* break out 'by

---

* Britain, France, the Benelux states, Italy, Eire, Denmark, Norway, Iceland, Sweden, Portugal, Greece, Turkey, Switzerland and Austria.

accident' (through the failure to manage a diplomatic crisis properly) and a US guarantee – even if it only existed on paper – could provide a major psychological boost to West European morale. The Americans, reluctant to be accused of seeking 'domination', and cautious about giving the Europeans a 'blank cheque' for costly military assistance in future, insisted that the Europeans should take the first steps towards defending themselves. This was one reason why the British, still hoping to maintain their own influence in world affairs, joined with France, Belgium, Holland and Luxembourg in the Brussels defence pact of March 1948. Talks between the Brussels powers, America and Canada on an Atlantic Pact finally began in July.

Meanwhile, in April 1948 the US Congress approved the European Recovery Programme, as the Marshall Plan had become, which provided several billion dollars to European countries in 1948–52. This was only a fraction of the total size of the European economy, but it gave assistance in some key areas, was of particular importance in strengthening the French and Italian governments and forced the Europeans to work together in overcoming their problems. The Marshall Plan also encouraged West Germany's revival as an integral part of the continental economy. The political future of Germany, on the other hand, was settled in June, after months of talks, by the 'London Accords' which foresaw the creation of a federal West German state. It was probably through fear of Germany's revival, and with hopes of forcing the West to back down on this, that Stalin in late June began to blockade land routes into the western sectors of Berlin. The former German capital, which had been under joint administration since 1945, lay deep within the Soviet occupation zone and at first it·seemed that the Western sectors would be starved into submission. But a massive airlift of supplies succeeded in keeping the city alive throughout the winter and the Berlin Blockade turned from a major Soviet challenge into a great triumph for the Western powers. In May 1949, after almost a year of crisis, Stalin conceded defeat and reopened land access to the city. The fears generated by the blockade had only served to strengthen Western suspicion of Russia and to deepen Europe's division. In April 1949 ten European nations* joined America and Canada in signing the North Atlantic Treaty in Washington, an alliance which ended any lingering fears that America might slip again into isolationism, as she had so disastrously after 1919. In September, the Americans approved a Military Assistance Programme to build up European armed forces, but the explosion of a Soviet atomic bomb at the same time highlighted European vulnerability in a world increasingly dominated by only two superpowers. September also saw West Germany elect its first government, an event which led Stalin to form his own German state in the East. By then Europe and, at its heart, Germany, were rigidly divided on the ideological, political, economic and military levels.

---

* Britain, France, the Benelux States, Italy, Denmark, Norway, Iceland and Portugal.

## The Cold War 1950–62

By 1950 the dividing line between East and West in Europe was clearly drawn but war on the Continent was unlikely. Berlin was a potential 'flash-point' and few believed that Germany could remain divided forever, but in a sense both sides were satisfied with what they held: Russia had its defence *glacis* in the East; America had given confidence and protection to Western Europe through Marshall aid and the North Atlantic Treaty Organisation (NATO). Despite the Soviet explosion of an atomic bomb, America maintained a marked advantage in atomic weapons. However, whilst the origins of the Cold War had principally been found within Europe tension was always apparent elsewhere. Moscow resented being excluded from the post-war occupation of Japan for example, whilst Washington was disturbed at the Communist victory in China in 1949, and in June 1950 the invasion of pro-Western South Korea by the Communist North dramatically demonstrated that Cold War tensions outside Europe could have a major impact within Europe. The Korean War shifted the world's attention to the Far East, led to a massive US rearmament effort once President Truman decided to aid the South, increased support in America for the rabidly anti-Communist views of Senator Joe McCarthy and, at the end of the year, brought Communist China into the war as an implacable new foe of the West. Fortunately Russia never became directly involved and the war was limited to the Korean peninsula, but its effect on Europe was considerable. By stimulating demand in the world economy it both added to inflation and, on the positive side, helped European industrial output to continue growing even after post-war reconstruction was achieved. The political results were equally far-reaching. Britain and France, both with colonial possessions in Asia, sent small forces to fight in Korea and in Germany there were fears that the Communists might use 'hot war' tactics closer to home: Korea, like Germany, had become divided after a joint East–West occupation; it seemed that the East Germans could emulate North Korea and try to reunite Germany by force. Konrad Adenauer, West Germany's Chancellor, suspected that Korea was intended by Stalin as a ruse, to draw attention to the Far East whilst he launched into violent action in Europe.

Worries such as this forced NATO to address its military weakness. NATO as a military alliance in 1950 was little more than an empty shell. Europeans had few military resources and the only significant American forces were scattered on occupation duties in Germany. The Red Army's conventional strength in Europe was overwhelming. Even as a demonstration of America's long-term commitment to European security NATO was a disappointment. The US would only aid its Allies, should they be attacked, in accordance with its constitution, which left decisions on war and peace to the Senate. It was because of this that Europeans were anxious to keep US troops permanently on the continent, almost as 'hostages', the logic being that the Senate was bound to declare war on an aggressor if US soldiers were killed in Europe. With Korea came the added fear that America could become involved in Asian affairs to the detriment of European interests. It was in order to reassure its Allies, and to balance the Red Army, that the Americans proposed in September 1950 to send extra divisions to Europe and to appoint a US Supreme Commander for NATO. In return, however, America wanted a major concession in the form of West German rearmament. From the US viewpoint this request seemed logical. Russia, not Germany, was now the West's enemy; Adenauer was emerging as a loyal ally who could provide substantial armed forces in the front line against Russia; and American people wanted to see that Europeans would help to defend themselves (not least because Congress had been assured in 1949 that NATO did *not* imply a costly, long-term commitment to Europe's defence).

For Europeans, however, the German rearmament proposal, so soon after 1945, came as a profound shock. Even Germans themselves had grave fears of a revival of militarism in their country and America's proposal began a long-running argument in NATO. The French were particularly opposed to the re-creation of a German Army and, in October, Premier René Pleven announced that France would rearm German troops only as part of a 'European Army' which, by creating federal defence institutions, would prevent Germany regaining any military independence. Despite doubts about the military efficiency of a European Army, it was agreed in December, to proceed with the Pleven Plan as the only way forward on German rearmament. More US troops were then sent to Europe and in 1951 Dwight Eisenhower became NATO's first Supreme Commander. A major rearmament effort was promised by the members of NATO, who were joined in 1952 by Greece and Turkey. A treaty to establish the 'European Defence Community' (EDC), as the Pleven Plan became known, was eventually signed by France, West Germany, Italy and the Benelux States in May 1952. The Americans hoped that it would come into force as quickly as possible, allowing German military forces to be recruited. To come into being, however, EDC needed to be ratified by all its members, and this soon proved very difficult, particularly in France. Many Frenchmen remained suspicious even of arming Germans within a European force, and many did not see why the French army should lose its own military independence by joining EDC. There were also worries about the effect of German rearmament on Soviet behaviour.

The Russians bitterly opposed West German rearmament, pointing out that this broke the 1945 Potsdam agreement. In March 1952 Moscow, in the so-called 'Stalin Note', had revived its pressure for discussions about a German peace treaty. This seemed like an attempt to prevent the signature of the EDC treaty and the West would not be drawn on it. However, the death of Josef Stalin in March 1953 seemed to bring a better chance for talks and revolutionised the international situation. The dictator's successors, led by Georgi Malenkov, talked of the need to resolve East–West differences and there were signs of a relaxation in tension, not least with the end of the Korean war in July. One of those interested in the opportunities for détente was Winston Churchill who was British premier once more and became the first major European statesman to advocate a relaxation of tensions with Russia. Churchill's support for détente may seem odd in view of his earlier criticisms of the 'iron curtain', but Churchill was concerned at the dangers of global war (especially after the explosion of hydrogen bombs by America and Russia in 1952 and 1953); he had hopes of establishing a reputation as a peacemaker, to match his reputation as a war leader; and he believed Britain could play a major role as the arbiter between Moscow and Washington. In May 1953 he proposed a meeting of East–West leaders and in 1954 wanted to hold a personal meeting with Malenkov. There were many reasons why such proposals failed to progress. Churchill himself was nearly 80 and increasingly unwell. The Soviets damaged their own case by, for example, crushing a brief workers' rising in East Berlin in June 1953, and America, whose friendship was always essential to Churchill, was still in its McCarthyite period. Eisenhower, who had become US President in January 1953, was interested in ideas for atomic arms control but his Secretary of State, John Foster Dulles, was an uncompromising anti-Soviet. Dulles believed the Russian leaders wanted détente for selfish reasons, to help install themselves in power after Stalin's death, or to sow division in the West. The last danger seemed very real because French critics of EDC did now argue that German rearmament should be abandoned so that détente could succeed. After all, if peace with Russia were now possible, why need Germany be rearmed?

Foreign ministers' talks were held with the Russians in Berlin in early 1954, but progress on a German peace treaty again proved impossible. Another conference was held a few months later at Geneva, when France's colonial war in Indochina was brought to an end. But a new crisis then broke out in NATO which made further talks with Russia impossible: after four years of discussion about West German rearmament, on 30 August the French parliament finally rejected EDC. Dulles had already warned that the defeat of EDC would provoke an 'agonising reappraisal' of US defence policy, hinting at a retreat from Europe to 'Fortress America'. Americans were exasperated that they should be paying for Europe's defence when the Europeans were not doing their utmost to help themselves. Konrad Adenauer, who had staked his reputation in Germany on loyalty to the West, also felt betrayed by France's action and Britain's foreign minister, Anthony Eden, made enormous diplomatic efforts to hold NATO together. In October, after conferences in London and Paris, the alliance was saved, ironically by an agreement to rearm Germany as a member of NATO, the very thing France had rejected in 1950. But French premier, Pierre Mendès-France, won various concessions: the French army would not now be placed under federal European controls (instead the European Army was abandoned); German forces would voluntarily desist from using certain categories of weapons, including atomic, bacteriological and chemical devices; Britain would maintain its current level of forces in Europe, and could therefore help France in controlling Germany in future. It took until May 1955, however, to ratify these Paris Agreements and bring West Germany into NATO. Meanwhile the alliance was in no state to 'negotiate from strength' with Moscow. In any case, Nikita Khruschev and Nikolai Bulganin, who ousted Malenkov from the Soviet leadership in early 1955, roundly condemned German rearmament. In May 1955 they responded to Western policies by forming the Warsaw Pact, defining a military structure for Eastern bloc countries similar to NATO's. Détente seemed as far off as ever.

Nonetheless, later in May, a major change took place. The new Soviet leaders decided not on a more bellicose response to German rearmament, but on an attempt to steal the limelight from NATO's success. Specifically, Russia agreed to sign a peace treaty with Austria which, like Germany, had been under four-power occupation since the war. The treaty was made on the basis of the country's reunification, the withdrawal of all foreign troops, and an Austrian policy of neutralism in international affairs. The Soviets believed that similar principles might be possible in a German peace treaty. In July, because of the new Soviet approach, Khruschev, Bulganin, Eisenhower, Eden (Churchill had now retired) and France's Edgar Faure met in Geneva for the first summit of East–West leaders since Potsdam, exactly ten years before. Germany was predictably the most important European issue. The Western powers had no interest in Russia's idea of a reunited and neutralised Germany however. West Germany was now part of the Western alliance, even pursuing a policy of co-operation with France through the policies of European unification. Furthermore, NATO's 'forward defence' strategy was based on the Elbe. The West believed, in any case, that Russia would try to exploit the process of German reunification to install a Communist government over the whole country. Whereas Moscow tried to pose as the champion of German unity therefore, the West posed as the defender of German liberty, arguing that reunification must only come after free nation-wide elections, and that Germany should be able to choose its own Allies. (This remained the Western position on German reunification until 1989.) With these proposals the Russians could not possibly agree, since a liberal-democratic Germany would almost certainly join NATO. Although East–West contacts continued after Geneva, the 'spirit of détente' remained simply that. Foreign Ministers' discussions later in the year failed to make any breakthrough. Adenauer, despite a visit to Moscow in September during which Russia and West Germany recognised each other's existence, remained deeply suspicious of Soviet intentions.

By the mid-1950s the Cold War had taken on an inexorable logic in Europe, which made divisions hard to break down. Mutual distrust in Germany had, it is clear, bred a situation in which each side's peace proposals had no chance of being accepted by the other. Each side was determined to hold onto what it had and to negotiate only from a 'position of strength'. But the unity of each bloc was largely based on enmity with the other and when talks did occur they tended to accentuate differences *within* the two blocs, which in turn made further dialogue difficult. For example, the events surrounding the collapse of the European Army in 1953–4 clearly showed how a lowering of Cold War tensions could expose divisions within NATO, which then undermined East–West contacts. In 1956 there was a similar experience in the Eastern bloc when, alongside the policy of détente with the West, Khruschev pursued a policy of 'destalinisation'. Khruschev's condemnation of Stalin in February 1956 led to hopes of radical change in Eastern Europe. As a result, there was serious unrest in Poland over the summer and in Hungary Imre Nagy took steps to create a multi-party state and withdraw from the Warsaw Pact. Such policies were far too extreme for the Kremlin and in November the Red Army ruthlessly crushed Hungary's bid for independence at the cost of thousands of lives. Although Dulles had often talked of 'liberating' Communist states, the West was powerless to help the Hungarians without provoking Armageddon. Worse still the crisis coincided with the Suez expedition, the ill-fated Anglo–French invasion of Egypt, which was itself condemned by Moscow as an 'imperialist' venture. Hungary served once again to offend Western democratic sensibilities and began a more difficult phase of the Cold War.

Despite talk of 'peaceful coexistence' with the West after Stalin, Russian leaders never intended to give up the ideological struggle with capitalism. Soviet leaders knew that war with America was unthinkable: NATO had been unable to match Soviet conventional strength in Europe because of the cost, but Dulles threatened 'massive retaliation' with nuclear weapons in the event of a Soviet threat to US vital interests and it was understood by 1955 that an atomic exchange in Europe would devastate the continent. The Kremlin therefore wanted to pursue competition short of armed conflict, and the mid-to-late 1950s saw the Cold War take on new dimensions and a truly global nature as Khruschev adapted to changed circumstances, proving ready, for example, to ally with groups in the emerging 'Third World' who opposed the capitalist and colonial West. In 1957 Russia stunned the West by launching an Inter-Continental Ballistic Missile (ICBM) and the first space satellite, 'Sputnik'. These technological successes gave credibility to Khruschev's claims that Communist states could eventually overtake capitalist economic growth. They also killed off any hope of US–Soviet 'disengagement' in central Europe and instead provoked a nuclear build-up by America.

In Europe the deepest Cold War problem remained Germany. Since 1954 the Soviets had developed a new proposal to resolve European security problems, whereby all existing European borders would be recognised in an arrangement involving Eastern and Western bloc states. The West had shown little liking for this. A European security agreement would legitimise Soviet domination of Eastern Europe and might be used to undermine America's commitment to West European defence. Moreover, it also meant recognising the independent existence of East Germany, which the Soviets had declared to be a sovereign state in 1955. Konrad Adenauer was adamant that West Germany was the only true Germany, bitterly opposed the Soviet action and, under the 'Hallstein doctrine', broke off relations with those countries – like Yugoslavia in 1957 (but excluding Russia) – who recognised East German sovereignty. It was probably in order to force movement on the German problem that Khruschev decided to exert pressure once again on the most exposed Western position in Europe, Berlin. In November 1958 he told the Western powers that they must leave Berlin within six months and make it a 'free city', or he would sign a separate peace treaty with East Germany. West Berlin's existence was still a thorn in the side of the Soviets, but Khruschev can have had little real hope that the West would abandon it. In fact, in December, America, Britain and France re-stated their determination to remain there. But the Soviet leader had rather more success in prising discussions out of the West in that a foreign ministers' conference was held about Germany in mid-1959 in Geneva. The two sides remained as far apart on the German problem as ever, however, and there was actually no threat the Soviets could make, short of military action, which could force concessions. Harold Macmillan, the British premier, maintaining Churchill's policy of détente, proved willing to visit Moscow early in 1959. But other NATO leaders, especially Charles de Gaulle who had returned to power in France, supported Adenauer's desire for firmness. Khruschev's threats over Berlin came to nothing. In May 1960 more talks began at leaders' levels in Paris, with Eisenhower anxious to play the role of peacemaker in his last year in office, but the conference collapsed when a US spy aircraft was shot down over the USSR.

Another summit meeting was not possible until June 1961 when a new President, John F Kennedy, met Khruschev in Vienna. Khruschev sensed a chance to humiliate the young President, who had recently failed in an attempt to overthrow the left-wing government of Fidel Castro in the Caribbean island of Cuba. Among other threats Khruschev said the West must settle the Berlin problem and recognise East Germany or face the consequences. This time, after more threats, he followed his ultimatum with action. In August 1961 the Soviets and East Germans erected barriers around West Berlin, preventing movement between the western sectors and the areas outside. The Berlin Wall came to be seen in the West as a symbol of the oppression of Communism, the most visible example of the 'Iron Curtain'. Despite Khruschev's bluster, it did not threaten the existence of West Berlin, but the wall put an end to the unedifying spectacle (for Communists) of thousands of East Germans travelling to Berlin and escaping to the West, an exodus underway throughout the 1950s which had seriously threatened East Germany's political and economic stability. Khruschev had succeeded too in demonstrating the West's powerlessness in certain local situations. Although Kennedy increased the size of US forces in Germany there was nothing he could do to bring the Berlin Wall down, or to stop those who tried to cross it from being shot.

Kennedy's inaction may have contributed to Khruschev's decision to build nuclear missile bases in Cuba the following year. If so, he miscalculated. Cuba, on America's doorstep was not Berlin, surrounded by Communist territory. In October 1962 Kennedy blockaded Cuba and forced Khruschev to withdraw his missiles in a crisis which seemed to take the world to the brink of nuclear war. Fourteen years after the first Berlin crisis the world seemed no nearer to a relaxation in Cold War tensions. Europe, and Germany, remained divided down the middle.

## The Rise of European Détente, 1963–75

October 1962 had seen the gravest of Cold War crises but was followed by a growing move towards détente in Europe. There were many reasons for this, not least the fact that the Cuban Missile crisis itself, by highlighting the dangers of nuclear war led to a relaxation in Superpower tensions, most notably in the August 1963 Test Ban Treaty, which restricted nuclear tests to underground explosions. A year later, in October 1964, Khruschev's fall from power also helped create a calmer atmosphere. Despite his talk of 'peaceful coexistence' Khruschev's brash personal style had provoked many dangerous moments in world affairs, and his own colleagues now accused him of 'harebrained scheming . . ., rash decisions and actions based on wishful thinking'. In part his actions had been designed to impress Russia's allies, especially the Chinese who continued to preach revolutionary Communism and a harsh anti-Western line. Khruschev's successors, Leonid Brezhnev and Alexei Kosygin, could not heal the Sino–Soviet breach, but they did pursue a less erratic foreign policy, preferring to build up Russia's nuclear arsenal (whose inferiority the Cuban crisis had demonstrated) rather than to bluster, rage and threaten the West. Their policy proved a success. Whereas, in 1964, the Russians had only about a quarter of America's total of ICBM's, six years later they had achieved parity. This was due in part, however, to America's decline into difficulties in the mid-1960s.

In November 1963 Kennedy was assassinated and the new President, Lyndon Johnson, lacking experience in foreign affairs, became increasingly involved in a war in Vietnam in South-east Asia. In 1964 Johnson won Congressional approval for aid to pro-Western South Vietnam in its struggle against 'Viet Cong' guerrillas who were supported by the Communist North. Between 1965 and 1969 US troop levels in South Vietnam mushroomed to over half a million, but proved of limited use against a determined guerrilla army whose members were indistinguishable from the people America was trying to defend. By 1968 the war was recognised to be 'unwinnable', it divided US society and was proving an enormous drain on economic resources. The policy of 'containment', which had guided Washington's foreign policy since 1947, was now undermined, because America seemed incapable of defeating Communism wherever and whenever it threatened. In Europe, meanwhile, America's reputation as the moral leader of the West suffered enormously because of the war. Vietnam helped to fuel student discontent over the state of Western society. European leaders who had feared since Korea that America's relentless anti-Communism would end in disaster gave Johnson little support and he did not stand for re-election in 1968. Instead Richard Nixon came to the White House with promises to end the Vietnam War, the intention of reshaping US policy to match its resources, and a desire for a new relationship with Moscow.

By 1961 the emergence of newly-independent states in Africa and Asia, the development of China as a powerful, independent Communist state and America's economic decline relative to Western Europe and Japan, all pointed to the emergence of a more sophisticated 'multi-polar' world. Even without Vietnam Western European nations would have taken a more independent line from America. By the late 1950s European states had not only recovered from the war, but had achieved remarkable economic growth. This allowed the development of freer trade with America, on lines envisaged at Bretton Woods in 1944, but it also created problems in Atlantic relations. Europeans were concerned at the expansion of American investment into Europe; Americans began to see the Common Market (created by France, Germany, Italy and the Benelux states), as a trade rival and argued that Europe should pay more for its own defence. Differences also grew on military-political issues. By the late 1950s some European leaders, including (to Soviet concern) the West Germans, believed that Europeans should share in the control of NATO's nuclear arsenal, and in 1958 General de Gaulle proposed a US–British–French 'directorate' to define the West's global strategy. The Cuban missile crisis heightened fears on the Continent that a US–Soviet nuclear conflict could occur without any European control over events and de Gaulle decided that France, which had exploded its first atomic bomb in 1960, must develop its own independent nuclear force. Growing Soviet nuclear capabilities over the decade also led Europeans to ask whether America really would risk a war with Russia to defend them. In the 1950s Dulles' threat of 'massive retaliation' in the event of war, did not seem unrealistic but by the 1970s a position of 'mutually-assured destruction' was reached between the Superpowers. NATO planning had accordingly to be adjusted in 1967 to a policy of 'escalated' response in the event of Soviet attack: conventional weapons, then short-range nuclear weapons, would be used before engaging in full nuclear exchange.

The greatest exponent in the 1960s of a European policy independent of Washington was Charles de Gaulle who never accepted that France should be subsidiary to US ideological leadership. Raised amidst memories of defeat by Prussia in 1870, de Gaulle had become a soldier and developed an almost religious belief in French greatness. In the 1950s he had condemned the French Fourth Republic as a weak regime, vacillating in its policies, too often a victim rather than a shaper of international events. In 1958 he founded a new Republic which would reflect French *grandeur*. De Gaulle's romantic notions were balanced by a harsh realism. He gave France stronger armed forces, insisted that she be respected on the world stage and believed that she must rely on her own resources for survival. Yet he recognised too that France was no Superpower, he was ready to retreat when necessary and he knew that, in the last analysis, Europe needed America to balance the USSR. He was a *realpolitiker*, believing nation-states were the prime actors in world affairs and that they operated by the logic of the balance of power. In general it can be said that he sought to maximise France's role, and her freedom of choice in any given situation. He gave the French people a new pride in themselves, especially with such successful developments as the nuclear *force de frappe* (even though this did not become a realistic deterrent until the later 1970s). So far as NATO was concerned, de Gaulle recognised the value of alliances in traditional diplomacy but believed that they should also preserve the military and diplomatic independence of their members. He felt NATO was too restrictive in this sense and subject to domination by the Anglo-Saxon powers, America and Britain. So far as Cold War issues were concerned, de Gaulle was an anti-Communist but he believed that the bi-polar world of the 1950s had brought an ever-present threat of nuclear conflagration and effectively left the Superpowers as the only states with true independence in foreign affairs. He looked back to the Yalta conference as the beginning of a betrayal of European interests by the Superpowers and was determined to assert a new 'European' role in world affairs, which would also reduce East–West tensions.

De Gaulle's pressure for a US–British–French directorate in NATO in 1958 showed his resentment of 'Anglo-Saxon' predominance and his desire for a leading role in events. When the Americans and British refused to grant his request he pulled the French Mediterranean fleet out of NATO. In 1961–3, he was completely unenthusiastic about Kennedy's desire to improve US–European co-operation and did most to undermine an American proposal for a 'multi-lateral nuclear force' within NATO. De Gaulle saw all such plans as a way to reshape US domination of Western Europe. By 1963 de Gaulle was securely in power as French President and had settled his most pressing original problem, the colonial war in Algeria. He was ready therefore to pursue a more forthright foreign policy. In January 1963 he vetoed an attempt by America's closest ally, Britain, to join the European Common Market and made a treaty with West Germany which provided for consultation on military, diplomatic and cultural issues. Such an alliance, with France's age-old enemy, showed de Gaulle's ability to adjust to new realities, and strengthened France's hand in Europe and the Western alliance. In 1964 came another example of the General's realism when, to the displeasure of both America and Russia, he entered into diplomatic relations with China. China's rift with Moscow, and other evidence of the breakdown of Soviet control in the Communist bloc, had given encouragement to de Gaulle's own policy of greater independence within the Western alliance. In Eastern Europe Yugoslavia had long since broken free of Soviet domination and by the mid-1960s other countries, most notably Romania, were successfully showing independence in their foreign policy. As well as the link to China, de Gaulle established economic and cultural ties with Eastern European countries. In the long-term he hoped that Soviet control over them would break down, allowing the re-creation of a common identity in Europe 'from the Atlantic to the Urals'.

On 7 March 1966 de Gaulle, in his most dramatic action so far, informed President Johnson that France, whilst remaining a signatory of the Atlantic Pact, was quitting the alliance's military organisation. NATO was thrown into turmoil. French forces left the integrated command, NATO forces left French soil and the alliance headquarters had to be moved from Fontainebleau to Brussels. Opponents pointed out that, if everyone behaved as de Gaulle had done, US troops would be forced out of Europe altogether and the alliance would disintegrate. The sense of crisis was made worse in the middle of the year when, as the pinnacle of his détente policy, de Gaulle visited Moscow. NATO, however, survived. Johnson chose not to argue with de Gaulle and no other state followed de Gaulle's path. The US, increasingly troubled in Vietnam, was itself developing détente in the mid-1960s: Johnson and Kosygin met in June 1967 and another step in arms control was taken in July 1968 when America, Russia and Britain signed a Non-proliferation Treaty to prevent the spread of nuclear weapons to other States. Then, however, in August 1968, détente stalled as Soviet tanks, emulating the Hungary operation of 1956, invaded Czechoslovakia to put an end to the liberalising government of Alexander Dubcek. Once more the West could do nothing to oppose the Russian action. Again the fundamental ideological differences between East and West were confirmed, further steps towards détente were set back and, whatever de Gaulle's hopes, Soviet predominance in eastern Europe was confirmed. This predominance was justified after November 1968 by the 'Brezhnev doctrine', a statement by the Soviet leader that any move away from Communism in an Eastern bloc state would be treated as a menace to all states in the bloc.

When the opportunities for détente revived after 1969 de Gaulle had left office and West Germany, not France, became the driving force in contacts with Russia. After the Berlin Wall crisis the Bonn government had had to accept that Adenauer's hope of reuniting Germany on Western terms was impossible to fulfil in the foreseeable future. In 1963 the ageing Adenauer finally resigned and the new Chancellor, Ludwig Erhard, began to establish tentative trade links with eastern Europe. Erhard was succeeded in 1966 by Kurt Kiesinger in a coalition which included the Social Democrats. Their leader, Willy Brandt, became foreign minister. Brandt was determined to develop co-operation with eastern Europe in the hope of reducing tension in Europe and building up the independence of eastern states, and he believed that East Germany's existence must be treated as a reality. Most importantly he abandoned the increasingly untenable 'Hallstein Doctrine',* and began to enter into diplomatic relations with countries who recognised East Germany. Under West German and French pressure the NATO countries made an important decision in 1967 to change the alliance's function. Following the Harmel Report members

---

* The Hallstein Doctrine – so called after Dr Walter Hallstein, a confidant of Adenauer – led to the severance of relations with Yugoslavia in 1957 and with Cuba in 1963, however, relations with the Soviet Union remained unaffected.

agreed that NATO should have a political role, negotiating for détente with the eastern bloc, as well as its traditional defence role. In 1967 too the Warsaw Pact states declared that West Germany should recognise East Germany as the first step to meaningful détente but Brandt could not yet go so far: most West Germans still hoped for the reunification of Germany. Soon after becoming Chancellor in 1969, however, he said that contacts with East Germany must be developed and offered to settle past differences with Russia and Poland.

Brandt's *Ostpolitik* (eastern policy) did not please everyone. The East German government was suspicious of Western intentions and two meetings between Brandt and the East German premier, Willi Stolph, in 1970 – though dramatic events in themselves – failed to make much progress. In France and elsewhere there were fears that West German independence in foreign affairs could lead to a resurgence of extreme nationalism. There were also doubts about Brandt in America. President Nixon, and his National Security Adviser, Henry Kissinger were themselves realists ready to pursue détente with Russia. The two men knew that the USSR had matched them in nuclear terms, believed that the Soviets could help to extricate America from the 'unwinnable' Vietnam war, and hoped to deal with Russia on rational, balance-of-power terms instead of the ideological rivalry of the past. Leonid Brezhnev, now the undisputed Soviet leader, was keen to accept a position of equality with America and to seek agreements which would legitimise Moscow's position in Eastern Europe and limit the economic burden of military spending. But there were important differences between America and Russia in the Middle East and other areas of the Third World in 1970, the year in which Brandt signed non-aggression treaties with the USSR and Poland. Kissinger in particular believed that there must be a 'linkage' between Western concessions to Russia and Soviet good behaviour in the Third World, but Brandt did not keep Washington fully informed of developments in *Ostpolitik*. It seemed therefore that he might outrun America in making agreements with Moscow and provoke a breach with Washington. In fact this did not occur for a number of reasons. Brandt never intended to disrupt the American alliance, on which West German security rested, and his Western allies in any case had one important pressure-point to use against him: US–British–French approval was needed, as occupation powers, for any agreement with East Germany on Berlin, which was a vital part of *Ostpolitik*. Also, in 1971–2, US support for détente increased until, at Moscow, in May 1972, Nixon and Brezhnev finally met and signed a Strategic Arms Limitation Treaty (SALT) limiting the number of inter-continental range missiles on each side. In September 1971 an agreement between Russia and the Western powers acknowledged the division of Berlin, and recognised West Berlin's status as an area linked to, but constitutionally separate from, West Germany. This paved the way to the ratification of the Soviet and Polish non-aggression treaties with Bonn and to the signature, in December 1972, of a 'Basic Treaty' between East and West Germany which, without ending hopes of reunification, accepted the divided nature of Germany and the need for closer personal and commercial ties between the two halves.

*Ostpolitik* brought great rewards for Brandt. He won the Nobel Peace Prize in 1971 and was re-elected Chancellor in November 1972. The acceptance of the 'two Germanies' and of a divided Berlin helped remove the gravest threat to peace and stability in central Europe. It paved the way for expanded West German trade with the Eastern bloc and for greater personal links between the two. More than this, it also paved the way for wider talks on European security. In 1969 NATO had agreed that progress in Germany should lead to a conference on European security which Moscow had wanted since the 1950s. In July 1973, after months of preliminary exchanges, a meeting of foreign ministers agreed to proceed with such talks which took place over the next two years. Thirty-five countries eventually signed the August 1975 'Helsinki Accords' which resulted. The signatories included NATO states (America amongst them), Warsaw Pact members, and neutrals. The Accords were negotiated despite great problems within NATO in the early 1970s. America's deepening economic problems had forced Nixon to introduce import restrictions in 1971 and to end the system, founded at Bretton Woods in 1944, whereby all Western currencies were valued against the dollar. These measures, introduced quite suddenly, led to considerable economic problems in the capitalist world. They simply reflected the decline in America's ability to shape world events since the Cuban Missile Crisis ten years before. The continued strengthening of the European and Japanese economies in the 1960s, the costs of Vietnam and of a large military arsenal, and demands for social reform at home had all taken their toll on American power. The US still carried much of the burden of NATO defence and undoubtedly remained the most powerful state in the world, but its relative superiority to other states was not what it had been in the 1950s. Some Americans wanted to cut down their force levels in Europe.

Nixon and Kissinger sought to readjust to new realities through the policy of détente, accepting Russian nuclear parity and satisfying Western Europe's desire for a relaxation of tensions. Kissinger even hoped to make 1973 the 'Year of Europe' in which the Atlantic alliance could be restored to full health, ending the distrust between America and Europe which had developed in the 1960s. But 1973 instead became most significant for the October Arab–Israeli War and a quadrupling of oil prices which further deepened the West's economic difficulties. Even the process of détente caused NATO problems, since some Europeans feared that US–Soviet co-operation would merely lead the Superpowers to control the Continent by 'condominium' (co-operation) rather than competition. The Helsinki Accords were significant in part because they showed that America and the Europeans *could* work together in defining Western aims, especially in the field of détente, and gave hope of lasting stability in Europe. The Accords included items to please both East and West. The Soviets obtained what they had hoped for since the war: an agreement that European borders should be changed only by

19

peaceful means, which in effect recognised the post-war settlement in Eastern Europe. For the West, however, there were promises of greater respect for human rights in the Soviet bloc and of increased East–West contacts, all of which could lead to an easing in Russian domination of Eastern Europe. Taken together the 1972 Basic Treaty on Germany and the 1975 Accords seemed effectively to provide Europe with what it had lacked since 1945: a post-war peace settlement based on the acceptance of the Continent's division.

## The 'New' Cold War and the Survival of European Détente, 1976–89

Despite the successful negotiation of the Helsinki Accords the years after 1975 saw the decline of détente and the reassertion of Cold War attitudes, even though strong support continued in Europe for East–West contacts. In themselves the Helsinki Accords had many flaws. The Helsinki 'Final Act' was not a binding treaty but rather a series of pledges. Critics argued that it had legitimised the Soviet system in Eastern Europe without providing anything meaningful in return. The promises on human rights seemed as tenuous as the Declaration on Liberated Europe, issued at Yalta 30 years before, and it was difficult to reconcile the Helsinki pledge to refrain from interference in other countries' affairs with the Brezhnev doctrine. In fact the principle of non-interference was invoked by Brezhnev himself after 1975 in response to Western criticisms about human rights violations in the Communist bloc. Russian dissidents, like the nuclear scientist Andrei Sakharov, continued to be harassed and in Czechoslovakia leaders of the 'Charter 77' group, set up to monitor human rights, were arrested in 1979. For all that, Helsinki did have its defenders. West European governments never expected the Final Act to work an instant revolution in international affairs and it was always understood that many questions lay beyond its scope. On military issues, for example, detailed discussions on 'Mutual and Balanced Force Reduction' (MBFR) in central Europe were handled by quite separate talks, begun in Vienna in 1973, which were to prove exceedingly long and complex. Helsinki was intended to be a step towards further conversations and, like Yalta, its recognition of European borders was not so much a 'betrayal' of those under Soviet domination as a recognition of hard facts. After all, no one had actually been ready, in 1956 or 1968, to help East Europeans fight for liberty. By providing Moscow with reassurance on the question of borders it was hoped to pave the way to greater contacts across the iron curtain and evolutionary changes in Eastern Europe.

Even before Helsinki, however, many Americans concluded that détente was beneficial only to the Soviets. Nixon's three summits with Brezhnev in 1972–4, SALT and the end of US involvement in Vietnam (January 1973) seemed to show the benefits of a relaxation in tension, yet many agreements with Russia drew criticism. SALT, for example, gave the Soviets an advantage in the number of ICBM's (even if the US maintained predominance in total numbers of warheads); grain sales to Russia helped Brezhnev solve his agricultural problems but upset US markets; Jewish emigration from the USSR increased but not enough to please the critics so that the US Congress (under the Jackson–Vanik amendment) decided to tie economic deals with Russia to greater Jewish emigration. There were worries too about the success of 'Euro-Communist' parties in France and more especially Italy, who had increased their appeal after 1968 by becoming more independent of Moscow and there were fears that the Kremlin would exploit political instability in Portugal in the mid-1970s. A basic, underlying problem was that the Soviets never accepted Kissinger's concept of 'linkage' whereby the Kremlin would desist from harming Western interests in return for concessions. For Moscow, agreements in certain areas, such as arms control, did *not* preclude competition in others, especially Third World conflicts. To US annoyance, Brezhnev supported the Arab cause in the 1973 Middle East war and helped a Marxist government come to power in Angola in 1975. In this situation the US government could not maintain the inflated hopes about détente which had built up in 1971–3. Nixon's forced resignation over the 'Watergate' political scandal in 1974, together with the fall of South Vietnam to Communism in 1975, were major blows to US self-confidence, and the 1976 election revealed two clear alternatives to the *realpolitik* of Nixon and his successor Gerald Ford. On the Right, Ronald Reagan represented a desire to return to a position of military strength and simple 1950s-style anti-communism, whilst the eventual victor, Democrat Jimmy Carter represented a new accent on liberal-idealism.

Carter's intentions were, in many ways, laudable and he had some successes, notably in bringing an Israeli–Egyptian peace treaty in 1978. However, his desire to secure human rights in Eastern Europe led to immediate arguments with Brezhnev and Soviet–American relations continued to be troubled in other areas. Carter upset Russia by establishing full diplomatic relations with China; Brezhnev upset America by supporting Ethiopia in a war against Somalia in 1977. Carter did try to maintain détente and the continuing Soviet desire for arms control led to a SALT II treaty being signed with Brezhnev, in Vienna, in mid-1979. But Vienna proved to be the last summit for six years and SALT II was never ratified by the US Senate, for in December the Red Army invaded neighbouring Afghanistan in order to prop up a weak Marxist government. For Americans, faced, they believed, with Communist expansionism throughout the Third World, this was the last straw. The Cold War was renewed.

As so often before, Europe found it difficult to escape the effects of a deterioration in US–Soviet relations. The moves towards European détente since the 1960s had nonetheless preserved the institutions of Cold War intact. NATO and Warsaw Pact forces faced each other across the Elbe, Germany was still divided, the Red Army remained in Eastern Europe and, despite the rise of the Common Market, Western Europe relied on the US as a military guarantor. It was easy therefore for East and

West to divide once more. The Belgrade conference on security and co-operation in Europe (CSCE) of 1977–8, designed to follow up the 1975 Helsinki decisions, proved how difficult it would be to break down East–West suspicions. Its lengthy sessions failed to achieve anything of note. Meanwhile, military questions in Europe continued to sour both détente and relations within NATO. Under President Ford leading Western states had begun to tackle their economic differences with greater determination. The first 'economic summit' of the major capitalist powers was held at Rambouillet in November 1975. Carter came to office determined to improve relations with Western Europe (and Japan) but his tendency towards indecision and contradictory actions soon had its effect on NATO. In late 1977 Carter successfully pressed NATO to deploy a new 'neutron' bomb on the Continent. The bomb, whose 'clean' radiation could kill humans without harming buildings, was morally repulsive to many but seemed the ideal weapon to use against the Warsaw Pact's armoury of tanks. Hardly had West European leaders accepted the proposal – risking popular opposition – than Carter changed his mind and cancelled the weapon. The French and German leaders, Giscard d'Estaing and Helmut Schmidt, who had a good personal relationship were especially concerned at Carter's vacillating behaviour. On the one hand Europe favoured détente, but on the other, they also needed US protection and were concerned that, if the worst came to the worst, Carter would not be prepared to go to war to save Europe. Such fears, which were particularly strong in West Germany, were heightened when the USSR deployed new SS-20 missiles in Europe at a time when NATO's intermediate range nuclear missiles (that is missiles of less than inter-continental range) were becoming outdated. The policy of 'escalated' response was under threat: the Soviets might be able to threaten Western Europe without NATO having any credible response.

In December 1979 NATO tried to resolve its dilemmas over détente and nuclear weapons with the adoption of a 'dual track' policy. The alliance was ready to hold talks with Russia on intermediate-nuclear force (INF) reductions in Europe, but at the same time would update its own defences by introducing 'cruise' missiles to Europe. 'Cruise', with its ability to penetrate Soviet radar, was seen as a riposte to the SS-20, and might also force meaningful concessions from Moscow. Immediately afterwards, however, came the Afghanistan invasion, which produced more problems for détente and US–European relations. Many Europeans were prepared to treat the far-off Soviet operation as a defensive action in line with the Brezhnev doctrine. Giscard d'Estaing even went to meet Brezhnev in May 1980 to ease the sense of crisis. Brezhnev himself probably hoped Afghanistan would be a swift, successful operation, like Czechoslovakia in 1968, which would do no lasting damage to Russia's world standing. In America, however, there was consternation at this, the first advance by the Red Army beyond the conquests made in World War II, and one which signified a threat to the already troubled Persian Gulf. Carter openly admitted that his past faith in Russia had been misplaced and the critics of détente seemed vindicated. As the Soviets became involved in a long struggle with Afghan guerrillas, similar in some respects to America's involvement in Vietnam, Carter began to take punitive measures against Moscow but without fully consulting his NATO allies. His most public action, the boycott of the 1980 Olympic Games in Moscow, won little support outside America.

However, if Europeans were exasperated with Carter, many had little liking either for the man who beat him in the November presidential elections. Ronald Reagan, with his crude, moralising attacks on Russia's 'evil Empire', his readiness to engage in military action (such as the invasion of the Caribbean island of Grenada in 1983), and his massive increase in military spending (which helped drive America deeply into debt) seemed disturbing to many Europeans. Differences soon arose between Reagan and, in particular, Helmut Schmidt, on a growing crisis in Poland, where a series of strikes, sparked off by high prices and food shortages, had broken out during 1980. The strikes had taken on an important political dimension when workers formed a free trades union 'Solidarity', and in 1981 it seemed that Soviet tanks would be needed to restore order. An invasion was avoided when, in October, Poland found its own military leader, General Wojtech Jaruzelski, who introduced martial law. But this harsh action was condemned by Reagan who called for punitive measures against the Eastern bloc, threatened to cut off all talks with Moscow and asked that Western aid be ended for an oil-gas pipeline which was being constructed from Soviet Siberia into Europe. To this the West Germans and others responded that Poland should be left to resolve its own internal difficulties. West Europeans had no wish to end their growing economic ties with the Eastern bloc, nor did Schmidt wish to damage the relationship built by Brandt and himself with East Germany.

In retrospect Reagan's policies could be positively judged. He gave renewed confidence and certainty to America after two troubled decades, his military actions were limited in scale and he eventually proved ready to talk with Moscow. The 'new' Cold War of 1979–85 had no war crises equivalent to Berlin in 1948 or Cuba in 1962 which pitted the Superpowers directly against one another. Reagan's anti-Communism did find sympathy in Europe, from Britain's Margaret Thatcher and, after 1982, from the new German Chancellor, Helmut Kohl. Furthermore the new Cold War did not end all East–West contacts. Another conference on security and co-operation in Europe (CSCE) to follow up Helsinki was held in Madrid in 1980–83. It saw little more than arguments over who had done most to break the 1975 Final Act; but the fact that it continued to meet held out the hope of more fruitful conversations in future. It even proved possible, in late 1981, to begin the INF talks which NATO wanted, and it was Reagan who took the most dramatic initiative in these with a proposal to destroy all US and Soviet intermediate-range missiles in Europe, the so-called 'zero option'. Despite the failure to ratify SALT II both Superpowers adhered to the terms of the treaty (they continued to do so until 1986) and in mid-1982 a new round of talks on strategic weapons began, called START, which aimed not simply to place limits on strategic arms but to *reduce* them.

If Reagan did prove bellicose during his first terms as President he was amply repaid by the Kremlin whose ageing leaders appeared unable to take any positive initiatives. Brezhnev died in November 1982, his successor, Yuri Andropov lasted little more than a year, and Konstantin Chernenko survived only until March 1985. Foreign policy remained throughout in the hands of the veteran foreign minister Andrei Gromyko, in office since 1957, who favoured a tough line with Washington. In the early 1980s Moscow refused to accept that its new SS-20s upset the military balance in Europe, relying perhaps on widespread anti-nuclear protests in Western Europe to prevent the introduction of new American weapons. When the deployment of 'cruise' missiles began nonetheless on schedule in 1983, the Soviets walked out of both the INF and START talks and in 1984 tensions seemed worse than ever. Eastern bloc states refused to attend the Los Angeles Olympic Games, East Germany's Erich Honecker cancelled a visit to West Germany, and Reagan was re-elected as US President. There were signs, however, of a continuing desire for détente even in Eastern Europe. East Germany and Hungary, for example, clearly wished to develop economic ties with Western Europe and were dissatisfied with Kremlin policies, whilst Romania broke ranks and sent an Olympic team to America.

In March 1985 two important changes on the Soviet side helped to relieve the image of an unremitting East–West struggle. First, having failed to prevent the arrival of 'cruise', Moscow reopened the INF talks. Second, and more important, came the succession of Mikhail Gorbachev to the Soviet leadership. Like Khruschev 30 years earlier, Gorbachev was a relatively young and dynamic individual, who combined a determination to reform inside the Soviet Union with a desire for détente outside. Unlike Khruschev, Gorbachev had been raised after the 1917 revolution, was less concerned with ideological radicalism and more interested in the protection and strengthening of the USSR than in an active Third World policy. His moves within Russia towards 'openness' (*glasnost*), accompanied as they were by freer elections and the release of dissidents, including Sakharov in 1986, impressed Western public opinion. Gorbachev eventually proved willing not only to condemn Stalin for the imprisonment and execution of loyal Russians in the 1930s, but also to concede that Stalin had secretly divided eastern Europe with Hitler in 1939. The new leader reduced Soviet involvement in Third World conflicts, and even withdrew the Red Army from Afghanistan in early 1989, leaving the Communist regime there to fend for itself.

In his dealings with Washington, Gorbachev soon proved adept at public relations, adopting a US-style Presidential image, and announcing such dramatic, unilateral concessions as a moratorium on nuclear tests. Within a few years some observers even began to sense in his reforms the triumph of capitalism over Communism, in that the USSR seemed to be adopting

Western methods. To others, however, Gorbachev's policies marked a skilful attempt to gain the initiative in the international field, to end Reagan's massive rearmament effort, and allow the USSR to reform and strengthen itself for continued competition with the West. Faced by such diverse interpretations of the new adversary, the Reagan Presidency in 1985, rather than return to Kissinger's ideal of 'linkage' in a period of détente, decided to pursue a policy of 'constructive confrontation' with Moscow, accepting that certain agreements with Russia were possible even if she remained a rival on the world stage. In November Reagan met Gorbachev in Geneva, and though only minor agreements on bilateral co-operation were made this, the first summit since 1979, proved surprisingly friendly. In September 1986, another round of European security talks, in Stockholm, ended with an extensive agreement on the notification of military manoeuvres between NATO and the Warsaw Pact. The road to agreement was far from smooth. In October 1986 the second Gorbachev–Reagan summit at Reykjavik, ended in failure when the American refused to abandon his 'Strategic Defense Initiative', launched three years earlier, which aimed to create an anti-ballistic missile system. Progress only resumed in 1987, when the two leaders succeeded, at last, in signing an INF treaty in Washington in December. The treaty which entered into force in June 1988 was the most far-reaching arms agreement to date. It removed all missiles from Europe with ranges between 300 and 3000 miles, including the SS-20s and cruise. There was full provision for verification with each side able to investigate the other side's compliance with the treaty. The agreement excluded the British and French nuclear arsenals, and it came as welcome news to advocates of nuclear disarmament, but ironically the INF treaty upset NATO planners and Europeans like Chancellor Kohl who feared, once again, that the agreement would harm the policy of an escalated response to any Soviet attack. To obtain true security in Europe, NATO still wanted to see a reduction of Russia's conventional strength, which remained overwhelming, and as in the 1970s there was some concern that Moscow and Washington could together decide the fate of Europe without European representation.

Gorbachev himself tried to reassure West Europeans about his intentions by developing the idea of a 'common European house'. This term was first used in a speech in Prague in April 1987 which recognised Europe, despite its deep ideological rift, as a single cultural and historical entity 'from the Atlantic to the Urals', a phrase which echoed de Gaulle's vision of the 1960s. In April–July 1989 the Soviet leader visited West Germany, Britain and France and again talked of a common European home, but it was still not clear what, in practical terms, this amounted to. More reassuring in terms of Soviet policy was Gorbachev's dramatic decision to allow a non-Communist premier to come to power in Poland. This not only marked the end of the Brezhnev Doctrine, it also heralded a rapid disintegration of the Soviet position in Eastern Europe,* and brought the

* See Chapter 8, Section four.

25

Cold War very definitely to an end. The system created in 1945–9 – when Stalin had established a series of puppet regimes in power in the East, and Europe had become ideologically, economically and militarily divided – now unravelled itself with astonishing speed. In most countries 'market economics' were now the aim, democratic elections were planned and the word 'communism' was frequently abandoned, even by the Communist parties. Radical change was embraced most enthusiastically in Poland, Hungary and, after a critical interlude, in Czechoslovakia, whilst in East Germany there were moves towards reunification with the West. In contrast to 1956, when Khruschev's call for reform in the East had soon led to a Soviet clampdown, Gorbachev's desire for change included an acceptance of political pluralism.

In America the debate at the end of 1989 was no longer whether Gorbachev's desire for reform was sincere, but whether he could survive its repercussions and President George Bush, the former Vice-President, who had succeeded Reagan in January 1989, was cautious about defining his Soviet policy. Bush and Gorbachev did not hold their first summit until December 1989 in Malta. By then it was clear that the relaxation of tensions between East and West had gone far beyond the détente of the 1970s, when the Atlantic alliance and Warsaw Pact had remained strong and tensions had been eased only against a background of continuing ideological competition between the two sides. There was some debate about whether Western policy had contributed to the Communists' demise. Supporters of détente in the 1970s could argue that personal contacts, trade and the Helsinki agreements had undermined the Soviet hold on the East, but opponents of détente could counter that Reagan's Cold War policies had helped to put unbearable strains on the Soviet economy, which now seemed on the verge of collapse. At all events it seemed that the Cold War, if it had a victor, had been won by the West. Khruschev's boasts in the late 1950s, that Communism would outstrip capitalism by the 1980s, had proved as empty as his threats over Berlin. The US State Department's Francis Fukuyama even dared to talk of the 'end of history' by which he meant that the ideological struggle between Marxist-Leninism and liberal democracy had resulted in such a clear victory for the latter that its predominance in future could not be challenged. Not only in Europe, but also in Afghanistan, Africa and East Asia, the Soviet Empire now drew in its horns.

Yet talk of a Western victory did not mean that Europe's problems could be solved easily. The Warsaw Pact might no longer be a threat to the West, but what was the future of NATO in the new era where Allied nations sought to realise the so-called 'peace dividend' by cutting defence spending? Cold War tensions might be at an end but did the Soviets not retain a huge nuclear arsenal, and how quickly could Strategic Arms Reduction Talks (START) be expected to progress? And could the CSCE talks be turned into a forum for meaningful co-operation between the two halves of Europe, plus America, leading perhaps to Gorbachev's 'common European house'? The international agenda in Europe may have changed beyond belief in the closing months of 1989 but the leaders of East and West were as unprepared for this as anyone else. Those who had to live with the legacy of Cold War did not necessarily have a future that was any clearer or simpler than those who inherited the remains of Hitler's Europe four and a half decades earlier.

# 2
# Western European Unity

## The Birth of the Ideal, 1945–50

The ideal of European unification existed long before 1945, at first arguably in the mediaeval notion of 'Christendom', and political philosophers, like Jean-Jacques Rousseau and Jeremy Bentham, had sometimes devised schemes for European co-operation. Yet the European political reality until the twentieth century was one of disunity and conflict, culminating in the two World Wars. It was these wars, unsurprisingly, which did most to give life to the ideal of unity. In 1918, liberal-internationalists proposed the League of Nations as a forum in which to resolve disputes by peaceful means on a *global* scale, but specifically European unity was also proposed by individuals like the Austrian Count Coudenhove-Kalergi. In 1929–30 the ideal finally reached the political agenda as a serious proposition when the French foreign minister, Aristide Briand, proposed a study of a United Europe as a way, first, to match the growing economic might of the USA and, second, to control the political strength of Germany within Europe. Unfortunately Briand's scheme was rapidly overtaken by the effects of the 'slump' and the rise of militant nationalism in the 1930s.

The Second World War brought unity proposals more securely to the fore in surprisingly diverse places. Hitler sought to create a 'New Order' in Europe and to portray his invasion of Russia as a latter-day crusade against Bolshevism. In June 1940 Britain proposed an 'indissoluble union' to France, in a last desperate bid to keep the latter in the war. Resistance groups on the Continent frequently produced schemes for a European structure which could prevent another war and some were ready to create a political federation. In London representatives of the Belgian, Dutch and Norwegian governments-in-exile all hoped for British leadership of a post-war alliance system, and many British officials and ministers came to believe that a 'western bloc' could both control Germany in future and bolster British standing in the world *vis-à-vis* America and Russia. The British, like Norway's Trygve Lie (who conceived of an 'Atlantic' defence system), at first thought mainly in terms of a military alliance, but others, like Belgium's Paul-Henri Spaak, wanted to see economic co-operation.

In September 1944 the leaders of Belgium, Holland and Luxembourg declared their intention to form the Benelux customs union. Meanwhile Charles de Gaulle's Free French also looked at European co-operation. His officials were particularly interested in the economic potential of European unity, which could help French post-war reconstruction, and also in ideas for controlling Germany within a European framework.

Despite these proposals the world in 1945 seemed likely to return to old ways of thinking. The great powers, America, Britain and Russia, dominated the peace-making process and hopes for world peace rested on the global UN. Britain and France, the two countries who seemed essential to European co-operation, bickered over their interests in the Middle East and over the peace conditions to impose on Germany, so that an Anglo–French alliance was not made until March 1947. Even the modest Benelux union was greeted with scepticism by Belgian civil servants and a single customs system was not established by its three members until January 1948. A treaty to create a full Benelux economic union was not finalised until ten years after that. In 1945 West European leaders were very reluctant to pursue co-operation because of fears that this could antagonise the Russians – who might see it as an alliance against them – or the Americans – who were opposed to spheres of influence and to closed trading blocs.

It was only after late 1946, inspired in part by a speech in Zurich by Winston Churchill, that support for European unity really began to gather pace. This was for a number of reasons. Most obvious was the breakdown in US–Soviet relations and the failure of the UN to keep the peace. Europeans feared being overwhelmed by Cold War terrors and some hoped that, through greater unity, they could form a 'third force' to match America and Russia. In September 1947 Britain's foreign secretary, Ernest Bevin, and France's premier, Paul Ramadier, talked of uniting their colonial empires together, and socialist politicians including British premier Clement Attlee* hoped to give the third force an ideological dimension: against American capitalism and Soviet communism, Europe would stand as the champion of democratic socialism, combining liberal political rights with radical social reform. European economic integration was widely expected to bring enormous benefits since an extensive single trading area (such as existed in America) might allow larger-scale industrial production and greater efficiency.

Ideas of a third force proved impossible to realise at least in the short term. Europe was too shattered by war, too demoralised psychologically and too devastated materially, to match America or Russia in the near future. Proposals to tap the colonial resources of the West European powers had, furthermore, no chance of fulfilment. Pressures were now underway for decolonisation and, in any case, the economic exploitation of the colonies would have required a massive capital outlay which Europe could not possibly finance. A socialist third force on the other

* Who dedicated a radio broadcast to the issue in January 1948.

hand proved impossible because, to widespread surprise, it was Christian Democratic parties which emerged as the predominant political force in Western Europe after 1945. The fundamental problem with the third force, however, was that Cold War tensions became too pressing in 1947 for Europe to escape them. In 1946 some still believed that the unity of all Europe, East and West, might be possible. Within months this proved an illusion. Rather than seeking to match American strength Western Europe soon looked to Washington for protection from the Soviet Union. This did not mean that unity was ruled out however, for the Americans, far from opposing European economic unity, began to see this as the only way to create a firm barrier to communist expansion. Ironically it was an American proposal, the Marshall Plan, which really began the concrete moves towards West European integration in the summer of 1947 even though, at the same time, it hardened the division of the Continent between East and West. US Congressmen believed economic unity, by leading to greater efficiency, would guarantee that Marshall aid was well spent and even demanded evidence of greater integration before agreeing to support Marshall aid payments.

In 1949 many West European states joined America in making the NATO alliance and there were some at that time who believed in forging an 'Atlantic community'. But the US was determined to maintain its independence of Europe. Notwithstanding accusations that they had imperialist designs on Europe, Americans hoped that the Continent would soon be able to stand on its own feet, free of US support. In January 1948 a US official told the British ambassador that Europe must soon be able to say 'no' both to America and Russia. Marshall aid was intended to create European stability by 1952, making further aid unnecessary. In 1949, Congress was also assured that NATO did *not* imply a costly long-term commitment to Europe. As it transpired hopes of European economic recovery were amply fulfilled after 1948. But the continuation of the Cold War and Europe's reluctance to surrender American military protection, meant that substantial amounts of US military aid and large numbers of US troops became committed to the Continent on a permanent basis after the Korean War.

A major question in the late 1940s was the exact *form* which European integration should take. Amidst the myriad of small pro-unity organisations formed after 1946 there were many who favoured a continental federation, with a common parliament, cabinet and economic policy. But these were a tiny minority of the West European population and European governments did not take kindly to idealists who believed that a European parliament and an American-style single market could be created swiftly on a continent whose linguistic, cultural and socio-economic differences had been ingrained over centuries. Many countries, including the Scandinavians, Portugal and Greece, wished to go no further than traditional inter-governmental co-operation in Europe, preserving the sovereignty and independence of member states. When, in April 1948, West European states met in Paris and created the Organisation of

European Economic Co-operation (OEEC)* to supervise the Marshall aid programme, the Americans were upset that it was an inter-governmental body, working on a basis of unanimity. Many believed that the OEEC was inadequate to achieve far-reaching changes in economic conditions, yet actually it did succeed in lowering trade barriers and smoothing inter-European payments. Among the alternatives to inter-governmental co-operation some talked of creating a 'confederation' in which there would be certain central institutions whilst most authority rested with member states. A more popular idea by 1950 was 'functional' co-operation. 'Functionalism' was a pragmatic, evolutionary approach to co-operation which simply meant that integration should be pursued in certain selected areas (or 'sectors') of the economy. A common European institution might be created, for example, to supervise the production and marketing of iron and steel. Functionalism in itself, however, did not answer a key question: whether there should be a continuation of inter-governmental co-operation or a loss of sovereignty to 'supranational' institutions, able to make *binding* decisions on their members.

By early 1950 it was clear that certain countries, foremost among them France, Italy and the Benelux states, *were* ready to consider a partial loss of sovereignty to supranational institutions. This was not through any idealistic belief in unity for its own sake, but because of the way these states viewed their national interests. The Benelux states had by then progressed with their own customs union and found that, by acting together, they could have a greater impact on international events. This was best demonstrated when they negotiated the Brussels Pact military alliance with Britain and France in March 1948. Italians, like premier Alcide Gasperi, sought an active, co-operative role in Europe in order to restore their international reputation after the Mussolini era, and believed their backward economy would gain from European links. The most important advocate of supranational co-operation, however, was France. It has been seen that French wartime planners believed that France could gain from European economic co-operation. This would provide access to larger markets and raw materials, and make industry more efficient. In August 1947 talks were initiated on a Franco–Italian customs union and in 1949 were extended to the Benelux states, in the so-called 'Fritalux' talks. France also wanted to give supranational powers to the OEEC.

What strengthened French commitment to European unity enormously in 1948–50 was the German problem. After three German invasions in living memory, French foreign policy was deeply concerned with Germany's future after 1945. Originally de Gaulle hoped to sever important economic and strategic areas from Germany: the Ruhr industrial basin would become an international asset, its resources tapped for the benefit of all mankind; the coal-rich Saarland would be in economic union with France; the Rhineland would be under permanent military

* In 1961 the OEEC was joined by America and Canada and became the Organisation of Economic Co-operation and Development.

occupation. Such a draconian policy would both weaken Germany and provide resources (especially coal) to France to transform her into a heavy-industrial power. Unfortunately, except for the separation of the Saar from Germany, which was carried out in December 1946, none of the French aims proved acceptable to the other Allies. Instead in 1948–9 France, by then economically-reliant on America, was forced to accept the creation of a West German state, whilst German industry was revived as part of the Marshall Plan. All this was extremely disturbing and the French desperately sought a new way to control Germany's revival. Some foreign ministry officials (like Briand 20 years before) saw European unity as the only solution: France and Germany could join in European institutions as equals, with no need for special controls on Germany; but at the same time German economic independence would be restricted and German resources would be used for the good of a greater whole. German political ambitions would then be turned away from nationalism to Europeanism, and Western European co-operation would also prevent Germany being lured into the Soviet camp. Robert Schuman, the French foreign minister after July 1948 who had been raised on the Franco–German border, was attracted to European unity as a way to bring a *rapprochement* between the two countries.

The French interest in European unity was not shared to the same extent by Britain. It has often been asked why Britain, whose reputation stood high in Europe after 1940 and which was the Continent's wealthiest state in 1945, failed to take up the leadership of European unity. In fact, in 1945, foreign secretary Ernest Bevin was interested in economic, military and political ties to Western Europe, took a keen interest in proposals for a customs union during 1946–8 and encouraged European co-operation in January 1948 by calling for a 'Western Union' through which Europe, backed by America and the Empire–Commonwealth, would match the Soviet Union. Britain had a close affinity with the liberal-democratic and colonial states on the Continent, to whom she provided large-scale military and economic aid after the war. Furthermore Britain did take a leading role in the acceptance of Marshall aid from America, creating the Brussels Pact and forming NATO. However there were many reasons for British reticence regarding European co-operation. Britain had extensive non-European links to the Empire–Commonwealth, which were practical as well as emotional. About half British trade was with the Commonwealth and Sterling Area (countries trading in British currency) whereas only about a quarter was with Europe. Psychologically Britain, having escaped occupation during the war, felt separated from Europe and still thought in terms of maintaining her independent status as a great power.

In British eyes close co-operation also seemed difficult because of problems on the Continent. Post-war governments in France and Italy, the most important states, were weak coalitions, short-lived and threatened by strong communist parties; a Soviet invasion of continental Europe was not out of the question; and Labour politicians disliked the Christian Democratic predominance on the Continent. Studies of a European customs union in 1947–8 suggested that this would demand a revolution in British economic practices without necessarily bringing dramatic results. European economies were competitive, rather than complementary, in economic terms, and were all in debt to America. Uniting them would merely compound their dollar deficits into a larger whole. Neither – importantly – did Britain share France's obsession with the German problem. If Britain had an interest in European co-operation it was as a way to withstand Soviet pressure and underpin British independence, not as a way to control Germany. In January 1949 the British cabinet ruled that co-operation with Europe should not be taken so far that it compromised Britain's ability to survive as an independent state. By April 1949, when NATO was formed, Bevin had decided that British security was best founded, not on co-operation with the weak and irresolute Europeans, but on the 'special relationship' with America. Co-operation with Europe in inter-governmental institutions was still desirable, but Bevin now rejected all idea of a third force because this could undermine the US commitment to the Continent.

Differences between Britain and France were highlighted in 1948–9 in discussions leading to the foundation of the Council of Europe. In May 1948 numerous European political figures met at the Hague and called for the creation of a European parliament as well as an economic union. The parliament idea was taken up by the French. They saw a European Assembly as a way to mobilise public opinion behind European co-operation in general, and did not wish to give the new body any sovereign authority over governments. Britain's Labour party had shown no interest in the Hague Congress however and Ernest Bevin viewed the Assembly proposal as an impractical scheme. Long arguments between Bevin and Schuman followed before, in 1949, Bevin agreed to an Assembly being created. The Council of Europe, which most European states joined, met annually, went on to create the European Court of Human Rights and provided an early step towards co-operation with West Germany, which joined in 1950. At Bevin's suggestion, the Council was seated in Strasbourg as a symbol of Franco–German *rapprochement*. But the Assembly had purely consultative powers and real authority rested in a Council of Ministers, created at the same time, in which Britain could rely on support, from the Scandinavians and others, for strictly inter-governmental co-operation. The Assembly's first meeting, in September 1949, disappointed both Britain's Labour leaders (who condemned it as a 'talk shop') and European federalists (who recognised its powerlessness).

## The Foundation of the European Community, 1950–57

In Spring 1950 Britain remained the most powerful European state. Her vision of inter-governmental European co-operation within a wider

'Atlantic' framework seemed to have won out over schemes for more radical co-operation. Furthermore mutual antagonism between France and Germany was so great that it was commonly assumed that only Britain could act as an 'honest broker' to draw them together. It was then, however, that the French revolutionised the situation with the 'Schuman Plan', announced by the foreign minister on 8 May. The Schuman Plan was based on ideas which had been circulating for some time but was devised in detail by Jean Monnet, who was in charge of France's economic modernisation programme. The basic scheme was for a supranational High Authority to control the coal and steel industries of France, Germany and any other states which wished to join. The plan was intended to achieve several French objectives *vis-à-vis* Germany. By tying together the two most important heavy industries in a modern economy, the Schuman Plan would make war between the two countries unthinkable and foster a *rapprochement* between them. It would guarantee continued German coal to France's steel industry in Lorraine but would do this by a voluntary system, which Germany would join as an equal, rather than through the draconian controls which France had earlier favoured. The plan was designed to give France the initiative in German affairs which had been slipping away from her. Yet the Schuman Plan also had wider potential. It proved a major step towards effective supranational co-operation in Europe. It allowed coal and steel production on the Continent to be managed more effectively without the need for a restrictive 'cartel' of businessmen, such as had been formed by steel producers in the inter-war years. And the Plan would give Europeans a framework for activity which was removed from the institutions created to deal with the Cold War. France now offered Germany a road to the future not as part of a German–Soviet alliance or as an American bastion in Europe, but as part of a European entity. A final significant point is that the Schuman Plan did not require British membership in order to succeed and could proceed whether she joined or not.

Italy and Belgium were immediately interested in the Schuman Plan. Earlier talks on a Franco–Italian–Benelux customs union had come to little, partly because the economies involved were too competitive. France and Italy, for example, directly competed in wine and automobile production. But by extending co-operation to Germany a larger better-balanced economic union could be created. The Dutch were somewhat reluctant to enter an organisation without Britain, but in practice followed Belgium's lead. Holland in any case had a vested interest in Germany's revival as a market for her agricultural products. The US, having failed to persuade Britain or the OEEC to pursue a customs union, gave strong support to the Schuman Plan. Most important of all was the attitude of West Germany, whose membership was fundamental to the plan's success. Germans were resentful of France's post-war attempts to keep them under close control, and it could not automatically be expected that they would agree to join European institutions. That Germany did join the Schuman Plan had much to do with Chancellor Konrad Adenauer, who had been interested in European unity between the wars. He believed that only by tying Germany to the other liberal-democratic states could the country's nascent democracy be strengthened. Like Schuman and Italy's Alcide de Gasperi, Adenauer was a Christian Democrat who talked of the need to protect Western Europe's Romano–Christian culture from the 'barbarism' of the East. He had already made speeches in favour of European co-operation and even of a Franco–German union.

Adenauer gave the Schuman Plan his blessing even before it was announced. Ernest Bevin, however, was given no advance warning. The British studied the Plan and appreciated its importance for better Franco-German relations. But London disliked the condition, which Schuman had made a *non-negotiable* basis for talks on his Plan, that all member states must accept the principle of supranational co-operation. Why the French insisted on this condition was obvious: supranationalism was essential in order to create strong institutions which could limit Germany's industrial independence in future. The British however, as has been seen, did not share France's concern with Germany to the same extent and were reluctant to compromise their own independence in supranational bodies. By the beginning of June France, West Germany, Italy and the Benelux states, henceforward known as 'the Six', were ready to enter talks on the Schuman Plan. The Dutch, still reluctant to act without Britain, reserved their right to withdraw from the talks if they disliked the outcome. Some argued that Britain should join on a similar basis. The Labour government, however, argued that it would seem like an act of 'sabotage' if Britain entered the talks only to walk out at a later date.

By late July a conference between 'the Six' in Paris had agreed in principle on the basics of a High Authority. A treaty was signed in April 1951 and the European Coal–Steel Community (ECSC) was founded in August 1952 in Luxembourg, with Monnet as its first President. The ECSC treaty created the High Authority as an executive institution, with control over the members' coal and steel industries which would pursue common policies on prices, working conditions and the like. But the treaty also created a Council of Ministers, which met regularly and had to be consulted by the Authority. There was also a Court, to resolve disputes, and an Assembly (which met in the Council of Europe's chamber in Strasbourg) to provide a democratic element in what was already criticised as an over-bureaucratic organisation. The ECSC undoubtedly marked an important step in supranational co-operation. It drew together several countries in a common body which controlled important areas of the economy; it was a sign of Franco–German *rapprochement* and it paved the way for the full removal of post-war industrial controls on West Germany by the Western allies; it succeeded in overcoming doubt and opposition from politicians and industrialists; and it created a workable machinery. Common markets between the Six in coal and steel began to function during 1953. Yet the ECSC was a very restricted 'Europe', which excluded most OEEC members, and fell far short of a full federation.

By 1952, however, the attention of 'pro-Europeans' was focused not on the ECSC but on the European Defence Community (EDC). The US wish to rearm Germany in September 1950* had put the French policy of controlling Germany through European institutions at risk almost as soon as the Schuman Plan was launched. America's readiness to revive West Germany militarily and bring her into NATO terrified the French, who opposed the idea. Franco–German distrust then seemed as intense as ever but Jean Monnet suggested that the situation could be saved by extending the supranational principle from coal and steel to the defence field. Under the 'Pleven Plan', announced by premier René Pleven in October, France, Germany, and other interested states would join in a European Army. The most important point in the Plan was that there would be no independent German General Staff and therefore no German military menace. Again Adenauer, himself keen to avoid any revival of militarism in his country, proved ready to enter talks on the plan, which began in Paris in February 1951. So did Italy, Belgium and Luxembourg. The Dutch, still reluctant to act without Britain, eventually signed the EDC treaty with the rest of the Six in May 1952. In September 1952 the same countries began to discuss a European Political Community (EPC), which was provided for under the EDC treaty. Alcide de Gasperi was particularly interested in the EPC proposal which was initially vague but could eventually lead to a common parliament, a joint foreign policy and a full 'common market'. Despite such ambitions, the story of EDC was one of slow progress, continued Franco–German distrust and ultimate disaster, which also destroyed the EPC.

From the outset, despite the talk of 'equality' with Germany, the French were determined to be the prominent power in EDC. Whilst Germany was prevented from establishing an independent military command, other community members would retain their separate defence structures. West Germany's contingent in the European Army was restricted in size and in the types of weapons it could use, and the guarantees against German misbehaviour were so ornate that the EDC treaty had more than 150 articles. The French also insisted that, until the treaty was ratified by all the member states, West Germany should remain a state under Allied occupation. The EDC treaty signature in May 1952 was followed by a series of problems. It took almost a year before the German supreme court judged that membership of the EDC was legal under the country's constitution. Meanwhile opposition to the treaty in France mounted. By 1953 the international situation and the French political situation differed radically from that of 1950 when the Pleven Plan was launched. The Korean War, which had caused the US to propose German rearmament in the first place, had settled into stalemate and the danger of a Soviet invasion of Western Europe had receded: German rearmament no longer seemed necessary. France's commitment of troops to the Indochina war brought fears that she would be outnumbered by German forces in the European theatre. Furthermore the 1951 French elections had brought

* See p 9.

a considerable number of Gaullists into the National Assembly who opposed EDC, not so much because it meant arming German soldiers, but because it would 'surrender' the command of the French Army to a supranational institution. This was an important line of argument which showed that many French people did not relish the idea of losing their independence to European bodies. The growing discontent over EDC led to the replacement of foreign minister Schuman by the more nationalist Georges Bidault at the end of 1952.

In June 1954 a more dynamic nationalist, Pierre Mendès-France, became both premier and foreign minister of France. He found the country to be bitterly divided over EDC. In August he tried to win the rest of the Six over to major changes in the treaty which would reduce its supranational content and allow French forces greater freedom of action to please the Gaullists. But Adenauer, Spaak and the others were exasperated with French delays and would not agree. Finally, on 30 August, the long and divisive debate was brought to an end when the French Assembly refused to ratify EDC.

The collapse of EDC was a bitter blow to the European movement, made worse by the fact that in October, after a crisis which threatened to rend the Atlantic alliance apart, France accepted West German rearmament within NATO, the very thing she had rejected in 1950. Mendès-France thereby demonstrated that it was more important to him to keep the French army free from supranational controls than it was to prevent German rearmament. What is more, Mendès-France agreed to join in a new, non-supranational organisation proposed by the British in the midst of the crisis, called the Western European Union (WEU). In effect the WEU marked the resuscitation and expansion of the 1948 Brussels Pact. It tied together Britain and the Six and so provided a potentially strong European dimension within NATO. But for the federalist movement it was small compensation for the loss of EDC and the EPC. The Coal–Steel Community survived of course, and in December 1954 Britain became an 'associate' member of it. But even in the ECSC Mendès-France tried to strengthen the hand of member states in the Council of Ministers, against the supranational power of the High Authority. In view of all these problems Jean Monnet decided to quit his position as ECSC President, and in 1955 left to found an 'Action Committee for the United States of Europe', a pressure group of leading pro-Europeans.

Even before Monnet left his post the so-called 're-launch of Europe' had begun. EDC, by embracing co-operation in the military field, an area fundamental to national pride, had proved over-ambitious. So, in early 1955 attention shifted back to the economic field. Mendès lost office early in the year to leaders who were better-disposed to supranationalism, Adenauer was all too ready to rebuild co-operation, and both Spaak and Monnet believed it would be possible to extend the principle of supranational links in 'sectors' of the European economy. Two possible candidates for the 'sector' approach were transport co-operation and atomic energy. The latter was particularly appealing because it was a new industry, where few vested interests existed but which was nonetheless important for the future. The French government, predictably, was eager to forestall independent German developments in the atomic field and very interested in the possibilities of Europoean co-operation here. The most dramatic proposal for co-operation, however, came not from Spaak and Monnet, the so-called 'fathers of Europe', but from the Dutch foreign minister, Johan Beyen. Beyen argued that in the long term the 'sector' approach to co-operation would have to face up to the need for an all-embracing 'common market' reducing all trade barriers between the Six. Why, he asked, should the common market not be studied *now*? The various ideas for progress were discussed by ECSC ministers meeting at Messina in early June. After the EDC débâcle they were reluctant to move quickly, reluctant even to use the word 'supranationalism'. But they decided to establish a study committee in Brussels to look at both a common market and the possibilities for 'sector' co-operation. Spaak was made chairman of these studies and Britain, as an associate member of ECSC, was asked to take part in the work.

The British, following the successful foundation of the WEU, had hopes of steering the new ECSC talks in the direction of inter-governmental co-operation, and therefore sent a representative along. But the work of the Spaak committee soon revealed that, even if the word 'supranationalism' was no longer used by the Six, the Messina decisions would probably lead to a loss of sovereignty to common institutions. Spaak proved a determined and businesslike chairman, and formed a number of smaller study committees, including one on a common market. To widespread surprise there was strong support for the common market idea from West Germany. Before the talks many had expected that the West Germans, especially their economics minister, Ludwig Erhard, would have little interest in a common market. Their economy was strong and could gain sufficiently in commercial terms from freer trade measures carried out through the OEEC – without any loss of sovereignty. But Adenauer's faith in supranationalism, as a way to guarantee democracy in Germany, was as strong as ever. It was confirmed, furthermore, by the failure to advance far with détente with Russia in 1955. Closer co-operation with Western Europe was ideally suited to Adenauer's policy of distancing himself from the Eastern bloc after September 1955, when Moscow upset him by recognising East Germany as a sovereign state. The French were certainly taken aback by Adenauer's support for the common market. For whilst France *was* interested in pursuing an atomic energy authority (EURATOM) she had little interest, at first, in Beyen's idea of common market. Feeling in the National Assembly was still unsympathetic to supranationalism and France had a tradition of protectionist trade barriers. The French were only ready to discuss a common market if it provided them with a high tariff 'wall' against outsiders and if there were complicated measures to guarantee equality of competition between members.

It was the belief that France and Germany would not prove ready to join a common market, and that the scheme would collapse, that led Britain to distance itself from the Spaak committee late in the year. The British then publicly advocated inter-governmental co-operation in the OEEC as an alternative. Spaak and Beyen were bitterly upset by Britain's action. None of the Six believed that the OEEC provided a meaningful alternative to the proposals discussed at Messina. In 1956 Britain drew up a scheme for a free trade area of OEEC states, but it was not put forward until November and by then the work of the Six, to British surprise, had progressed well. The French elections of early 1956 had strengthened the pro-Europeans in the National Assembly and, behind the scenes, the Americans continued to support greater unity. In May the Spaak committee finished its work by recommending two treaties among the Six, to create both a European Economic Community (EEC), or common market, and an atomic energy body, EURATOM. A ministerial meeting in Venice agreed to this and in June work began to draft the treaties. France still wanted EURATOM more than she wanted a common market, and in September 1956 caused a new crisis in the negotiations, with various demands to ease her own position in a six-power customs union. But the Suez crisis in November confirmed France's desire for European co-operation whilst damaging her relations with Britain. The Euratom and Common Market treaties were signed, by the premiers of the Six, in Rome on 25 March 1957. In stark contrast to the problems over EDC, both treaties were ratified by the end of the year. The French now seemed fully committed once more to a future of European co-operation.

## The Community of the Six, 1958–72

The European Economic Community, which came into being on 1 January 1958, was much less supranational in form than the ECSC. The central administrative body in the new organisation was the Commission, based in Brussels, which federalists hoped could become the motor of greater unity, working by majority votes and able to initiate policy. The Commission's president, five vice-presidents and commissioners* were nominated by the member governments but were supposedly loyal to the EEC itself and had departments created under them, just like a government. In 1967, under the Merger treaty, the Commission acted as the executive body of the whole European Community (EC), for Euratom and the ECSC, as well as the EEC. Yet the Commission could only do what member states allowed it to do, and it lost real power to other institutions which protected national interests. Like the ECSC, the EEC had a Council of Ministers as its main decision-making body. The Council held monthly meetings, later becoming more frequent, with different ministers attending according to the subject being discussed. Chairmanship of

* The number of Commissioners grew as new states joined the Community and stood at seventeen in 1986.

the body revolved every six months. Despite the provision for votes (weighted broadly according to members' population size) the Council usually tried to establish a unanimous position among the member states. The position of member states was further strengthened by the creation of a Committe of Permanent Representatives in 1958, though this did not become a fully legal Community institution until 1967. The Committee, made up of officials from each country, discussed policy proposals by the Commission and, again, tried to establish a unanimous view. The development which really strengthened the governments, however, was the tendency, beginning in Paris in February 1961, for European leaders to meet in 'summits' where major decisions were taken, even though no provision for this existed in the Rome treaty.

Other bodies created by the Rome treaty had limited powers. The Economic and Social Council of 144 members drawn from public life – businessmen, trades unionists, and others – was supposed to be consulted on Community policies, but actually had limited influence. The Assembly, though renamed the 'European Parliament' in 1962, had no effective control over the Council or Commission. The Parliament could not sack individual Commissioners, or force amendments on legislation, nor did it develop much influence over budgetary matters until the 1970s. Ultimately it could censure the Commission and so dismiss the whole body, but such an action was so extreme that its use was not even threatened until 1972. Practical problems were caused for parliamentarians by the fact that Community bodies were scattered in Strasbourg, Luxembourg and Brussels. The last important institution, the Court of Justice, based in Luxembourg, was designed to ensure that Community laws had 'equivalent effect' in all member states and it established the primacy of 'Community Law' among the Six. This last was an important function, which set the EEC apart from other international organisations. But Community Law existed *alongside* national legal systems, which there was no attempt to harmonise.

The EEC treaty though running to 248 articles and looking forward to an 'ever-closer union', left many elements of economic co-operation to be worked out in detail later. The basic aim was to create a customs union, with free and equal competition among the Six and a 'common external tariff' against the rest of the world. It was planned to establish this common market in transitional stages over 12 years: actually this process was speeded up and a full customs union was achieved, triumphantly, on 1 July 1968. The 'Community method' therefore was pragmatic, but it aimed at great things. On the economic side it was believed that customs union, by creating healthy competition and allowing for large-scale production, would have a dynamic effect, leading to higher growth and better living standards. On the political side, federalists hoped that there would be a gradual shift of decision-making to European institutions and that economic co-operation would have a major political impact, forcing unity at all levels – economic, social, financial, foreign affairs – until states merged into one. Many of the economic hopes were achieved in the 1960s. Between 1958 and 1970 trade among the Six increased five times over, exports to the rest of the world expanded two and a half times, and Gross Domestic Product grew within the EEC at an average of five per cent per annum. The common market in 1972 included 190 million people. Not all this success could be credited to the EEC however. In the 1950s West European economies had already recovered from the war, trade amongst all advanced states was growing in the 1960s and Western trade expansion was helped by the 'Kennedy Round' of tariff reductions involving Europe and North America. Neither can the Six be said to have achieved all that they set out to do. In 1970 the ideal of free and equal competition was actually far from realised: the movement of people, goods and capital around the Six faced numerous impediments, and genuinely 'free' movement on the EC was not finally planned until the 1990s. A 'Social Fund' was created to help tackle unemployment, but it was small in size and common social, regional and transport policies proved very difficult to achieve.

The one area which the Rome Treaty had ignored, but where the Six did create a common policy, was in agriculture. Although about one fifth of EEC workers were in agriculture in 1958, it was largely at the insistence of France that the Common Agricultural Policy (CAP) came into being. Indeed General de Gaulle, the French leader after 1958, insisted that the policy must be introduced if France was to remain committed to the Community. The first regulations were introduced only in January 1962 and a full policy was not effective until 1968. CAP had many positive effects, not least in showing that the Six could work together on a very complicated issue. It gave a better living standard to farmers, helped an area of the EEC economy which (except for Holland) was labour-intensive and inefficient, and it led the Community to grow more of its own food, guaranteeing supplies to consumers. However, the way the CAP worked made it the subject of intense criticism. Basically the policy protected farmers by guaranteeing a price for their products and by setting up barriers against imports. The EC Commission bought up any agricultural surpluses within the Community, stepping in once prices reached a certain 'intervention' level. This helped to prevent a price slump but it also led to 'butter mountains' and 'wine lakes' which were expensive to store. Sometimes the excess products could be released back onto the market, but at other times they were sold abroad at a loss or simply destroyed. The CAP favoured farmers over consumers, encouraged overproduction and high prices, forced members to buy food at prices higher than the world market, tended to benefit well-off farmers rather than the poor, absorbed most of the Community budget* and distorted the world food market. Yet once created it proved impossible to remove and difficult to reform.

One sign of the success of the EEC was the change it brought to

---

* As will be seen later, the budget was greatly extended in the 1960s simply to finance the CAP.

British policy. In 1958 Britain still hoped to embrace the Six and other OEEC members in a free trade area, holding most of Western Europe together. For the Six, however, a free trade area was too loose a form of co-operation and General de Gaulle opposed the British plan, which offered France no special concessions in the agricultural field. After the foundation of the EEC a number of states agreed, in 1959, to create a separate free trade organisation. The European Free Trade Association (EFTA) was created by the Stockholm Convention of January 1960, and included Britain, Denmark, Norway, Sweden, Switzerland, Austria and Portugal, sometimes known as 'the Seven'. It was later joined by Iceland (1970) and Finland (1985).* EFTA, like the EEC, involved the gradual reduction of internal trading restrictions, but it had no common external tariff, was geographically-scattered, had a much smaller population, and was economically dominated by Britain (which represented two-thirds of EFTA's industrial output). The British, facing the decline of Commonwealth trade and the loss of its Empire, found EFTA of limited use. After the Suez crisis Britain had rebuilt its foreign policy around the US alliance but in 1960 the Americans seemed concerned with the rising power of the Six rather than Britain. In July 1961, therefore, the Conservative government of Harold Macmillan announced that Britain would apply to join the EEC and a Cabinet minister, Edward Heath, was sent to handle the entry negotiations in Brussels.

The negotiations on British entry became fused with a wider debate in 1960–3 about the future of the Community. In May 1960 the Six had agreed to quicken the process of economic co-operation, so that internal EEC tariffs were already reduced by half in July 1962. Such success led to hopes that the Six could play a greater political role in the world, but this raised questions about how exactly to create a common political outlook. In contrast to the 'Community approach' leading eventually to full union, General de Gaulle believed in a *Europe des Patries*, that is a Europe of nation-states. He wanted greater co-operation among the Six in the political field, but his motives were to resist US predominance in Europe and to give Western Europeans, especially France, a greater say in world events. He did not want his own country to lose its identity in a supranational body. In the 1950s de Gaulle had opposed the EDC, and many feared that he would destroy the EEC too after 1958. In September 1960 the General spoke of nation states as 'the only realities upon which one can build' and proposed to develop economic, cultural and defence co-operation through inter-governmental, not supranational, bodies. He found an ally in Konrad Adenauer. This may seem surprising in view of Adenauer's previous support for supranationalism, but the Chancellor saw Franco–German co-operation as the vital element in his European policy. He was concerned about de Gaulle's anti-Americanism, but was pleased by the support he had received from the French leader in 1958–61 over the Berlin crises with Russia.

* Later certain members left to join the EC.

In 1961, after two leaders' summits in Paris (February) and Bad Godesburg (July), it was agreed to set up a study committee under France's Christian Fouchet to explore future political unity. By December 1961 the Fouchet committee, which met independently of EEC institutions, had devised a plan that aimed to build up cultural, defence and foreign policy co-operation among the Six in a Union of States. As de Gaulle wanted, this should only be developed on the basis of unanimous agreements, with a new Commission being created in Paris, made up of national civil servants, not officials loyal to European institutions. The Six agreed to draft a treaty on these lines, but as a compromise de Gaulle was asked to accept that the Atlantic alliance with America should be safeguarded and that 'Community co-operation' on economic issues in the EEC should continue to be developed. This the General proved unwilling to do. In January 1962 he produced a new plan (known as 'Fouchet Plan II') which went beyond his previous proposals and suggested that, under a new Six-power treaty, economic co-operation should also fall under the control of the Union of States. This was too much for his opponents who now clearly saw that de Gaulle was opposed to the 'Community approach' in all areas, including economics. By spring the Six had become bitterly divided. De Gaulle condemned supranationalism as 'a myth and a fiction' whilst his opponents in other EEC governments talked of proceeding towards an 'Economic Union'. Consideration of the British application to enter the EEC was then used as a convenient excuse to put aside further formal discussion of the Fouchet Plan.

The failure of the Fouchet Plan did not end de Gaulle's disagreements with his European partners. In 1962 he remained concerned about America's role in Europe, via NATO, he disliked President Kennedy's 'Grand Design' for the improvement of Atlantic co-operation, and he became gravely upset when the British purchased a new nuclear weapons system, 'Polaris' from Washington. This provided the General with the excuse, in January 1963, to veto Britain's application to enter the EEC, arguing that Britain would be a 'trojan horse' for America in Europe. The veto gravely upset all the other Community members, especially Belgium and Holland. Almost immediately, however, the General was able to reassert his position by confirming his 'special relationship' with Konrad Adenauer in a Franco–German treaty of co-operation. By April the sense of crisis among the Six receded when it was agreed to quicken the pace towards a customs union still further. It was in this period that de Gaulle was anxious to proceed with devising the CAP and it seemed because of this that he might make concessions to his partners. In early 1964, however, relations worsened again when the Six failed to adopt a scheme, known as the 'Mansholt Plan' to advance more rapidly on the CAP. De Gaulle was also disappointed with West German policy after Adenauer's resignation from office in 1963 and was especially offended by German interest in an American plan for a 'Multilateral Nuclear Force' in NATO. Partly because of French opposition to closer US–European links, the US abandoned this plan at the end of 1964 and in December the Six managed to agree on an important element of the CAP, common cereal prices. But by then there was deep distrust between France and the rest of the Community.

De Gaulle in early 1965 was clearly less interested in general economic co-operation than he was in the CAP and measures to limit US power in Europe. His latest scheme was for European scientific co-operation to enable European companies to challenge the US in world markets. Above all, however, de Gaulle was worried that under the terms of the Treaty of Rome, the EEC was supposed, in January 1966, to take more of its decisions by majority votes, which could force France to accept policies she did not want. It was at this time that the European Commission under its President, Walter Hallstein, produced a plan to finance the CAP. Such a plan was vital because, up to now, the Community budget had been small and was paid for by national contributions. CAP would add enormously to the budget. But the Hallstein Plan offended de Gaulle on two counts. Firstly because, by giving the EEC its own resources from agricultural levies and customs duties, it would give the Commission greater independence; and secondly because it proposed to widen the budgetary powers of the European Parliament, again strengthening the supranational element in the EEC to which the General was opposed.

At a Council of Ministers meeting in late June the French vigorously opposed the Hallstein Plan, then, on 6 July they began to boycott Community bodies. This policy known as the 'empty chair', lasted for six months and was the EEC's greatest-ever crisis. De Gaulle showed, in a press conference on 9 September, that his most serious concern was the introduction of more majority voting in the Community in future and that this was where he most wanted changes. His five partners, however, were reluctant to give way to the General. They offered some concessions to France, including the final resolution of CAP, but they also threatened to use majority votes in January without him, and even talked of admitting Britain to the Community whether he agreed or not. Such dangers, along with evidence of pro-European sympathies in the French elections of December 1965, brought de Gaulle back to the negotiating table. At the Luxembourg foreign ministers' meeting in January 1966 France agreed to rejoin Community bodies. In return de Gaulle secured new limits on the Commission's powers, the abandonment of the Hallstein Plan, a timetable for the start of a CAP, and – most importantly – an agreement that on 'very important issues' the principle of unanimity should be maintained. This last undertaking became known as the 'Luxembourg Compromise'.

The EEC had survived the 'empty chair' crisis intact and the Rome Treaty remained fundamentally unchanged. Yet de Gaulle had given the Community a shock and under the 'Luxembourg Compromise' he retained a power of veto over future important decisions. In the wake of the crisis summit meetings between the Six lessened in frequency. 1967–8 saw the merger of the EEC, Euratom and ECSC, and the achievement both of a full customs union and CAP, but these represented the fulfilment of past agreements rather than new departures. In 1967 the British government, now led by Harold Wilson, applied to join the Community and once again de Gaulle vetoed the attempt. Wilson left the application 'on the table' in Brussels, but it was only in late 1969 that progress became possible on the extension of the EC to new members. By then de Gaulle had left office and his successor, Georges Pompidou, was concerned at the growing strength and independence of West Germany, particularly because of Chancellor Willy Brandt's *Ostpolitik*.\* Once again the desire to control Germany gave France a powerful motivation for supporting European unity. Franco–British co-operation could reinforce such a policy. Other forces were at work. By now, thanks to the Luxembourg Compromise, France was less fearful of the European Commission; the completion of the customs union led to hopes among the Six of further developments in the EEC; and there was still the need to settle the long-term finance of CAP, a question which had been papered over after de Gaulle's 'empty chair' policy. So it was that, at a highly important summit in the Hague in December 1969, several major decisions were taken which breathed new life into the Community and gave something to both France and her partners. It was agreed at the Hague to enlarge the Community to include Britain and others, to finance CAP by giving the EC its own resources and to look at new areas of co-operation in the economic and political fields.

Talks on the enlargement of the EC began with Britain, Eire, Denmark and Norway – all north European democracies – in June 1970. The new members had to accept previous EC agreements, but were allowed a five-year transition period to adjust to them. Problems with Britain over Commonwealth trade, the position of sterling and the cost of CAP, were overcome in May 1971. Difficulties with Norway over fisheries policy took longer to resolve and, although a Treaty of Accession was signed by all four applicants on 22 January 1972, the Norwegians rejected the idea of entry nine months later in a referendum. Meanwhile, without damaging the prospects for enlargement, the Six had continued to improve the EC. In April 1970, to pay for the CAP, it was agreed to provide the Community with its own financial resources from payments of agricultural levies, external customs duties and one per cent of the Value Added Tax raised by members.† As the Hallstein Report had wanted, the European Parliament's budgetary powers were also strengthened. Furthermore, in November 1970, following the 'Davignon Report', the foreign ministers of the Six began to meet together in a European Political Co-operation body. This was outside the framework of the Community institutions established by the Rome Treaty, but it was hoped that it could bring about a common European attitude to international problems.

More dramatic was the October 1970 report by a group under Luxembourg's premier, Pierre Werner, on economic and monetary union (EMU). Willy Brandt, in particular at this time, was interested

---

\* See pp 17–19.
† This necessitated the introduction of VAT in several member states in the 1970s.

in EMU as a way to create closer European co-operation, bring greater equality to all West Europeans and ensure stability between the value of EC currencies. In 1969 there had been major changes in the value of the German mark and French franc which threatened to damage EEC internal trade. The Werner Report proposed the gradual harmonisation of economic, taxation and budgetary policies among EMU members. In the long term there would be a centralised body for monetary policy, supervised by the European Parliament, though in the short term members should simply try to limit the fluctuations betwen their currencies. These were dramatic proposals indeed. In October 1972, at a Summit in Paris, the Community leaders committed themselves to EMU, which was to be achieved by 1980. They also agreed to pursue a common external trade policy towards Eastern Europe and the Third World, and to take joint action on scientific, social and environmental issues. Three years after the Hague summit the Community seemed on the brink, not merely of a major enlargement, but of a leap towards full economic union.

## The Enlarged Community 1973–89

The 'northern enlargement' to Britain, Denmark and Eire on 1 January 1973 brought over 60 million more people into the Common Market, which now totalled 250 million, and was similar in population size to the US and USSR. In commercial terms the EC accounted for over one-fifth of world trade and was comparable in importance to the USA and Japan. In contrast to the 1940s and 1950s, Americans came to resent the success and, as they saw it, the protectionism of the new European bloc. Despite common values, close trading links and shared security concerns, America, Japan and the Community had become intense trading competitors. The EC also proved successful in developing trade with the Eastern bloc, with West Germany playing the leading role. Ideological differences did not prevent the Community from taking more than half of the Eastern bloc's exports to the non-communist world, whilst the Eastern bloc absorbed high-technology goods from Western Europe. In addition the EC developed important trading links to the Third World. In 1963 the Yaoundé Convention had linked former French and Belgian colonies in Africa to the EEC, and provided aid to them. Charles de Gaulle had wanted such an agreement as a way to maintain French economic links to their former colonies, and it represented yet another important concession to him by the rest of the Six. The Convention was criticised as 'neo-colonialist' because of its insistence on reciprocal trade concessions from the Africans. It was improved in the later 1960s and in 1975 the first Lomé Convention also included British ex-colonies. This convention, re-negotiated in 1980 and 1985, provided greater aid to the Third World states, but its value to them was limited by the effects of inflation and the restrictions on agricultural trade with Europe caused by CAP.

The commercial power of the EC was not, unfortunately, matched by greater political influence in the 1970s. This was principally because of the failure to develop greater economic and political union. Various areas of co-operation experienced difficulties in the 1970s. European defence co-operation had been made less likely in 1973 by the admission of neutral Eire to the EC. The Common Fisheries Policy was a relatively new EC development which gained greater significance with the enlargement. It was designed to ensure non-discrimination among members and to control fish catches, and caused little controversy when it was begun in 1970. It caused resentment in Britain, after 1973 however, because Britain had an extensive coastline and a large fishing industry. Although the new members were given ten years before they had to accept the Fisheries Policy, the problem was exacerbated in 1977 by the extension of international fishing limits to 200 miles, giving the EC a huge area to control. The British complained when they were only given a quarter of new EC fishing quotas despite providing sixty per cent of the fishing grounds. A complex settlement of this problem was not reached until January 1983, when Britain effectively got one-third of the fishing quotas. In another new initiative in 1974, under Italian and Irish pressure, the EC agreed to establish a Regional Development Fund. The need to reduce regional disparities had been stated in the Treaty of Rome, and a regional policy appeared the ideal way to create a fair and healthy European economy. In the 1960s regional policies had remained in national hands. There were vain hopes that EC growth rates would automatically raise standards in poorer areas, but by 1970 certain areas of southern Italy were six times poorer than rich EC areas, such as the Paris region. The creation of the Regional Fund in March 1975 failed to have a dramatic effect. It amounted to only a fraction of the EC budget and was designed to supplement, not supplant, national policies. Only in 1984 did the Commission obtain real power to direct aid at specific projects in poorer regions.

The bulk of the Community budget continued to be spent after 1973 on the CAP, which became more costly than ever. EC agricultural production continued to grow despite the tendency of workers to move from the land to the industrial and service sectors. This growth simply added to the burdens on the CAP. Propaganda actions, such as Christmas sales of excess butter, failed to stop the complaints about the policy: that it tended to help large farms, which could adopt intensive production methods, rather than the needy; that it distorted world markets and upset the US, which threatened a trade war with the EC over CAP in 1986–7;\* and that it harmed the environment by encouraging the use of chemical fertilisers. Only in the mid-1980s did the Commission determinedly begin to tackle the problem of overproduction. Once again the country which complained most about the policy was Britain, which found itself in the position of being a 'net contributor' to the EC after 1973, paying far more into the EC than it received back. This was partly because Britain, as a major world trading

* Because of the loss of maize exports to Spain when she joined the EC.

power, provided a substantial amount of the EC's earnings from customs duties. But it was also because Britain, as a heavily industrialised nation, got little in return from Brussels under CAP payments. The Conservative government of Edward Heath was criticised for accepting this position in 1973, and in 1974–5 the new Labour government renegotiated British membership. The terms were then, successfully, put to a referendum. Yet the new terms failed to prevent Britain becoming the largest net contributor to the EC budget by 1979, when Margaret Thatcher came to office and began a determined campaign to cut Britain's payments.

Other members argued that it was not the EC's fault if Britain paid more money than others under the terms of membership, and there were bitter arguments before a temporary (three year) settlement of the issue was reached, at the Luxembourg summit of April 1980, when Britain got some repayments. In May 1982 Britain tried to force concessions by delaying a review of CAP prices, but was defeated by a majority vote of the other members, an event which called into question the Luxembourg Compromise and showed that Thatcher could not simply act as a new de Gaulle. A final settlement of the British problem was not reached until the June 1984 Fontainebleau summit, when a rebate system effectively halved the net contribution. By then British economic growth rates since 1973 had undergone a transformation and were better, over the years 1981–5, than all the rest of the EC except Denmark and Luxembourg. Also, half of Britain's trade was with the EC, compared to about one-third in 1973. Yet Britain's GDP per head remained behind most of the Six original EEC members, much of Britain's trading improvement with Europe was in oil exports and she was actually in deficit, especially to West Germany, in manufacturing trade. British industry had not therefore responded well to the European challenge, and Bonn and Paris remained the strongest elements in the EC.

The greatest failure for the EC in the 1970s was the failure to progress towards EMU. Even before the ambitious decision of the 1972 Paris summit to seek EMU by 1980, the chances of successful monetary co-operation were undermined by instability in the world economic and financial system. In April 1972, in the Basle Agreement, the central banks of the Six, Britain, Denmark and Eire had formed a currency 'snake', by which they valued their currencies within a certain percentage of the US dollar. But the system of fixed exchange rates established after the war and based on the dollar had already disintegrated by that time. The US, faced by the revival of European and Japanese competition, by inflation and the costs of the Vietnam war, could no longer remain the foundation stone of a world currency system and the dollar had been 'floated' in August 1971. The British, Danes and Irish almost immediately left the 'snake', which continued to be troubled by the growing world recession and virtually collapsed in 1973 due to increasing oil prices after the October Arab–Israeli War. The 'snake' did not have any provision for strong currency nations to help the weak, nor did it provide for the harmonisation of national economic policies. A Monetary Co-operation

Fund, to give support to weak currencies, was set up in April 1973, but proved of limited value. The enlargement of the EC had, quite simply, come at the worst possible time so far as global economic conditions were concerned, and did not bring the dynamic improvements that had been hoped for.

Interest in the 'snake' was eventually revived and in March 1979, after difficult negotiations, a much better European Monetary System (EMS) was established. It included the Monetary Co-operation Fund and it created a European Currency Unit (ECU), made up of a trade-weighted 'basket' of currencies, as a measure for certain EC activities, including for example, the 'intervention price' under CAP. The main element in EMS though, was the Exchange Rate Mechanism (ERM), in which member states valued their currencies within a certain percentage of the ECU. Under ERM strong currency nations were forced to help the weak to re-establish the equilibrium of the system, although large-scale fluctuations could lead to an alteration of the 'central rate'. The system survived the new depression of 1979–81 and succeeded in creating some degree of stability by the later 1980s, though not without many problems. Eire and Italy had to be given special concessions in order to take part, Britain refused to join the ERM, and French economic policies caused five changes in the 'central rate' in 1981–3. Indeed Mitterand's Socialist government had to change its economic policies in 1983 partly to save EMS and good relations with West Germany, which was the dominant force in the ERM. Yet for many years most Europeans did not know the system existed and it was no substitute for full EMU. After 1986, therefore, interest in EMU revived and in 1988 the Hanover summit set up another committee to look at the idea. Jacques Delors, the Commission President, gave his name to the new Report which was produced in April 1989. Like the 1970 Werner Report this looked forward to a full EMU in the long term, with free capital movements, fixed exchange rates (or maybe a common currency) and a central budgetary institution. In the first stage, however, it proposed only the closer co-ordination of EC currencies through the ERM. The EC summit in June 1989 agreed to achieve this first stage in July 1990 but set no dates for further progress and, yet again, the British had important doubts about the proposal.

Other efforts to strengthen the political and economic role of the EC also proved difficult to realise. At the December 1974 summit of Community leaders in Paris the Belgian premier, Leo Tindemans, was asked to draw up a personal report on the future shape of a European Union. It was also agreed in principle to strengthen the European Parliament by making it an elected body. This came after years of French opposition, and despite British and Danish doubts. The role of governments was also strengthened at Paris by the formal creation of a 'European Council', made up of heads of government and foreign ministers to meet three times per year. Leaders' meetings had already, of course, become commonplace, and had gained primacy over both the Council of Ministers and the 'Eurocrats' in Brussels. The Tindemans Report appeared in January

1976 and recommended a widening of EC activity in economic, social and regional policies. It wanted the Community to pursue a common foreign policy, to develop a 'Citizen's Europe' through such measures as freedom of movement, and to strengthen the powers of the Commission. Yet it also conceded that there might have to be 'differentiated progress' among members towards common goals. The Report was welcomed by federalists but soon faced numerous difficulties. The economic depression had bitten deeply into European morale, in practice governments were reluctant to extend the powers of Community institutions, and the Plan itself was both over ambitious in its general aims and too vague on specific actions. In November 1976 the European Council, meeting in the Hague, merely expressed 'great interest' in the Report. A similar fate befell other proposals over the following years. In 1981, for example, the West German and Italian foreign ministers, Hans-Dietrich Genscher and Emilio Colombo, put forward a Plan to strengthen and restructure the EC. This simply led in June 1983 to a 'Solemn Declaration on European Union' by the European Council, which did no more than restate existing practices in flowery language. Activity on political union in the 1970s and early 1980s thus involved words rather than deeds, and the power of national governments remained paramount.

Attention in the later 1970s centred on the Paris summit's decision to hold direct elections to the European Parliament. The decision was confirmed in 1975 and elections were finally held in 1979, the same year that EMS was created. There were 518 seats in all, shared out in proportion to members' population size. Different electoral systems were used in different states, there was limited popular interest, and votes tended to go to national political parties. But the elections did strengthen the hand of Parliament *vis-à-vis* the other EC institutions. In 1978, furthermore, the Parliament was given the right to reject the whole EC budget. This weapon was not as significant as it seemed: a two-thirds majority was needed for the vote to succeed; the EC budget, despite the costs of the CAP, only amounted to one per cent of the Community's GDP; and, if the budget was rejected, the Commission would still have the right to spend money on a month-by-month basis. Immediately in December 1979, however, Parliament rejected the 1980 budget, criticising it for spending too much on CAP and too little on social and regional policies. This at least forced the Commission to be careful in future. Parliament showed its power further in the mid-1980s by delaying the budget for three years in succession. It was also able to press the governments for swifter progress towards an Economic Union. In 1980 the Italian Attiero Spinelli and other parliamentarians founded the 'Crocodile Club' (named after a Luxembourg restaurant) to draw up plans for institutional reform, and in 1981 Parliament established an Institutional Committee with Spinelli as a member. As a result, in February 1984, a Draft Treaty of 87 articles was approved by the Parliament, embodying institutional reforms for the EC, to make it more democratic and efficient, and the extension of its role over more areas of the European economy. The treaty was not, predictably, adopted by the member states but it encouraged the governments to look again at reform.

Greater urgency was given to the question of reform of the EC in the 1980s by the so-called 'southern enlargement' to Greece, Spain and Portugal. All these states were poorer than the previous members, with less industrialised economies and less secure democratic traditions. Greece had been the first EEC 'associate' member in 1962 and had already reduced tariffs and harmonised agricultural policies with the Community. The rule of the Greek military junta in 1967–74 had damaged relations but it was partly in order to stabilise Greek democracy that a treaty of accession was signed in 1979, leading to membership in 1981. It was a similar story with Spain and Portugal, who had both become democracies in the mid-1970s, and who joined the EC in 1986. In so far as the 'southern enlargement' extended the European ideal, created a larger market for goods, and protected democracy it could be seen as a success. But there were many problems. The Greek economy, despite a five-year transition period, could not compete equally with the EC and soon faced a massive trade deficit, and the Socialist government in Athens pursued a negative policy towards the EC for several years. Spanish and Portuguese membership came only after long talks, and was expected to put greater pressures on the Social and Regional Funds, as well as increasing the costs of the CAP. Spain was a large producer of wine and olive oil, which the EC already had in abundance. Portugal became the poorest EC member with almost a quarter of its people living off the land. In 1984, therefore, VAT payments to the EC were increased on all members to cope with the added costs of Spanish and Portuguese membership. Despite a ten-year transition period, both countries suffered balance of payments problems on entering the Community.

The 1986 enlargement was only one element in the revival of EC fortunes in the mid-1980s. After the disappointments of the 1970s and early 1980s, the EC seemed to find real forward momentum once more, helped by improving economic circumstances. In 1984 the Economic Council, as well as settling the British budget problem and agreeing to Spanish and Portuguese membership, had established two committees. One, under Pietro Adonnino, produced a report in 1985 on the idea of a 'People's Europe' and suggested such developments as European television, the harmonisation of election systems and a common system of driving licences. Progress on these ideas was slow. Far more important, and partly in response to pressures from the European Parliament, was the committee under an Irish Senator, James Dooge, to study EC institutions. This committee, made up of government representatives, was sometimes grandiosely referred to as the 'Spaak II Committee' (after the body which had drawn up the Rome Treaties in the 1950s). It reported in 1985 in favour of establishing an Inter-Governmental Conference to carry out institutional reforms and to widen the EC's objectives. These would include stronger political co-operation. The British, Danes and Greeks were unenthusiastic about much of the Report and the Milan summit, in June, agreed only by a majority vote – not unanimity – to set up an Inter-Governmental Conference. Italy and the Benelux states were ready to proceed without their more reticent partners, but in the event all EC members entered the Conference in September, and by the end of the year a number of changes to the Treaty of Rome had been defined, which were contained in the so-called 'Single European Act'. In the Act the objective of EMU was stated; the Regional Fund was defined; the legal scope of the EC was extended to such areas as environment, technological co-operation and social policy; the system of foreign ministers' meetings, held since 1970, was formally drawn under the EC umbrella; the use of majority votes was extended (although the vexed issue of the Luxembourg Compromise was not tackled); and most importantly, under pressure from the Commission, it was decided to achieve a genuine 'common market' in 1992 with the free movement of people, goods and capital throughout the EC. The last, it should be remembered, was an aim which should have been achieved, under the Rome Treaty, in 1970.

The Single European Act disappointed many federalists because it tended to codify practices which had developed since 1958, rather than to reform the EC in any radical way. It said nothing about educational or cultural co-operation, it did not do anything to bring EMU nearer (that was left to the Delors Plan) and it effectively left foreign policy co-operation in government hands. The Italian government was particularly disappointed by it. However, it did mark the first major overhaul of the Treaties of Rome, it reformed EC institutions to some extent and it succeeded in keeping the members united. This was a major change from the failures of the 1970s. In February 1986 a referendum was needed in Denmark before that country was able to join the other signatories to the Single European Act, but a split was avoided. The aim of achieving a genuine common market was a major commitment and though it relied on the voluntary co-operation of member states, complex legislative measures were soon underway to carry it out. By ending non-tariff barriers, such as customs controls, restrictive business laws and technical regulations, it was hoped to bring a new boost to the European economy with greater competition and expanded trade after 1992.

A speech by Margaret Thatcher in Bruges in September 1988 confirmed her opposition to greater supranationalism. Britain also refused to sign a Social Charter in 1989 which guaranteed certain minimum social rights to EC peoples, and it had to be said, thirty years after the Rome treaties, that European unity had not really fulfilled the high hopes of Schuman, de Gasperi or Adenauer. Member governments continued to take a primary interest in the views of their own people, the EC was slow to make decisions and was not subject to proper democratic control, CAP was unreformed, and the Community lacked the political cohesion to act as a single 'force' in world affairs. The EC customs union, however, was undoubtedly a major success and greater economic unity did have a beneficial social and political impact in Europe. Despite US–European commercial rivalry, the American hopes of 1948 for the creation of a stable, thriving, anti-communist Europe had arguably been fulfilled. The Six original EC members, along with Spain, were committed to further developments like the Delors Plan, and Franco–German co-operation remained the back-bone of the unity movement. The friendship between Giscard d'Estaing and Helmut Schmidt in the late 1970s and the more formal relationship between Francois Mitterand and Helmut Kohl in the 1980s, was in stark contrast to the enmities of the two world wars.

The dramatic events in Eastern Europe in late 1989 called into question even the Franco–German relationship. Fears were raised that West Germany, by far the strongest EC economy, might concentrate on reunification with East Germany and slow down EC unity. Yet, with the dangers came also opportunities. Proposals to extend the EC to Eastern Europe raised the possibility that EC institutions, forged amidst the divisions of Cold War, might become the vehicles for pan-European unity. At the Strasbourg summit in December 1989 it again proved possible to satisfy both Paris and Bonn. It was agreed that a new Intergovernmental Conference would be called in December 1990 to discuss further steps towards monetary union as set out in the Delors Plan, which particularly pleased President Mitterand. On the other hand, to satisfy Kohl, financial assistance to Eastern Europe was promised and it was affirmed that the German people had the right 'to regain its unity through free self-determination.' British doubts about EMU were brushed aside and Franco–German co-operation was confirmed as the foundation stone of the Community.

# 3
# West Germany

## Founding the Bonn Republic, 1945–9

In May 1945 Germany faced complete defeat at the hands of the Allies. In contrast to November 1918, when most of the country had escaped invasion, Soviet and Western forces advanced into the German heartland. America, Russia, Britain and France divided the country into occupation zones, destroyed the last vestiges of Nazi authority and set up their own military government. German civilians especially suffered mistreatment at the hands of the Red Army in the East, but there was little sympathy for them after six years of war. Adolf Hitler's ruthless occupation policy across Europe and the discovery of the concentration camps ensured that Germans were loathed and hated and the destruction they suffered was seen as deserved. Some cities, such as Dresden, had been virtually destroyed by 'saturation bombing'; three-quarters of buildings in the capital, Berlin, were damaged. East of the Oder–Neisse river, the Allies had agreed to place lands 'under Polish administration' and most Germans living there fled their homes, creating a daunting refugee problem in western Germany. Over six million Germans had lost their lives during the war, about half of them soldiers, and most of those in the age group 18–35. Millions of soldiers were made prisoners of war, and many other Germans were interned under the Allied policy of 'denazification' whilst their activities under the Third Reich were investigated. Leading Nazis were tried at Nuremberg in 1946 and several were sentenced to death. Meanwhile the removal of Nazi officials from their posts caused administrative havoc and the 'denazification' process proved slow to carry through and unjust in its results. The four occupation powers executed the policy in different ways and innocent people could spend months in prison whilst many of the guilty escaped. There was a positive side to Allied policy, with the attempt to 're-educate' Germans towards democratic values, but faith in Nazi ideology was arguably destroyed not by re-education but by Hitler's suicide, defeat and the problems which followed. Most Germans now took little interest in politics, becoming cynical about the authoritarian and military values of the past, and uncertain of what to put in their place. In the early post-war years it was difficult even to stay alive, with low rations, a fuel shortage and an economy which worked by barter in the absence of a stable currency. The Allies took reparations and industrial output was much reduced: even in 1947 production was less than half pre-war levels.

Economic hardship, the death and destruction brought by war, and a lack of faith in themselves, all made the task of reconstruction a formidable one for Germans. The ghosts of war continued to haunt the country for decades to come. Trials of leading Nazi war criminals, like that of Klaus Barbie in France in 1987, kept memories of wartime atrocities alive. Over ten million expellees from east of the Oder–Neisse were living in West Germany in the 1960s. And some Allied occupation rights still survived in Berlin in 1989. Germans had to try to come to terms with the problem of 'collective guilt' for the events of the Hitler period. Despite talk of 'liberation' rather than 'defeat' in 1945 few Germans had actively resisted the Nazis. Many tried simply to deny all memories of the Third Reich or else to question the notion of collective guilt; others were concerned that the old authoritarian values *did* survive beneath the surface, that civil servants remained in office despite serving the Nazis and that the basis for a genuine new democracy was not therefore laid after the war. Just as significant as the legacy of the Third Reich was the division of Germany brought by the occupation. For, by 1947, the country had become a victim of Cold War tensions and was effectively split in two. Even in defeat Germany was too valuable – strategically and economically – for either East or West to let it fall into the hands of the other. Whilst the Soviets carried through the redistribution of land, the nationalisation of industry and the transfer of political authority to German Communists, so the three Western powers increasingly co-operated in the creation of a federalised, liberal-democratic state in the West. In 1946 the Americans and British agreed to unite their occupation areas into a 'Bizone'; in 1947 western Germany was embraced in the Marshall Plan for European economic recovery; and in June 1948, after a conference in London, the decision was made to create a West German government.

The need for German support ensured that the Allies' original determination, to exact vengeance for wartime sufferings, melted away. In 1943 the American Treasury had conceived the 'Morgenthau Plan' to turn Germany into an agricultural economy, but in the summer of 1947 the Americans and British agreed to increase steel production in the Bizone. Attempts were made to root out those businessmen who had supported Hitler and to break up the industrial cartels which had provided the materials for the German war efforts. At the Potsdam conference in July 1945 all the occupation powers agreed to disarm Germany, and limits were placed on the types of goods which German factories could produce, to prevent her regaining any war potential. In western Germany, however, private businessmen soon returned to their old positions. Business confidence was greatly boosted after June 1948 by the introduction of a new, stable currency and heavy industrial output was accelerated under the Marshall

Plan. In 1947 German coal and steel production stood at 130 million tons and 3 million tons respectively – by 1952 the figures were 208 million tons and almost 16 million tons. American and British policy makers saw western Germany as an important bastion against Soviet Communism, a country which, being in the front line against the Red Army, must be tied securely to the West. The French, having been victims of German occupation, were much less certain about this policy. They wished to use German resources but without recreating a strong German state. But France's own reliance on US financial support made it difficult to resist the Anglo–American policy. In June 1948 France was promised various limits by America and Britain on German independence: industrial restrictions would remain, an 'International Authority' was established to control the coal and steel resources of the Ruhr valley – Germany's industrial heartland – and a Military Security Board was set up to guarantee disarmament. The concessions paved the way for the 'fusion' of all three western zones into a single unit and the foundation of a West German regime.

Democracy was being rekindled in Germany long before a West German government was created. The first free election after the war was in the Bavarian village of Wohlmutschüll, in the US zone in August 1945, for the position of Mayor. Democracy continued to be refounded 'from below' with such elections, gradually building up to *Länder* (provincial) level. The *Land* (province) of Prussia, with its historic domination of Germany and its association with militarism, was abolished, and *Länder* borders were redrawn. *Länder* parliaments were elected with German Minister-Presidents at the head of the provincial administrations. In 1947, to strengthen the German role in policy-making an 'Economic Council' was established in the Bizone.

The London conference decisions of June 1948 to elect a Constituent Assembly and devise a West German constitution provoked a sharp Soviet protest, in the form of the Berlin blockade. The western sectors of Berlin (entirely surrounded by the Soviet core) were cut off from all access by land to the West, as the Soviets tried to force concessions from the Western powers on the future shape of Germany. Equally disturbing for the Western powers at this time was that the German Minister-Presidents did not relish the idea of creating a West German government either. Reviving the economy and allowing local elections was all very well for west Germans, but to create a government only in the western zones would be to divide the nation: German people might well be appalled by this and turn against their new leaders. Soviet propaganda had been trying, since 1946, to portray the Western powers as wanting to divide Germany. The Soviets, with control of the eastern zone, could pose as the champions of German reunification and try to win West Germans over to their side.

After a critical few weeks of talks with the Minister-Presidents a compromise was reached by which a German government would be created, but without giving the impression that this meant a permanent division. Instead of a Constituent Assembly, a 'Parliamentary Council' met in Bonn in September 1948 to devise, *not* a constitution but a 'Basic

Law'. Effectively the Basic Law *was* a constitution. However, it was intended only to be a 'provisional' arrangement until Germany could be reunited. The deliberations in Bonn were guided by rules laid down by the Allies. West Germany was to have a liberal-democratic constitution, with important powers decentralised to the *Länder* (to prevent a strong central *Reich*) and guarantees of democratic freedoms. Representatives from West Berlin were allowed to attend as 'observers' but Berlin was to remain under four-power occupation, legally separate from the rest of Germany. It took until May 1949 to draft the Basic Law. Meanwhile, the Western allies had successfully kept Berlin supplied by an airlift throughout the winter, which forced the Soviet Union to call off its blockade and strengthened West German faith in the Western powers.

The Basic Law was devised in the knowledge that Germany, since being unified in 1870, had been ruled by an authoritarian government under the Kaisers before 1918, and by a totalitarian system under the Nazis after 1933. The previous experiment in liberal-democracy, the Weimar Republic (1918–33), had ended in disaster, undermined by the harsh Versailles peace treaty, the survival of strong imperialist elements in the army, civil service and judiciary, economic problems and the alienation of both the Communists and the far Right. A new constitution could not promise to bring an end to all these problems but it was at least hoped to correct some of the flaws in the Weimar constitution, which had been marked by unstable governments, numerous political parties, an over-powerful Presidency and inadequate constitutional guarantees. The Basic Law, devised in intense debates, created a two-chamber parliament with an upper *Bundesrat*, made up of *Länder* representatives, able to amend and delay legislation but not initiate it. The lower *Bundestag* was elected every four years and under the electoral law of 15 June 1949 had half its members from constituencies and half its members elected under proportional representation. Germans had a double vote: one for each type of representative. This system ensured reasonably fair representation for each party, whilst preventing a large number of parties being elected to parliament. To help the latter aim further, no parties could be represented in the *Bundestag* unless they won five per cent of the vote in a *Land* or won one seat outright. (In 1956 the system was changed so that parties needed five per cent of the vote at *national* level, or three direct seats.) The Chancellor was to be elected by a majority of the *Bundestag* to act as the head of the executive, and could only be removed from office by a 'constructive vote of no confidence': that is, if the *Bundestag* voted a Chancellor out, they also had to put forward an alternative to replace him. The Chancellor was thus in a much stronger position than under Weimar, and, additionally, he could request an early election if he asked for a vote of confidence and this was rejected by the *Bundestag*. The powers of the Federal President, elected every five years by the *Bundestag* and *Länder* parliamentary representatives, were reduced mainly to the ceremonial functions of a head of state.

Other major elements in the Basic Law included the decentralisation of authority over cultural and religious affairs, education, local government and the police to *Länder* level. The *Länder* had considerable financial independence and their position in the *Bundesrat* further strengthened their powers. However, in due course more and more authority (over defence and foreign affairs for example) went to the central government. Federal law was always superior to *Länder* law and the *Länder* were restricted in many areas to carrying out the policies of the Bonn government. Civil rights were defined in the Basic Law, including freedom of expression, assembly, religion and of movement, and the government was obliged to respect these. As a further important guarantee against the subversion of democracy, a Constitutional Court, separate from the government and parliament, was created\* to decide whether government actions were permissible under the Basic Law. The Court could also ban any political parties which it considered anti-democratic, a move partly designed to prevent a return of the Nazi party, though the Court also banned the Communist party in 1956. Such practices as the use of the term *Bund* (federation) rather than *Reich* (Empire) also emphasised the break with the past (as did the return of the old Weimar flag of red, black and gold). The Basic Law proved acceptable to the Western allies, who approved it in May 1949. To emphasise their changed attitude to Germany the Allies were politically represented in West Germany in future not by Military Governors, but by High Commissioners. The Allies kept certain reserved powers (including control of foreign policy) under an Occupation Statute but their practice was to give the new German government as much independence as possible. Such a government was finally elected on 14 August 1949 after an intense election campaign.

After May 1945 several political parties had been formed in Germany. The most confident was the Social Democratic Party (SPD), the strongest party under the Weimar Republic, with working-class support and hoping to take advantage of the anti-capitalist mood in post-war Germany to bring about a planned economy and social reforms. But the division of Germany had served to weaken the party. In April 1946 Otto Grotewohl, the SPD leader in the eastern zone, complied with the Soviet wish to unite his party with the Communists, who had also re-formed themselves in 1945 and were hoping to widen their appeal. The division of the country meant the loss of former SPD strongholds in the East, the development of the Cold War also undermined support for Marxist ideas, and the SPD alienated voters in the Western zones by poor tactics. The party leader, Kurt Schumacher, was a strong-minded social reformer and anti-communist, but his energies had been sapped by years in concentration camps under the Nazis, he refused to co-operate with 'bourgeois' political parties or the Catholic Church, and he had an abrasive, intolerant personal manner. His belief that the SPD would naturally become the majority party proved misplaced as another party emerged to rival him, in the form of the Christian Democratic Union (CDU), with its Bavarian offshoot, the Christian Social Union.

\* It actually came into being in 1951.

The CDU began in 1945 as an attempt to create a single, reformist yet non-socialist party, with support from both the Catholic and Protestant communities. It was thus intended to have a much wider appeal than the old Catholic Centre Party, which gradually faded away after the war. Its leading member by 1948 was Konrad Adenauer, Mayor of Cologne in 1917–33, an opponent of the Nazis, who had returned to his position of Mayor in 1945 only to be ousted by the British, who favoured the SPD. Devoting his energies to national politics, Adenauer had become President of the Parliamentary Council in 1948–9. Despite his age (he was born in 1876) his patient, practical and dignified leadership won wide respect. His supporters prevented the SPD from writing their ideas for social and economic change into the Basic Law, defeated SPD hopes for a more centralised government and later (in November 1949) ensured that Beethoven's birthplace, Bonn, would be the capital of the new Republic. Many had favoured Frankfurt, a larger town, a major business centre, and the seat at the first all-German parliament in 1848. Bonn was contemptuously referred to as the 'capital village'. The town, however, was closer to Adenauer's home, was not a centre of SPD support, and could more easily be seen as a 'temporary' capital until an all-German government was re-established in Berlin. Adenauer also succeeded, within the CDU, in rejecting socialist-style ideas for reform, such as nationalisation, which had been seen in the party's 1947 'Ahlen Programme'. Instead Adenauer supported a 'social market' economy which would end state controls and create a democratic form of capitalism, based on individual freedom, private property and the free market. These ideas were associated with Ludwig Erhard, who played a leading economic role in the Bizonal Council and joined the CDU in June 1949.

In the August 1949 election the German people favoured the CDU (31 per cent) over the SPD (29 per cent), and other parties too proved willing to support Adenauer for the Chancellorship. Most important were the Free Democrats (12 per cent), who had inherited the old Liberal mantle. They were non-religious, anti-socialist and supported *laissez-faire* economics. The Free Democrats (FDP) and the conservative German Party, based in Hanover, joined the CDU in a coalition, easily outmatching the SPD. Even so Adenauer was only elected Chancellor by a slim margin – 202 votes out of 404. There were twelve other, small parties in the *Bundestag*, ranging from the Communists through the remnants of the old Christian Centre Party to the extreme right-wing Conservatives. Despite the safeguards in the Basic Law some even feared a return to the parliamentary instability of Weimar. When the new Republic formally came into being in September it indeed had many difficulties to overcome. West Germany was still loathed abroad, economic reconstruction had only begun, large numbers of refugees had swollen the numbers of the unemployed, many politicians were inexperienced in office, the government lacked full sovereignty, and the division from the East had been a traumatic experience. There were no guarantees that the wealthy, stable, democratic regime of later years would emerge.

## The Adenauer Era, 1949–63

That West Germany achieved wealth and stability in the 1950s and 1960s was due in part to the prolonged and steady leadership of 'the old man' Konrad Adenauer. Despite his age and his narrow election as Chancellor he soon established himself firmly in Bonn, dominating his new Cabinet, whilst his political opponents were weak: the non-coalition parties in the *Bundestag* were divided among themselves and neither the Communists nor the various conservative groups proved willing to combine with the SPD, whose socialist programme alienated many. As the 1950s proceeded the smaller conservative parties faded away and their voters tended to support the CDU, which therefore gained an unassailable position in government. As in France under the Fifth Republic, West Germany moved away from a system of political parties based on class, religious and constitutional differences. The Weimar system of Communists, Social Democrats, liberals, Catholic Centre and conservative parties gave way to a broad two-party system, such as already existed in Britain, with the FDP running a poor third. Both the CDU and the SPD sought to give themselves a mass membership, a national organisation and wide popular appeal, though the CDU at first proved far better at fulfilling the last aim. The major difference between West Germany and Britain was that, thanks to Germany's partial system of proportional representation, the CDU had to rely on FDP support, thereby giving the 'third party' a major political role and an important moderating influence. One early sign of the rewards the FDP could expect from its moderating role was the election of one of its leaders, Theoder Heuss, as Federal President in September 1949.

Adenauer's programme as Chancellor had several main elements. Domestically he needed to integrate twelve million refugees into German society and to demonstrate the benefits of the 'social market' over the SPD's preference for nationalisation. Regarding relations with the Allies he hoped to extend his government's rights to full sovereignty, but by a policy of friendship and reconciliation rather than through the demanding style favoured by Schumacher. In pan-German affairs, Adenauer was determined to portray Bonn as the only legitimate German government: despite the foundation of an East German regime in 1949 West Germans continued to call eastern Germany 'the zone'. Internationally Adenauer wanted to restore his country's name, by giving compensation to Hitler's main victims, the Jews, by seeking a *rapprochement* with France and other European neighbours, and by making Bonn a loyal ally of the United States. Although West Germany was not supposed to have an independent foreign policy, the Chancellor effectively handled international affairs from his own office, helped by his assistant Herbert Blankenhorn. Their pro-Western policy soon had its successes. In November 1949 under the Petersberg Agreements, the Allies reduced the amount of reparations taken from Germany; in 1951, thanks to Adenauer's support for the new European

Coal–Steel Community,* reparations were ended altogether, and in May 1952, under the Treaty of Bonn, the Allies finally undertook to restore German sovereignty.

There was, however, a price to be paid for such concessions. In supporting the Coal–Steel Community, Adenauer had agreed to surrender control of two key industries to a supranational European authority. After September 1950 Adenauer had also agreed to a US proposal for German rearmament, despite the controversy this caused. Adenauer believed that a new democratic German army could be created but others were not so confident after the experiences of the past. The Interior Minister, the pacifist George Heinemann, resigned over the proposal and later joined the SPD. Many others opposed rearmament under the slogan '*Ohne Mich*' (Without Me). Then, in May 1952, the Bonn Treaty was made conditional on Germany drafting troops for service in a European Army. Adenauer's view was that West Germany must tie itself to the Atlantic Alliance in order to ensure Western support against Russia. At the time of the Korean War in 1950 he feared a Soviet invasion and he believed that the USSR would only agree to German reunification on its own terms, which could well result in Communist rule. Adenauer was determined to preserve Germany's nascent democracy, and its place in Romano–Christian culture by tying the country firmly to other Western democracies. If the West remained strong, he believed, the illegitimate East German regime would eventually collapse. However, his policies led to his being condemned by Schumacher as 'the Chancellor of the Allies'. The SPD believed that Adenauer should have taken up opportunities for talks with the Soviets, particularly Stalin's March 1952 proposal for a reunited but neutral Germany (which the Western powers saw simply as a Russian bid to prevent German rearmament). Adenauer's policies appeared to keep Germany divided. Some Germans were also upset by Adenauer's agreement to Israeli demands for compensation after Hitler's 'Final Solution'. Under the June 1952 Hague Agreements reparations were paid to Israel, and other payments to Jews followed in the Indemnification Laws of 1953. Nevertheless, Adenauer was determined to take responsibility for the mistakes of the past and to this end he also agreed to settle pre-1945 German debts.

Debt repayment was helped by the German economic boom of the 1950s which is often identified with Economics Minister Erhard. In 1950 the economic picture had looked very bleak. Unemployment stood at over ten per cent, German trade was in deficit, an IMF loan was obtained, there was still a serious housing shortage and over one-third of government spending had to go to covering Allied occupation costs. Adenauer's popularity in this early period was low and Erhard's policies seemed slow to work. Refugee groups were particularly disaffected and in January 1951 formed their own political party, the BHE, to represent their interests. However, the Korean War stimulated the German economy, as it

* See pp 34–5.

did the rest of Western Europe, and there was much unrealised potential after the years of occupation. In 1951 business investment began to take off, the IMF loan was repaid and the government and trade unions jointly encouraged the building of new accommodation, mostly in the form of cheap rented flats. Erhard concentrated on a policy of low taxes, a stable currency and liberal trade, but an important element in West Germany's success was the co-operation of workers and the trades unions. There were sixteen industrial trades unions, each linked to a particular industry, which simplified negotiations on pay and conditions. The unions joined together in the *Deutscher Gewerkschaftsbund* in October 1949. Old religious barriers, which had divided the unions between the wars, were ended and in 1951 the government established the right of 'co-determination' in the coal and steel industries. 'Co-determination' gave workers a legal right to sit on management boards, so as to influence management decisions. This was seen as a way to reward the unions for their opposition to Nazism, as well as a way to foster good industrial relations. The 1952 Works Constitution Law spread workers' powers more widely across German industry, although this act did not give the same degree of influence as was provided in the coal and steel industries. The Trades Unions themselves were not necessarily pleased with 'co-determination' since the policy tended to reduce the Union's role and make workers less militant, but co-determination showed that all classes in Germany could share in the benefits of the 'social market', helped create good industrial relations and reduced the danger of deep class-based divisions between the CDU and SPD.

By September 1953, when West Germany's second post-war elections were due, Adenauer's government could claim many successes. Allied controls had been reduced and the Constitutional Court had dismissed an SPD claim that German membership of a European Army was unconstitutional. German industry had laid the basis for its later success in producing steel, chemicals and electrical goods, trade was now in surplus and growth rates were over eight per cent per annum. Unemployment had fallen to six per cent, wages were higher and economic expansion helped to provide housing and unemployment for the refugees from the eastern lands. In May 1952 an Equalisation of Burdens Act provided compensation payments to refugees for the losses they had suffered as a result of the war. This was paid for by a special tax and payments continued until 1979. The BHE party, as a result, did not become the right-wing nationalist party which many had feared. (One neo-Nazi party which was formed in 1951, the Socialist Reichs Party, was quickly banned by the Constitutional Court.) In the election, the BHE won 27 seats but most other small parties, including the Communists, lost all their seats and the CDU (45 per cent of the vote) reaped the benefit. The FDP (9.5 per cent) stayed in coalition with the CDU, and the SDP (29 per cent) were again disappointed. The SPD was alienated both by Adenauer's determinedly pro-Western foreign policy and by Erhard's social market. But the Soviet's ruthless response to the June 1953 East

Berlin rising had seemed to prove Adenauer's pro-Western policy right and, after Schumacher's death in August 1952, the SPD were led by the well-meaning but colourless Erich Ollenhauer.

Fortified by his second election victory Adenauer adhered to his policies, which continued to pay dividends. Growth rates slowed somewhat in the mid-1950s, yet were still in excess of seven per cent. Over three and a half million more Germans fled from East Germany in the 1950s but were absorbed relatively easily, helped by the fact that generally many were young and skilled. Unemployment continued to fall and was constantly below one per cent in 1961–6. All signs of a housing shortage had disappeared by 1963. Such formidable economic successes gave the German people a new confidence and allowed the expansion of social services, with a major pensions reform in 1957, when old age pensions were made universal and tied to the cost of living. This important reform showed, once again, that the success of the social market could bring rewards for all Germans. Adenauer's foreign policy seemed threatened in August 1954, when a vote by the French parliament put an end to the European Army project and caused a delay in the restoration of German sovereignty. Nonetheless, in May 1955 West Germany was finally rearmed as an equal member of NATO. At the same time, exactly ten years after defeat in World War II, full West German sovereignty was achieved and a foreign ministry properly established. Until 1968 the Allies retained the right to use emergency powers to protect their armed forces, but otherwise the occupation was ended. Adenauer was also pleased that soon afterwards, in October 1955, the people of the coal-rich Saar, which had been separated from Germany in 1946 (at French insistence), rejected French plans for their future. Adenauer had earlier seemed to connive at French control of the Saar, in order to preserve his policy of friendship with Paris, but in January 1956 a new pro-German government in the Saar requested reunification with West Germany. This was achieved in January 1957.

Adenauer's foreign policy continued to cause some controversy and even to provoke divisions between the CDU and FDP by 1957. Many Germans were concerned after 1953 by the growing Western reliance on nuclear arms. The SPD and trades unions continued to oppose German rearmament and to express an interest in a reunited, neutral German state. Adenauer and the Western allies insisted that Germany could only be reunited through free, national elections, and with the freedom to pursue a pro-Western policy, and Adenauer utterly rejected the idea that East Germany could be a sovereign state, such as the Soviets declared it to be in September 1955. Adenauer in 1955 proceeded to set up a Ministry of Defence and to create a new *Bundeswehr*, whose first members joined up in November. Under the regulations of March 1956 the new army was to be made up of 'citizens in uniform', committed to defend democracy, preserving full civil rights and even able to join a trades union. Yet the force still provoked concern and the SPD opposed the introduction of conscription in May 1956. Many FDP members too, by then, had grave doubts as to whether Adenauer's policies on reunification and rearmament were the right ones. The FDP also questioned whether Adenauer's support for West European integration did not harden Germany's division. There was FDP resentment at Adenauer's domination of government, and over his consideration of an electoral reform which would make it even more difficult for small parties to be elected to the *Bundestag*. So great had the FDP's disaffection become by February 1956 that most of its members left the coalition. In April 1957, now in opposition, they condemned the idea of accepting nuclear weapons on German soil, thus joining with the SPD, religious and scientific groups who opposed Adenauer's pro-nuclear policy.

Fortunately for Adenauer enough FDP members continued to support the coalition after February 1956 (and eventually joined the CDU) that it survived in office. And in the September 1957 election the FDP seemed to have chosen the wrong course when its share of the vote fell below 8 per cent, whilst the CDU – strengthened by the 1957 pension reform – won just over half the votes cast. The SPD still led by Ollenhauer, and with policies largely based on negative criticisms at Adenauer, rose only slightly to 32 per cent. The FDP soon rejoined the government. For a time after this, its third electoral defeat in succession, the SPD continued to criticise the government on nuclear weapons and in 1958 began the 'Campaign against Nuclear Death', which held a number of rallies. However, the threatening policies of Nikita Khruschev as Soviet leader again aided Adenauer, and many SPD leaders now believed the party must give itself wider appeal. In December 1958, one month after Khruschev began to make verbal threats against the Western position in Berlin, the SPD's Willy Brandt was re-elected Mayor of the city, a post he had held since 1957. Brandt represented a 'revisionist' outlook in the SPD. He was ardently pro-Western and anti-Soviet, he wanted greater social reform in Germany but he was ready to accept a capitalist element in running the economy too. Other party leaders, such as the former Communist Herbert Wehner, agreed change was needed, and in November 1959 their views triumphed in the Bad Godesberg programme, drawn up at a special party meeting. The programme marked an attempt to widen the SPD's appeal away from its working-class bed-rock. Much about the programme was vague, but it ended the traditional reliance on Marxist rhetoric, talked of 'Christian ethics' and ended such symbolism as the red flag and raised fist. The SPD would use state planning where necessary but accepted that Erhard's social market had its successes. In June 1960, following this acceptance of 'realities' in domestic policy, Wehner told the *Bundestag* that the SPD also accepted the main elements of Adenauer's foreign policy, such as NATO and EEC membership. In November 1960 the SPD, armed with policies that were designed to win power and not simply to protect doctrinal purity, chose the popular Brandt as their candidate for Chancellor in the next election. (Under the German system a party's candidate for Chancellor is not necessarily the party chairman.)

By 1961, despite his continuing economic successes, there were signs that Adenauer's position was under threat. It was not so much his age, or any loss of physical energy that was the problem, but the fact that he was so domineering, had been in power too long and could upset even his closest colleagues. He had clashes on several occasions with Erhard, for example, who seemed his natural successor. When Theodor Heuss retired as President in 1959 Adenauer wanted Erhard to fill the vacant position, which would prevent him becoming Chancellor. As the East–West crisis over Berlin deepened German foreign policy also became troubled: even Adenauer feared that the Americans might prove ready to compromise with Khruschev. When the Berlin Wall was erected in August 1961 the Americans seemed powerless and it was Brandt, as Mayor of Berlin, who stole the limelight from Adenauer in opposing the Soviets and East Germans. Adenauer still emerged triumphant in the September 1961 election, but the CDU fell back to 45 per cent of the vote whilst the SPD advanced to 36 per cent and the FDP to 13 per cent. The FDP leader, Erich Mende, only agreed to form a new coalition with the CDU if Adenauer agreed, in writing, that he would resign within two years. Many FDP members had not wanted to save 'the old man' at all, but Adenauer was able to threaten Mende with the idea of a 'Grand Coalition', that is a coalition between the CDU and SPD, such as was being canvassed by moderates in both main parties.

In retrospect Adenauer's personal reputation would have been better served if he had retired gracefully in 1961. As it was the next two years proved very difficult. The building of the Berlin Wall seemed to show that Germany's division could not be broken down by the forceful anti-communist line which he favoured. The SPD's willingness to talk with the Eastern bloc, whilst maintaining the Western alliance, seemed a more realistic policy. Adenauer remained concerned that US President Kennedy would pursue détente with Moscow to Germany's cost, and the Chancellor drew closer to France's President de Gaulle. However, Erhard and foreign minister Gerhard Schröder, remained pro-American and were distrustful of de Gaulle's ideas for a more independent European policy. Erhard and Adenauer now clashed on other issues but in an argument in May 1962 over custom duties it was Erhard who won the *Bundestag*'s support. When in July 1962 Adenauer said he might not retire the following year, pressure rose in the CDU to find a replacement. Then the '*Spiegel* affair' broke which finally made the Chancellor's position untenable. The magazine *Der Spiegel* had long-criticised the defence minister (since 1956), Franz Josef Strauss, who was right-wing, abrasive, pro-American and had hopes of becoming Chancellor. In October 1962 the magazine printed an article, based on classified material, which exposed problems in Strauss's policies. In response, Adenauer and Strauss not only had the magazine's offices searched but also arrested its editor. This led to a public outcry, comparisons were made to the Nazi era and, in November, FDP ministers left the coalition. They only returned after Strauss resigned, his hopes of becoming Chancellor shattered. In February 1963 the CDU lost a humiliating third of their vote in the Berlin election, and in April Adenauer acknowledged that Erhard should succeed him.

Konrad Adenauer finally resigned in October 1963 and, despite the problems of his last two years, the historical judgement on him was generally favourable. He was, indeed, widely compared to Bismarck. From an unfavourable position in 1949 – greatly aided by Western support and the Basic Law – Adenauer had given West Germany political stability, won international respect, preserved peace abroad and democracy at home, prevented the rise of political extremism, brought *rapprochement* with France, and presided over a remarkable economic recovery. Particularly important were his decision to tie Germany into the Atlantic Alliance externally and his demonstration that the 'social market economy' could work internally: both policies had eventually been accepted by the SPD opposition, thus providing a fundamental consensus between the major parties regarding the shape of West Germany. Then again, his paternalistic leadership style, his willingness to bring ex-Nazis into office, his pro-Westernism and his fostering of materialism were to invite widespread criticism in Germany over the following years.

## The Rise of the SPD, 1963–74

Ludwig Erhard, who succeeded Adenauer as Chancellor in October 1963, was an experienced minister, the man held responsible for German economic success since 1949, deeply committed to the US alliance and who, at 66, could look forward to a long career as Chancellor – given the record of his predecessor. Yet Erhard's honest, calm, and fair-minded character reflected a lack of political acumen and an inability to wield authority which won him the nickname of 'the Rubber Lion'. In 1963 he made few changes to Adenauer's cabinet and emphasised the element of continuity in government, though his personal style was very different to that of 'the old man'. In contrast to Adenauer, Erhard always welcomed discussion and looked for consensus. At first, the new chancellor had his successes. In December 1963 his government made an agreement with East Germany to allow West Berliners to visit their relations in East Berlin at Christmas. Similar arrangements followed at other holidays. Bonn still refused to recognise East Germany's existence and remained diplomatically cut off from countries in Eastern Europe who did recognise her, but trade with Eastern Europe was expanded. In 1964 the CDU's Heinrich Lübke, originally elected President in 1959, was re-elected with SPD support, thus demonstrating the ability of the two main parties to work together. And in the September 1965 election, Erhard triumphed over Brandt, improved the CDU vote and hoped to lead Germany into a new era of economic and social progress.

Behind the scenes, however, the ageing Adenauer continued to criticise Erhard and there were signs of growing social and economic problems in Germany. Growth rates in the 1960s began to slow down to two or three per cent, still quite favourable, compared to other countries, but a blow to German self-confidence. Criticisms of the capitalist system, which Erhard had seemed to make so successful in the 1950s, increased. There were demands for higher wages, for social reform and for wider access to higher education, yet in 1966 the government felt the need to cut back on spending programmes as the economy moved into a minor recession. The same year radical students in Berlin, led by Rudi Dutschke, began protests against the Vietnam War and doubts grew about US foreign policy in general, particularly with its absorption in South-East Asia and lack of interest in Europe. Meanwhile the SPD kept up pressure for a policy of 'co-existence' with East Germany. Erhard's loyalty to the US alliance succeeded in alienating those elements in the CDU who preferred to build up West European co-operation through friendship with France. Yet ironically it was US President Johnson who finally ensured Erhard's downfall. In 1966 the Americans, and the British, both in economic difficulties themselves, pressed the Bonn government to relieve them of military costs in Germany. To offset these costs Johnson wanted West Germany to buy more military hardware from America. In September Erhard visited Johnson to try to resolve the issue, but the President would not make any concessions and Erhard appeared weak on the world stage. In late October, after the Chancellor proposed certain tax increases, the FDP left the coalition and on 30 November, without their support, Erhard was forced to resign, his party divided, his foreign policy questioned, and even his reputation as an economic wizard tarnished.

Erhard was succeeded at the end of 1966, not by a reconstituted CDU–FDP coalition, but by a 'Grand Coalition' of the CDU and SDP, the first time the SDP had shared in government since 1930. A new CDU–FDP combination had been considered but the FDP seemed fickle and unreliable: October 1966 was not the first occasion of course on which they had left the Cabinet. In any case the CSU (the CDU wing in Bavaria) insisted on the return of Franz Josef Strauss to the Cabinet, which the FDP could never accept following the *Spiegel* affair. The SPD too decided that they could not rely on the FDP to provide a solid, lasting majority in parliament and Herbert Wehner was all in favour of a 'Grand Coalition'. Such a 'Black–Red' combination would give strong government, provide a basis for tackling Germany's economic problems and allow the SPD some much-needed experience of power. The CDU and SPD had seemed close enough since 1960 on domestic and international issues to work together and the CDU were keen to rebuild themselves after a troubled period since 1961. The new Chancellor was Kurt Georg Kiesinger, a sensitive, able man, and a good orator, who had established a good reputation as Minister-President of Baden-Würtemberg in the early sixties. Brandt, who had become SPD chairman in 1964, was the new foreign minister, able to develop SPD ideas on links to Eastern Europe. Without formally recognising East Germany, Brandt stressed détente with the Eastern bloc as preferable to confrontation, and established diplomatic relations even with countries who recognised East Germany. It was hoped to reassure the Warsaw Pact about European security, to develop a strong German role in central Europe and eventually to break down barriers with East Germany. The Soviet invasion of Czechoslovakia in August 1968 proved a setback, however, and Brandt's 'Ostpolitik' did not fully become a reality until he himself became Chancellor.

The policies of the Grand Coalition were planned after August 1967, by leading CDU and SPD members meeting in the 'Kressbronn Circle' (so-called because the first meeting was held in Kressbronn whilst Kiesinger was there on holiday). Despite some differences the two parties co-operated reasonably well together at first. Nowhere was this more true than in the relationship between Strauss, who had become Finance Minister, and the SPD's Karl Schiller, who took charge of Economics. These two pursued a much more interventionist policy than had previously been the case, using government-directed investment policy, as well as certain spending controls and tax increases, to tackle unemployment, reduce the budget deficit and restore economic growth. Government representatives, employers and workers now met together to discuss economic policies. These efforts were not untroubled. The CDU would not let economic planning be taken as far as the SPD favoured, farmers protested against cuts in agricultural subsidies and defence cuts could not go far because of fears of weakening NATO. However, the Strauss–Schiller policy soon seemed successful. Unemployment peaked at over two per cent in 1967, then fell off, and Germany continued to absorb up to two million 'guest' workers from Turkey, Yugoslavia and elsewhere. Growth was back at a remarkable six per cent in 1968, inflation remained low and the budget was in healthy surplus by 1969. This probably helped undermine support for a new right-wing party, the National Democrats, whose anti-US, anti-Soviet and anti-immigrant policies had won it up to ten per cent of support in *Länder* elections in 1966–8.

Greater concern for the government was provoked on the left of German politics at this time. Many Germans were concerned that the very existence of the Grand Coalition meant that there was no effective opposition in parliament, save for the 49 FDP members. The SPD seemed to have compromised its principles in joining the 'Kiesebrandt' coalition and this was at a time of growing questioning of capitalist society by intellectuals, students and radical politicians. Problems which affected the whole Western world in the mid-1960s – the 'generation gap'; new moral and artistic values; alienation from technology, materialism and the consumer society; disaffection in factories and universities – were made particularly acute in Germany by the legacy of war. The younger generation, who had never known the Weimar or Nazi eras, still less the Wilhelmine Empire, had little understanding of those who had lived through earlier turmoils. Radicals accused the government of representing authoritarian, elitist, uncaring values, and of being a US puppet, influenced by ex-Nazis. Adenauer's paternalism and his willingness to rehabilitate ex-Nazis who renounced their former beliefs were now questioned. During the 1950s Adenauer had favoured such individuals as Hans Glöbke (who had been head of the Chancellor's office) and Theodor Oberländer (a Cabinet minister) despite their close involvement in shaping Nazi policies. Adenauer had taken the view that it was pointless to divide the country by too much emphasis on the Nazi era, and in the 1950s many Germans were all too ready to forget the recent past. In the 1960s, however, there was greater interest in the history of the Nazi period and questions were raised about the moral basis of the new Germany. Kiesinger himself was criticised for his Nazi party membership even though he had risked his life to help Jews during the war. Berlin was a particular centre of discontent because of the large number of young men who went there to escape conscription in West Germany itself.

Vietnam, the rise of the National Democrats, and the lack of reform in universities despite a rising number of students (over 400 000 in 1968) added fuel to the criticisms of society, as did the transfer of emergency military powers from the Allies to the Bonn government in 1968. The Socialist Students Union, expelled from the SPD in 1961 and controlled by the extreme left, had considerable influence; Rudi Dutschke formed an 'extra-parliamentary opposition' (the APO) to transform Germany into a libertarian society and a 'direct democracy'. 'New Left' thinkers, it should be stressed, rejected East European socialism as well as bourgeois democracy. Indeed, when the German Communists reconstituted themselves as a political party (the DKP) in October 1968, the Bonn government saw no need to ban them, because orthodox Communists did not seem a threat. Neither can the student unrest in Germany be said to have been as serious as it was in France. Nonetheless there were serious disturbances after June 1967, when police shot and killed a student protesting against a visit to Berlin by the Shah of Iran. Even more widespread demonstrations took place when Dutschke was shot and wounded by a right-wing extremist in April 1968. Over the next two years the protest movement, a mixture of genuine discontent, sincere concern and self-indulgence, petered out. Certain individuals, like Andreas Baader and Ulrike Meinhof, joined in the Red Army Faction to try to undermine the state by terror tactics. Many others joined the SPD, and eventually had a major influence on changing its policies back into a more radical line than the Bad Godesberg programme.

In September 1969 the SPD could face the elections reasonably united, with experience in power and well-championed by Brandt. The 'Grand Coalition' had managed to outlast the student unrest and to tackle Germany's economic problems, but its story had been a troubled one in 1967–8 and by 1969 differences between the two constituent parties were more apparent. The SPD, for example, had refused to support the CDU in its desire for electoral reform. The CDU had wanted to change to a system of simple majority votes in constituencies, a move which would prevent the National Democrats winning seats but which would also destroy the FDP. Some SPD leaders had shown an interest in the proposal when the coalition was founded, but in March 1968 the party deferred consideration of the issue and so won the FDP's thanks. Then in 1969 the FDP supported the SPD's Presidential candidate, Gustav Heinemann, who successfully triumphed over the CDU's Schröder. The Grand Coalition then became crippled and although the CDU emerged first from the elections with a respectable 46 per cent, they were outnumbered by the SPD (who rose to 43 per cent) and FDP (who declined to 6 per cent, their lowest vote ever). The National Democrats failed to win any seats.

After the election, despite some doubts about relying on the FDP, Brandt quickly moved to establish an SPD–FDP coalition. Social democratic policies of state intervention and Ostpolitik were now in favour with the electorate, especially among young people and, after the liberal reforms at the Second Vatican Council, even Roman Catholic voters were prepared to lend support to the SPD. There were those who believed that the new Chancellor lacked the drive and ability to head the government, which would be a far greater challenge than his experience governing West Berlin. Yet Brandt, born illegimitate, exiled under the Nazis, who had even become a Norwegian citizen for a time after the war, had come through many trials. He was moderate, sensible and tough. Appointing the FDP leader Walter Scheel as foreign minister and ably assisted by Egon Bahr, Brandt developed 'Ostpolitik' much more dramatically than had been possible under the Grand Coalition, in a situation where East–West détente was increasingly more welcome to the US and so need not endanger Western unity. Despite his high international profile, his determination to preserve the Atlantic alliance and his 1972 Nobel Peace Prize, Brandt's policy provoked concern amongst the CDU, who doubted that the 'Eastern Treaties' would actually lead to any relaxation of Soviet control in East Germany. The 1970 treaties with Russia and Poland included the mutual renunciation of force but they also marked an acceptance of the status quo in Europe (including Germany's division) and of the Oder–Neisse border. Then again Brandt's 'Ostpolitik' was popular with German voters and it was difficult for the CDU to oppose the greatest prize of all, the 1971 Berlin agreements, which led to much greater access between the two halves of Berlin.

Domestically, Brandt also went further than the Grand Coalition in extending state intervention in the economy, with the intention of fostering a more egalitarian, caring society. Spending at central and local level was expended on welfare, cultural and educational improvements. By 1974 public services took up over a quarter of the GNP, compared to 15 per cent 20 years before. The Education Act of 1971 improved financial support for students, the school leaving age was raised to 16, the voting age was lowered to 18 and worker participation in businesses was strengthened under a 1971 act. In 1972 pension payments were made more generous and there were also improvements in family allowances, health care, unemployment pay, the penal code and rent controls. Real incomes rose, the working week was now generally forty hours and paid holidays were more numerous. On the Left there was some dismay that the reforms were not more dramatic, and especially that wealth was not redistributed more equally. The Baader–Meinhof group remained active in 1970–2 with bank robberies and bombings, and government counter-measures led to renewed accusations about a 'police state'. But others became concerned that state spending was too high. Although the currency was strong (despite a revaluation in 1969) and the budget in surplus, wage demands were also high and inflation rose from 2 per cent in 1969 to over 5 per cent in 1972. Although this still compared well with other Western states, in May 1971 the Finance Minister, Alex Möller, resigned and his post was given to Schiller, who also remained as Economics Minister. Schiller's dual 'Superministry' attracted criticism however, his attempts to control public spending were unpopular and his bullying behaviour made him enemies. In June 1972 he too was forced to resign, the 'Superministry' being inherited by Helmut Schmidt.

Schiller's resignation came soon after the decisive Bundestag vote on the 'Eastern Treaties' and made mid-1972 a difficult time for Brandt. Since 1970 a number of FDP members, critical of domestic and foreign policy, had defected from the government coalition to the CDU. In January 1972 an SDP member, one born east of the Oder–Neisse, also defected and the CDU leader, Rainer Barzel, believed he could win a constructive vote of no confidence against Brandt. When such a vote took place on 27 April, however, it was amidst popular demonstrations in Brandt's favour and threats of strike action if he lost. Barzel's attempt failed by two votes and there were accusations of bribery being used to achieve the result. After the vote Brandt's position was stronger. The 'Eastern Treaties' were ratified on 17 May, with the CDU deciding to abstain, and Brandt then went on to negotiate the 'Basic Treaty' defining future relations with East Germany, on the principle of two German states existing in one nation. Despite inflation and Schiller's resignation, West Germany's economic performance was far better than her Western partners, and growth was still over 3 per cent. In September Brandt engineered a voting defeat in the *Bundestag*, enabling him to call an election to exploit the popularity of Ostpolitik and restore a firm parliamentary majority. His move proved a great success. For in the 19 November election, for the first (and last) time in West Germany's history the SPD (46 per cent) outstripped the CDU (45 per cent) whilst the FDP (8.5 per cent) also improved. It was the culmination of a remarkable advance by the SPD since the late 1950s, when they had lost election after election. The realism and moderation of the Bad Godesberg programme, the bankruptcy of Adenauer's Cold War policies, the change in popular attitudes on socio-economic issues in the 1960s, the alliance with the FDP and Brandt's own popularity had combined to put the SPD securely in office.

Like Erhard after the 1965 election, however, Brandt's apparently impregnable position soon disintegrated. Despite the completion of the Basic Treaty with East Germany, and the signature of a treaty with Czechoslovakia in 1973, Ostpolitik did not bring a major change in Communist rule in Eastern Europe. SDP left-wingers were more neutralist and anti-American than their leaders, and anxious to see more radical domestic reforms but Brandt feared that greater radicalism would alienate the FDP, on whom the SDP still depended in the *Bundestag*. The oil price rises of October 1973 came as a serious blow to Bonn, as it did to other Western European nations. There were cuts in the road-building programme and a ban on Sunday driving to try to reduce reliance on oil. Inflation and unemployment rose, as did wage demands. Then again, another election was not due for some time, the FDP remained loyal to the coalition and Brandt's international reputation stood high. The Chancellor's fall came very quickly in the end, after one of his personal staff was arrested on 24 April 1974 as an East German spy. Confidence in Brandt was hit; his critics in the SPD, like Herbert Wehner, were strengthened; and he himself was personally hurt by the mounting criticisms. On 6 May he suddenly resigned as Chancellor (whilst remaining as SPD chairman). Though criticised as the Chancellor who had accepted Germany's division, he had greatly helped his country's standing in the world, extended social welfare provisions on a large scale and placed his party in the leading role in Bonn.

## Schmidt and Kohl, 1974–89

Brandt's successor, appointed on 16 May 1974, was Helmut Schmidt, a pragmatic, intelligent man, who had been critical of Brandt's leadership at times, and who could be brusque and impatient. Schmidt, born in 1918, had been a Hitler Youth member and a lieutenant in the wartime army, but he had joined the SPD soon after the war and entered the *Bundestag* as early as 1953. In the 1950s he had failed to advance far in the party nationally, and had instead made his name as internal affairs minister in the *Land* of Hamburg after 1961. His return to the *Bundestag* in 1965 was followed by a rapid rise: Chairman of the Parliamentary Party in 1967; Deputy Chairman of the SPD from 1968; Minister of Defence, 1969–72; and Minister of Finance, 1972–4. He had supported the Bad Godesberg programme and was loyal to the Atlantic alliance. On becoming Chancellor he was determined to obtain more investment and jobs for the German economy, to maintain Ostpolitik and to withstand a new wave of terrorism from the Red Army faction. Since Walter Scheel had been elected President on 15 May, Schmidt's foreign minister was the new FDP leader, Hans-Dietrich Genscher who became, by 1989, the longest serving foreign minister in the Western world. Schmidt and Genscher could not repeat the dramatic advances in foreign policy made by Brandt, and some Germans remained disappointed by the lack of political change in the East, but Genscher's reputation grew enormously as foreign minister, helping the FDP's popularity. Personal contacts with East Germany continued to grow and West Germany was able to expand its trade and financial links to Eastern Europe.

The German economy in 1974 was still troubled by the 1973 oil price increase. Thanks to deflationary measures, Bonn did not experience the large-scale trade deficits and inflation of other Western countries, but unemployment rose to 4.7 per cent in 1975 and inflation was over 5 per cent, a poor performance when compared to the past. There was resentment against immigrant workers despite government attempts (since 1973) to reduce the number of 'guests' from abroad. The government's moves to widen abortion and to extend the principle of co-determination in industry both caused controversy, yet Schmidt's personal popularity remained high and he survived the test of the October 1976 election. The CDU, led by the apparently undynamic Helmut Kohl, increased their vote to nearly 49 per cent and this restored their leading position in the country, but the SPD (43 per cent) and FDP (8 per cent) retained their majority in the *Bundestag*. *Länder* elections had earlier suggested an even better CDU vote, but after October 1976 the party became more divided with the CSU branch in Bavaria, under Franz Josef Strauss, taking a more independent line. This eventually helped make Strauss the CDU's candidate for Chancellor in the next election, but he remained such a controversial figure in the country that his election was unlikely.

After 1976 unemployment in Germany was falling, inflation was under control and exports were expanded to offset the cost of oil imports. Yet other Western states, still grappling with the aftermath of 1973, pressured Schmidt to reflate the West German economy faster so as to help their own recovery. Schmidt played an important role in encouraging international agreement among the 'Group of Seven' leading Western countries* who began to meet annually after 1975. Working closely with President Giscard d'Estaing of France, the Chancellor also helped found the European Monetary System in 1979. After the bitter experiences of the past some Germans were reluctant to take a high international profile but Schmidt was keen to achieve exchange rate stability, to tackle the energy price problem and to prevent a policy of protectionism in the Western democracies. There were limits, however, to how far he was ready to stimulate German demand to help other countries and he was critical of the Americans, British and others for doing too little to tackle inflation. West Germany, like Japan, largely escaped the high inflation, unemployment and interest rates (collectively known as 'stagflation') which dogged the Western world in the later 1970s. But in Germany, nonetheless, it was a time of great apprehension and doubt after the boom years of the 1950s and 1960s. The moral confusion bred in the late 1960s lingered and the Left were gaining strength in the SPD with criticisms of the US alliance, authoritarianism in the state and environmental problems. In September 1977 the second wave of terrorism by the Baader–Meinhof gang reached its grisly climax: the businessman Hans-Martin Schleyer was kidnapped and murdered; Palestinian and German terrorists made a vain bid to get Baader and others released from prison, by hijacking a *Lufthansa* airliner; and when German police forcibly put an end to the hijack Baader and his colleagues committed suicide. The threat from the Red Army Faction then lessened, though murders continued to be carried out throughout

---

* The US, Japan, West Germany, France, Britain, Italy and Canada.

the 1980s and US bases in West Germany were bombed. Government security laws, passed to tackle terrorism, caused controversy especially when left-wing activists were excluded from civil service posts.

West Germany was still very prosperous in the late 1970s, improvements were being made in living standards and Schmidt was able to limit the difficulties in the economy, even if he often seemed to react to events rather than to give the country any real sense of direction. In 1979, however, came the second major oil price increase of the decade, followed by a general depression in the West. For the first time since the mid-1960s, Bonn faced a trade deficit. Investment was low, interest rates rose, there was concern over a fall in the population level from its 1974 peak of 62 million, and there were calls to cut back on the high social welfare spending built up by the SPD governments. In foreign affairs too there were problems. Schmidt was already upset by the vacillating policy of US President Jimmy Carter. Then, after the invasion of Afghanistan in December 1979, Carter's policy was suddenly reversed, the Cold War was revived and the Germans found that Ostpolitik was also put at risk. Schmidt, however, like Giscard in France, showed his independence of America by talking to Soviet leaders in Moscow in July 1980 and he returned to triumph in the general election. The CDU, with Strauss as a controversial candidate for Chancellor actually fell back to 44.5 per cent, whilst Genscher's FDP (11 per cent) advanced and the SDP (43 per cent) held firm. Nevertheless, it was always clear that Schmidt's third term in office would prove a difficult one.

Numerous problems arose after the 1980 election to ensure the demise of Schmidt and the SPD. In foreign policy, despite his respect for the consistency of the new US President, Ronald Reagan, the Chancellor continued to argue with the Americans. In November 1981 Bonn and Moscow signed an agreement to build a gas pipeline into Western Europe from Siberia, which provoked US displeasure. Meanwhile NATO's decision to deploy intermediate nuclear weapons in West Germany enraged the neutralists in the SPD, who became increasingly vocal and uncontrollable. Support also grew for a new political movement, the environmentalists or Greens. The Greens had grown only slowly in importance since the 1960s and they won less than 2 per cent of votes in the 1980 election. They wanted not merely to take anti-pollution and anti-nuclear measures, but also to change Germany back into a rural economy, yet they grew rapidly in appeal after 1981 and attracted the sympathy of leftists who were dissatisfied with the moderation of the SPD. Economic problems also continued to deepen. In 1980 unemployment was 3.8 per cent, but in 1981 it rose to 5.5 per cent and in 1983 was 9.2 per cent. Such figures had not been seen in Germany since the early 1950s and, as elsewhere in Europe, heavy industry was worst hit. German steel production had peaked in 1974 at over 53 million tons, in 1979 it was 46 million but by 1983 it had fallen to 36 million. Unemployment payments led to increased government spending and the trades unions wanted to tackle West Germany's problems by higher wages to stimulate demand, and shorter hours and a lower retirement age to ease unemployment. However, in the FDP (which was itself troubled by a financial scandal in 1981) certain elements believed that government spending must now be cut and taxes lowered. Otherwise, they argued, German industry would be completely strangled.

In April 1982 the SPD Congress voted for higher taxes and greater state control in industry but such demands alienated FDP moderates, and suggested that Schmidt was losing control of his party. Poor local election results led FDP leaders to believe that an alliance with the CDU was now more desirable and on 17 September they left the coalition. Schmidt, bitter at the FDP's desertion, tried to manipulate an early election but on 1 October the CDU leader Helmut Kohl succeeded in doing what Rainer Barzel had failed to do ten years earlier: he won a constructive vote of no confidence against Schmidt. The SPD were ousted from power after 16 years, amidst deep internal divisions and a confused economic scheme. The SPD left-wing remained concerned over nuclear weapons and the environment, and were keen to solve German problems by state intervention. The CDU however, like Margaret Thatcher's Conservatives in Britain, represented a resurgence of conservative values, a faith in the Atlantic alliance and a belief that state intervention must be reduced to allow the economy to resuscitate. The new Chancellor, Kohl, seemed personally mediocre but the 1 October vote showed that he could also be subtle and determined, and he had a formidable political record. He had joined the CDU in 1946, when aged only 16, had risen to become Minister-President of the Rhineland–Palatinate in 1969–76, was party chairman after 1973 and leader in the *Bundestag* three years later. His calm manner was underpinned by a deep religious faith.

Kohl's political wisdom and the change of mood in German politics were both confirmed in the elections of 6 March 1983. Kohl, like Brandt in 1972, engineered the vote by deliberately losing a confidence motion in the *Bundestag*. Unemployment was high, with little suggestion that the CDU's economic policies would reduce it quickly. There was also intense debate over nuclear weapons and environmental issues, with the Greens obtaining nearly 6 per cent of the vote and thus entering the *Bundestag*, the first time since the 1950s that a fourth party had had any electoral success. After Schmidt's fall, the SDP chose a moderate candidate, Hans-Jochen Vogel, for Chancellor, but the party was very divided, Vogel was uninspiring, and Kohl was so confident of CDU success that he even advised electors to give their second votes to FDP candidates. This was to avoid the elimination of the FDP from the *Bundestag* and to prevent any SPD–Green coalition government. The CDU's vote of 49 per cent was their second best ever, whilst the SPD (38 per cent) and FDP (7 per cent) dropped back. Kohl's old rival, Strauss, who was still detested by the FDP, was kept out of office but Genscher was retained as foreign minister and was able to preserve Ostpolitik. Most of the CDU were now prepared to accept Ostpolitik given its popularity, even if East Germany in the mid-1980s was as authoritarian as ever. More loans were extended to East Germany and telecommunications links were improved.

At home the Kohl government followed a policy of restraint in public spending, tolerated a high level of unemployment and sought to restore business confidence by tax changes and a belief in *laissez-faire* economics. This led to an improvement in trade and a fall in inflation, so that Germany in the late 1980s became once again a country of trade surpluses and a strong currency, at the cost of some social division. The FDP's radical wing was dissatisfied with these policies, but there had always been a strong *laissez-faire* economic tradition in the party and the SDP were now too divided to make suitable partners in government. With the departure of Schmidt and Herbert Wehner from the political scene in 1983, Brandt, the party chairman, was once again the leading force in the SPD but he failed to control the left. The rise of the Greens had placed the SPD in a difficult position, in that any attempt to capture moderate votes might alienate existing party supporters and drive them over to the Greens. Instead, in November 1983, at a time of massive demonstrations against nuclear weapons, an SPD conference voted to oppose intermediate-range missile deployments. The party continued to demand arms reductions in 1985–6. It was unsurprising that, with Johannes Rau as their candidate for Chancellor, they fared even less well in the 1987 election (with 37 per cent of the vote) than they had four years before. With unemployment still above two million there was also a decline in the CDU vote (to 44 per cent) but the FDP (9 per cent) were stronger. Support for the Greens (8 per cent) was probably boosted by the explosion of the Chernobyl nuclear power station, in the Soviet Union in April 1986, which caused widespread poisoning of the atmosphere across Europe.

Following its second poor electoral showing in a row the SPD remained divided. Brandt retired as party chairman amidst much criticism, to be succeeded by Vogel who, of course, had already failed in one bid to become Chancellor. However, Chancellor Kohl, too, soon seemed in difficulties. In foreign affairs East–West détente had revived after the rise of Mikhail Gorbachev in Russia and in September 1987 Erich Honecker made the first visit by an East German head of state to West Germany. Kohl himself went to Moscow in October 1988. But as a result many West Germans no longer saw the Soviets as a threat and there were growing signs of resentment about Kohl's pro-US policy and the presence of NATO forces in Germany. Then, paradoxically, the US-Soviet treaty of 1987 which removed intermediate nuclear weapons from Europe also led to renewed worries that Germany would be left undefended by America if war did break out. At home, meanwhile, Kohl faced a number of problems. In 1987–8 the CDU was rocked by scandal when Uwe Barschel, the Minister-President of Schleswig–Holstein, used illegal means to help his re-election. Barschel was eventually forced to resign and committed suicide. The Chancellor's appointment of non-party men to Cabinet posts caused resentment in the CDU and in November 1988 there was another embarrassing resignation, by the President of the *Bundestag*, Philipp Jenninger, who made a speech on the fortieth anniversary of *Kristallnacht* (the Nazi's anti-Jewish pogrom) which some took to be sympathetic to

Nazism. The old cloud of extreme nationalism had already reappeared when Franz Schönhuber formed the right-wing, anti-immigrant Republican party and won some successes in local elections. A number of government policies also ran into trouble. Kohl was forced to scrap a proposed tax reform (affecting interest payments) due to the popular outcry against it, and also reversed a decision to extend the length of conscription to 18 months, which was designed to cope with the falling population. The government continued to cut spending and introduced such controversial moves as increased charges for medical care. Kohl had always had to cope with the personal problem of appearing lacklustre and undynamic, and in 1988 even close colleagues doubted whether he could remain as Chancellor for long.

In autumn 1989, however, forty years after its foundation the future of the Bonn Republic was suddenly being revolutionised. Events in Eastern Europe and more particularly in East Germany opened up new dangers and opportunities. Kohl had been able to maintain his leadership of the CDU in 1988–9, helped by a Cabinet reshuffle and the death of his old rival Franz Josef Strauss. Then the Chancellor's energetic but careful response to events in the East boosted his flagging popularity. The SPD was tainted somewhat by its attempts during the 1980s to establish links with the ruling Socialist Unity Party (SED) in East Germany. It was possible to argue that Ostpolitik had, in the end, served to undermine the East German regime by reinforcing the liberal-democratic alternative to Communism in the minds of the East German people. But the SPD could now find little alternative to Kohl's policy of welcoming the SED's demise, allowing refugees in from the East and exploring possible routes to German reunification. At the end of 1989 the Chancellor's reputation had recovered. There was intense concern over the financial and social costs of absorbing hundreds of thousands of refugees who now flooded in from the East, but West Germany seemed in an excellent position to exploit the likely expansion of trade with Eastern Europe in future. More importantly, the door was now open to end the 'provisional' Bonn Republic, unite with East Germany and re-create a single German state.

Despite its difficult birth in the late 1940s, the instability of the regimes which preceded it, the deep scars left by the Nazi era and the divisions brought by the Cold War, the Federal Republic had survived for four decades as a stable, tolerant, secure and wealthy democracy, with one of the strongest economies in the Western world and a leading role in the European Community. Neither neo-Nazism nor left-wing terrorism had succeeded in undermining the foundations of the Republic, which had combined a strongly capitalist economic system with a good degree of social justice. Nevertheless, there were those for whom the changes of 1989 revived fears of nationalism, authoritarianism and expansionism in German policy. Bonn's power in the post-war world had, after all, been limited by the division from the East. The separation of West Germany from East Germany had helped guarantee Western security, given Germans an identification with Western values and aided the

Franco–German *rapprochement*, allowing Germans to be safely integrated into the Atlantic alliance. Now even France and Britain together could barely match the economic might of West Germany, and a reunified Germany could well become the dominant economic force in Western and Eastern Europe. How such formidable influence would be used depended in part on how deeply liberal-democratic values had become entrenched since 1945. However, the longevity of the Republic, the material rewards it had provided to the German people and the fact that Eastern Europeans hoped to emulate West German success in future, suggested that Bonn would act to promote, not threaten, democracy across Europe in the 1990s.

# 4
# France

## Resistance, Renewal and the New Republic, 1944–7

Although nominally a Great Power in 1945, with a seat on the United Nations Security Council and the second largest Empire in the world, France emerged from the Second World War as a much-weakened nation. In June 1940 the land of Louis XIV and Napoleon had experienced swift defeat at the hands of Germany. The Third Republic had survived the Great War of 1914–18 but its institutions were blamed by many for the humiliation of 1940. Under the Republic France had put an end to the frequent changes of regime since 1789, had achieved a good degree of social stability and guaranteed personal freedoms to its people. But the country, reacting to the authoritarianism of the past, was governed by an unstable *régime des parties* in which one short-lived coalition succeeded another, corruption was rife and strong, decisive government almost impossible. The nation had also become economically and demographically stagnant: heavy industrial production lagged behind Britain and Germany, nearly a third of people still lived off the land, and in 1940 the population (at about 40 million) was little larger than it had been in 1900. It can be argued that the major failings in 1940 lay not with the government but with the Army whose ageing generals were quite unprepared for the tactics of *blitzkrieg*. It was, however, the Right which emerged triumphant from the political crisis brought by defeat. Marshall Philippe Pétain, the hero of Verdun, became premier, signed an armistice with Hitler and established an authoritarian government, based in Vichy. Pétain followed a policy of collaboration with the Nazi 'New Order' in Europe, whilst claiming to be the defender of French independence.

That France emerged from the war with some pride restored was due to the existence of the Resistance, who insisted on maintaining the struggle against Germany. The Resistance had two main elements. Inside France the opponents of Vichy and of Nazism began to organise underground activities, and to plan France's post-war revival. Beyond France, General Charles de Gaulle, who had been Under-Secretary of Defence in 1940, formed the 'Free French' movement, based first in London and then (after 1943) Algiers, and claimed to be the 'true' representative of the French nation. Viewed by many as a vain upstart, de Gaulle's stand was in fact inspired not by ambition but by a deeply-held belief in the *grandeur* of France. Though a man of conservative, even authoritarian views, who had been a protege of Pétain's, de Gaulle rejected the Vichy regime because of its identification with surrender and collaboration, actions which were unworthy of France. The concept already existed in French politics of an 'eternal' nation which transcended the frequent changes of regime. De Gaulle saw himself, like Joan of Arc or Georges Clemenceau before him, as the embodiment of that eternal, spiritual France, who would save the country from its humiliation. Certain French colonies immediately accepted his leadership, his movement was supported by the British, and the Resistance within France also recognised him as leader. De Gaulle's haughtiness and his determination to protect French interests in the world, often provoked bitter arguments with his allies, the British and Americans. In the Summer of 1944, however, the liberation of France, aided by the home Resistance, left de Gaulle as the only possible French leader. He entered Paris on 25 August and in October his government was given full recognition by the Allies.

From the outset the story of the 'Fourth Republic'* was a troubled one. In 1944 the French people, already exhausted by defeat and occupation, still faced malnutrition, strict food rationing and inflation. Less than half the rail network was operable, industrial production was at a third of its pre-war level, overseas trade was at a standstill. The war had cut a swathe of destruction across northern France and killed over half a million people. Much ill-feeling was vented out on former collaborators, many of whom faced summary execution before government authority was fully established. One of those condemned to death legally, in August 1945, was Pétain, though his sentence was commuted to life imprisonment. With the old political Right destroyed, some expected to see a united Resistance party leading the country, with bold ideas for national renewal. But the facts were that most Frenchmen had *not* been in the Resistance and that the Resistance itself was divided into different groups. The Communists accepted de Gaulle's leadership, joined the government and supported the 'battle for production' in 1945, but were loyal above all to Moscow. Certainly the Communists' role since 1941 had expunged memories of the Hitler–Stalin Pact period when they had opposed the French war effort. This, together with their ability to organise clandestine activity and their promises of economic and social reform, helped the Communists to emerge as the strongest party in the first post-war elections in October 1945, when they won 26 per cent of the vote. Two other parties, however, were close behind. The Socialists (24.5 per cent) had considered merging with the Communists when the war ended to create a single working-class party but their leaders, like Leon Blum, believed that the road to socialism lay

* The Republic was not formally constituted until 1946, but the term 'Fourth Republic' was used before this.

through a liberal-democratic political system rather than a Soviet-style regime. The Christian Democratic Popular Republican Movement (MRP) had been formed in November 1944 as a new reformist party, but one committed to the defence of the individual in society. The Christian Democrats did even better than the Socialists in the election (25.5 per cent), partly by proving a refuge for conservatives. But the Radicals, the predominant party under the Third Republic suffered from being identified with the failures of the 1930s and attracted less than one vote in ten.

The economic problems, the exhaustion brought by war, and divisions between the political parties all caused difficulties for de Gaulle. The General's hope that France could play a major international role was undermined by the country's economic and military weakness. In 1944–5 de Gaulle's Minister of Economic Affairs, Pierre Mendès-France, proposed a bold economic programme to strengthen the country through the introduction of austerity measures and national economic planning. However, de Gaulle, whose knowledge of economic affairs was limited, was persuaded by other ministers that the French people were unprepared for the burdens of an austerity programme and that there would be a natural, if gradual, improvement in post-war conditions without Mendès-France's measures. In fact, whilst some economic areas, especially the transport system, did improve in 1945, inflation grew worse. True, in January 1946, de Gaulle approved a proposal by Jean Monnet, a businessman and international civil servant, to devise a reconstruction and modernisation plan. But, meanwhile, popular discontent with France's economic problems was widespread. By January 1946 de Gaulle was also disturbed by the growing influence of the main political parties, following the October elections of a Constituent Assembly, which was to devise a new constitution. De Gaulle was a soldier, not a party man. He despised most of the political leaders and hoped to give France a strong constitution with a powerful Presidency, a position which, of course, he would be well suited to fill. The new Assembly, however, was quite unsympathetic to these views. The Communists and Socialists wanted a weak Presidency and a strong one-chamber parliament, able to push through radical reforms. Already, in November, de Gaulle had had to threaten resignation to put an end to Communist demands for certain key cabinet posts. Then in December he was appalled by the Socialists' desire to cut the military budget. In January he surprised everyone and actually did resign. He evidently hoped that he would be recalled to power by popular acclamation and that the parties would be unable to work without him. If so, it proved a grave miscalculation. The main parties were pleased to have excluded such an authoritarian figure from government and de Gaulle did not return to power for 12 years.

With de Gaulle gone the Communists, Socialists and Christian Democrats continued to work together in a 'tripartite' coalition under the Socialist Felix Gouin. The Christian Democrats differed from the other parties by favouring a two-chamber parliament, a stronger Presidency and the protection of the Roman Catholic Church. Not all issues divided the Christian Democrats against the other two however. All the parties for example, after the trials of war, believed in the need to reform and expand the social security system in order to create a fairer society. They also wished to nationalise certain industries. Nationalisation was not new to France – the railways had been put into State ownership in 1937 – but support for economic planning had grown during the war as a way towards national renewal, greater investment and improved working conditions, and also as a way to punish businessmen who had collaborated with the Nazis. Nationalisation had begun under de Gaulle and embraced the coal, gas and electricity industries, airlines, major banking and insurance companies, and *Renault* cars. A new national insurance system, to provide health insurance, old age pensions and family allowances was also introduced in 1946, and at the end of the year the Monnet Plan for reconstruction and modernisation was finalised. Many industries, such as road transport or iron and steel, remained in private hands, and those which were nationalised continued to use old management methods. National insurance did not actually become a comprehensive scheme for about 20 years due to popular suspicions and lack of funds. The Monnet Plan however, committed France to economic growth, with the aim of surpassing the best pre-war levels of industrial output by 1950, and thus marked a revolutionary change in attitudes from the economic stagnation of the Third Republic. The Plan worked by setting targets for certain key sectors of the economy (such as steel, electricity and cement) rather than by close state direction, it tended to foster the return to industrial predominance of capitalist businessmen, and it relied on loans from abroad, particularly from America. By encouraging expansion, automation and innovation it proved vital in strengthening France despite the Fourth Republic's political weaknesses.

By May 1946 a constitution had been drafted which suited the Communist–Socialist approach to politics, with a strong lower house of parliament. But the Christian Democrats criticised this and the French people, called to give their view on it in a referendum, rejected the document. This led to elections for a new Constituent Assembly in which the Christian Democrats emerged as the strongest party, had one of their leaders – Georges Bidault – made premier, and were then able to draw up a constitution better suited to their tastes. Nonetheless the new document, approved by another referendum in October, still gave most authority to the National Assembly. An upper house was created, but its powers were limited, and the President had little real power. General de Gaulle, who had re-emerged onto the political scene, opposed the constitution and it was approved by only a minority of the electorate: 36 per cent voted 'for', over 31 per cent 'against', and 31 per cent abstained. It hardly amounted to a vote of confidence for the new regime.

The system of *tripartisme* (three-party co-operation) had survived the strains of devising a constitution and the elections to a National Assembly in November showed that stable government would continue to rely on the main parties working together: the Communists now had 29 per cent of the vote, the Christian Democrats 26 per cent and the Socialists 18 per cent. Nonetheless, the government became increasingly divided in 1947 on a range of issues, and it was the Communists who were usually at odds with their coalition partners. Traditionally the French nation was said to be divided on the basis of 'Three Cs' – the constitution, clericalism and class. This was a rather simplistic interpretation of the many disagreements which affected political life, but it contained some truth and helped to explain why France was unable to create a British or American-style two-party system: the question of authoritarianism and democracy in the constitution, which had divided Frenchmen since the Revolution, had again served to divide the country in the constitutional debates of 1946; the role of the Roman Catholic Church in national life divided the Christian Democrats from the other leading parties; and questions of class conflict were particularly apparent in early 1947 in differences over wage levels. The Communists favoured wage increases, whilst the other parties argued these would be inflationary. Even graver problems were provoked by the addition of two more 'C's' to the traditional political debate: colonialism and the Cold War. France was not unique in having to come to terms with East–West tension and pressures for decolonisation after the war, but for various reasons these two problems had a particularly important impact on her. The issue of decolonisation indeed was ultimately to do much to destroy the Fourth Republic. Most French people believed it was essential to hold on to their Empire in the late 1940s. The Empire had made a major contribution, in men and resources, to the French war effort, much national pride was invested in it, and it was seen as a source of continuing French influence in the world. After victory in 1945 there were hopes of creating a new imperial relationship. Even liberals believed that the colonies would remain loyal if they received economic benefits and shared in the ideals of liberty, equality and fraternity, which France provided through her 'civilising mission'. To this end a conference of colonial administrators at Brazzaville in 1944 had introduced such reforms as the end of forced labour and improved education. The 1946 Constitution turned the Empire into a 'French Union', supposedly of equals, represented in a Union Assembly.

It soon became clear that France's tradition of 'assimilation' and centralised control over her colonies had won out over any real desire to share power with native peoples. The Union Assembly was powerless and 'equality' a sham: the 'Ministry of Overseas France' in Paris controlled the French Union. Neither was the French Army, with its tradition of colonial service and following the humiliation of 1940, ready to surrender to nationalist demands for independence. Unrest in Algeria was quickly repressed in May 1945 and trouble in Madagascar was ruthlessly put down in March–April 1947. The greatest challenge arose in Indochina, France's major colony in South-east Asia. Asian and Middle Eastern areas generally gave more trouble to the colonial powers, than did their possessions in Black Africa at this time. The former regions were more developed and better educated, often with advanced civilisations of their own and with nationalist movements established before the war. Nationalists were encouraged to want independence by their resentment of European exploitation, by the spread of liberal and socialist philosophies among the emerging middle classes, and by the success of two anti-colonial powers, America and the Soviet Union in the war. In Asia native peoples had also seen the European powers defeated, in 1941–2, by an Asian power, Japan. France had particular problems in one part of Indochina, Vietnam, whose independence had been declared in September 1945 by Ho Chi Minh, the leader of the Viet Minh movement. He had fought the Japanese and also happened to be Communist. In 1946 he came to Paris to discuss independence, but he found the French government was determined to restore its authority in all Indochina. In November 1946 the French bombarded the Vietnamese part of Haiphong after unrest there. The Viet Minh responded in December with a massacre of French civilians in the city of Hanoi. A vicious colonial war then broke out which was to last until 1954, with increasing costs to the French in lives and money.

In Indochina, France became embroiled in one of the most complex of the post-war colonial conflicts, but it took time to accept that the days of European colonial rule were numbered. The adjustment was made more difficult by the fact that Vietnam also became part of Cold War tensions: the Chinese Communists, who triumphed in their own country in 1949, gave aid to Ho Chi Minh, and the following year the Americans extended aid to the French. Both colonial issues and the Cold War had by then had a major impact on French domestic politics, dividing the Communists from the other two major parties. In early 1947 the Communists were critical of the tough policy adopted towards native independence movements in Madagascar and Indochina. In foreign policy the Communists also favoured co-operation with the USSR at a time when relations between the Soviet Union and the Western powers were rapidly breaking down. The Christian Democrats and Socialists did not relish the idea of Cold War in Spring 1947 but their liberal-democratic sensibilities and need for US financial aid helped push them towards co-operation with America (whose support was also vital in resolving the future of western Germany). In May 1947, after mounting disagreements, the Communists refused to support the government in a vote of confidence and premier Paul Ramadier decided to expel them from office. *Tripartisme* was then at an end, and the problem of maintaining a stable government in the new Republic then became extremely difficult.

## The Decline of the Fourth Republic, 1947–58

The expulsion of the Communists from government helped France to obtain US financial support through the Marshall plan of June 1947, but it also led to a deep rift in French political life, in which the Communists, with support from over a quarter of the population, effectively became ostracised from the rest of the country (a similar position to that in Italy). For a few months the Communists hoped that a return to office might be possible, but the formation of the Cominform by Europe's leading Communist parties in September 1947, was followed by an intensified struggle against the government. The Communists denounced the 'bourgeois' Republic, inspired a series of strikes in late 1947, and summer 1948, and condemned France's growing links with the Western allies. In December 1947, amidst the first major strike wave, moderate trades unionists split from the Communist-dominated workers' confederation, CGT, to form a new movement, the *Force Ouvrière*. Nonetheless, the Communists continued to draw considerable sympathy from the working class and the intelligentsia, including such people as the painter Pablo Picasso, the writer Jean-Paul Sartre and the nuclear scientist Frédéric Joliot-Curie. Only gradually did sympathisers become alienated by such Soviet actions as the 1956 invasion of Hungary, which even the CGT refused to approve. Meanwhile the rupture with the Communists caused particular problems for the Socialists. Left-wingers accused the Socialist leadership of failing to support social and economic reforms sufficiently. This failure was seen as the reason for the decline in the Socialist vote between the October 1945 and November 1946 elections. In 1946 the left-wing Guy Mollet had become Secretary-General of the party. Mollet disliked Ramadier's expulsion of the Communists and, in November 1947, helped to bring down the government. Thereafter many other coalitions collapsed because of Socialist doubts about major policy decisions, especially regarding financial issues, defence spending and social reforms. In February 1950 the Socialists left a government under Georges Bidault which survived for several months without them. It was a sign of things to come.

Problems were also added to the Republic in Spring 1947 by the formation of a new political force on the Right, led by General de Gaulle. Supposedly 'above' party politics, the Rally of the French People (RPF) seemed to have neo-Fascist elements. It had a charismatic, nationalist leader, attracted right-wing, anti-communist support – ironically, from many of Pétain's old supporters – and aimed to create a more authoritarian government. Violence at certain of its gatherings, de Gaulle's lack of a coherent government programme, and an easing in the country's economic problems, eventually helped to reduce the RPF's popularity. But in the municipal elections of October 1947 it won a staggering 38 per cent of the vote, and there seemed a real danger of a collapse of government, perhaps leading to a civil war, with de Gaulle's followers pitted against the Communists. The coalition parties, describing themselves as the 'third force' between extremes of Gaullism and Communism, were able to hang on to power, partly because no general election was due until 1951. But the RPF had an impact on the National Assembly because certain deputies were willing to leave their own parties and give de Gaulle their allegiance. The Christian Democrats were especially vulnerable to attacks from the

RPF, which appealed to similar sections of the population for support: in fact it was a parallel situation to that faced by the Socialists in competing with the Communists.

Until 1951 the Christian Democrats remained the backbone of all 'third force' governments, usually with the Socialists. But in the June 1951 elections the MRP share of the vote fell to only 13.5 per cent, compared to 26 per cent for the Communists, 21.5 per cent for the RPF and 15.5 per cent for the Socialists. The rest of the vote was shared between smaller groups, generally on the Centre-Right. It was partly in order to compete with the RPF for Roman Catholic votes that in September 1951 the MRP, supported by other conservative groups, passed the Barangé and Marie Laws, which gave small amounts of state support to religious schools. This, however, helped to alienate the MRP from the anti-clerical Socialists. The two parties did not share power in a coalition cabinet again until 1957, although they both continued to give the 'third force' their support in parliamentary votes. In fact the Socialists were out of office for the whole period 1951–6.

The 1951 election increased the difficulties of forming a government. Even before this the Fourth Republic had presented a spectacle of political instability, all too similar to the Third Republic. The post-war electoral system had tried to move away from the pre-war system in which many independent, local representatives were elected to parliament. In 1946 candidates were elected on 'party lists' in multi-member constituencies. This succeeded to some extent. At least it reduced the number of independents and tended to help the three larger parties. In 1946 whereas it needed only 33000 votes to elect the average Communist deputy, a Radical required 45000 votes. Yet small parties still existed and in 1951, in a quite cynical move by supporters of the 'third force', the electoral system had been changed in order to reduce the seats won by the two extremist parties, the Communists and RPF. Under the new system parties could enter into electoral alliances in the constituencies, and would win *all* the seats in a constituency if they won a majority of votes. Again, this system fulfilled its main purpose: the Communists and RPF found it difficult to join electoral alliances, and so lost seats. Despite their large vote the Communists actually had the same number of seats as the Socialists in the new Assembly. The average Radical deputy now needed only 25000 votes, compared to a Communist's 51000. But such manipulation of votes did nothing to earn respect for the regime and resulted in a fragmented Assembly. In general cabinets were much more conservative than before, not only excluding Socialist members but also, after Antoine Pinay's premiership in 1952, drawing on support from some RPF members. The RPF, having failed to win the 1951 election outright, had itself become divided. In May 1953 indeed, de Gaulle disbanded the movement, but his followers remained an important equation in the arithmetic of parliamentary majorities.

The existence of two extremist parties and a multitude of 'third force' groups helped create a system of government based on ephemeral, insecure coalitions. Between December 1947 and May 1958 the Fourth Republic had no less than 21 premierships. Some premiers survived in power for a mere few days; only two survived in a period of office for more than 12 months. Many were members of smaller parties. Constitutionally, governments were only obliged to resign if defeated by an absolute majority in a vote of confidence or in a censure motion. As it transpired, however, particular coalitions were usually formed to tackle a certain set of issues and then disintegrated. Prime Ministers would resign if a particularly important vote was lost or if a party withdrew from the coalition. Sometimes too unnecessary risks were run. Premiers, for example, insisted on having their cabinets approved by the Assembly once they were chosen, even though this was quite unnecessary. Once governments fell it could take several days to form another and sometimes the air of crisis lasted for months. On 19 July 1948, for example, premier Robert Schuman resigned and on the 24th André Marie began to form another cabinet; Marie, however, was forced to resign on 27 August and Schuman was invested again on the 31st; Schuman this time survived only a few days and a stable government only emerged under Henri Queuille after 11 September. (All this during the early weeks of the Berlin blockade!) The elements of instability in the Fourth Republic can be exaggerated. Many ministers survived in the same position through several governments. The foreign ministry, for example, (except for one month) was in the hands of either Georges Bidault or Robert Schuman for almost ten years, 1944–54. Most premiers had been in the immediately preceding government and some were premiers on several occasions. Stability was also provided by the civil service and by the quite effective Presidency of Vincent Auriol between 1947 and 1954. Yet a system which relied on short-lived coalitions, colourless prime ministers, behind-the-scenes political bargains and frequent crises was not one to inspire public or foreign confidence.

The danger of losing votes in the Assembly meant that most premiers were loathe to tackle complex problems – hence the term *immobilisme* to describe the political system. A tough stand was taken against strikers in 1947, 1948 and 1953, but in general strong government was rare, government ministers frequently kept information from each other, and the Republic was sometimes prey to another old disease, political corruption. The worse scandal was the 'Affair of the Generals', which broke in September 1949 following the 'leak' of a top secret report on the Indochina War. The scandal led to the resignation of the army's chief of staff, General Revers. The Fourth Republic did have some able, energetic leaders, such as Robert Schuman, the 'Father of Europe' or Mendès-France, but the experience of the latter when he re-emerged from the political wilderness to take the premiership in June 1954 was a perfect illustration of the Republic's inability to foster strong government. Mendès came to power at a time when two problems, born of decolonisation and the Cold War, threatened to tear France apart and destroy her international standing. Most pressing was the war in Indochina in which, after eight years of costly warfare, the country had just been defeated by nationalist guerrillas at Dienbienphu. 92 000 French lives had been lost, France had to accept that its days as a colonial power in Asia were over and Mendès promised to settle the war within a month – or resign. Not only did he succeed in this apparently impossible task, making peace with the Viet Minh at a conference in Geneva, but he went on to tackle the long-running problem of German rearmament. Since 1950 the idea of German rearmament, proposed by the United States, had divided France so much that it was called a 'new Dreyfus affair'. Mendès resolved the difficulty by abandoning the idea of German rearmament within a 'European Army' and later accepting German entry into NATO. In the process Mendès alienated the Christian Democrats and others who supported the European Army. When he turned to deal with North African problems, in February 1955, they took their revenge and he lost power. Further evidence of *immobilisme* came when Mendès' successor, Edgar Faure, also tried to tackle North African problems and was defeated. Under the constitution if a government was defeated twice within 18 months, by an absolute majority, the prime minister had the right to appeal to the electorate. Yet when Faure exercised this right, calling an election for January 1956, his own Radical party expelled him from membership! Such was the determination of the parties to run the political system to their own satisfaction and to prevent any strong individual dominating government.

The 1956 elections saw a left-right split within the 'third force', with Mendès-France's Radicals joining the Socialists in an electoral alliance – the 'Republic Front' – against the MRP, Gaullists and other conservatives. The 'Republican Front' emerged triumphant from this contest and the Socialists (15 per cent) now proved more essential to coalition government that did the MRP (10 per cent). Indeed, Guy Mollet was able to form the longest-lived government of the Fourth Republic (February 1956–May 1957). The divisions within the third force, however, helped the Communists to win a larger number of seats in the Assembly, commensurate with their 26 per cent share of the vote. In addition, any relief brought by the demise of the RPF was offset by the rise of a new anti-Republican force on the extreme right: Pierre Poujade's followers, known as Poujadists, won 11.5 per cent of votes mainly from lower middle-class groups – shopkeepers, small farmers and the like – whose economic fortunes were in decline. Mollet's social reforms, including the extension of holidays with pay and pension reforms, were somewhat limited; Mendès-France quit the government after differences over foreign and economic policies; and all the time the colonial war in Algeria was proving more bloody, dividing the French nation and straining the economy.

Despite its defeat in the Indochina conflict France (like other European colonial powers) hoped to remain a major force in Africa for some time. Sub-Saharan Africa certainly seemed too underdeveloped for independence, even if some educated locals had begun to form political parties after 1946. In North Africa, part of the Arab and Muslim world, things were more complex. Independent Arab states already existed in Libya, Egypt and the Middle East and mounting violence in Tunisia and Morocco had led Edgar Faure to concede self-government to them. In 1956 they both became independent. This put intense pressure on France's remaining North African possession, Algeria, where despite growing unrest since October 1954, it was no easy matter to concede independence. Algeria had been the first major French colony in Africa in the early nineteenth century, it had served as de Gaulle's headquarters in 1943–4 and was still seen as a possible place of retreat if the Red Army invaded France. It was also important for French trade and had substantial oil reserves. But above all it had about a million French settlers (compared to eight million natives) and it was constitutionally a *département* of France. The settlers blamed the French government's liberal policy in Tunisia and Morocco for the Arab unrest in Algeria, and a crowd of French Algerians attacked Mollet when he visited Algeria in February 1956. The Army too, after its defeat in Indochina, opposed (and even sabotaged) talks with the anti-colonial National Liberation Front (FLN) which intensified its guerrilla actions against the French in 1957.

After the collapse of Mollet's coalition, Félix Gaillard's government (November 1957–April 1958) finally brought the Socialists and Christian Democrats together once again and tackled inflationary pressures by devaluing the franc and introducing higher taxes. But Algeria provided the Republic with a problem which, even more than Indochina and German rearmament in 1954, seemed insoluble. Even the Socialists were afraid to upset patriotic opinion in France which was in favour of the French Algerians. Meanwhile, in North Africa, the military increasingly took matters into their own hands, openly defying the government in Paris. The Fourth Republic which, despite its weaknesses, had survived the onslaught of Communists and Gaullists in 1947–8, found itself completely paralysed ten years later. In February 1958, after 16 French troops were killed in an FLN ambush, the French Air Force took its revenge by bombing Sakhiet, a town in Tunisia, where the guerrillas had set up bases. Sixty nine people were killed and the air raid, carried out without authority from Paris, provoked an international outrage. Gaillard did nothing to punish those responsible, but he was bitterly criticised by patriots for allowing the Americans and British to mediate in the dispute between France and Tunisia. When Gaillard's government collapsed in April and President Coty called on another moderate, Pierre Pflimmlin, to form a government, there were riots in Algeria which led the Army to take control there on 3 May. It was clear that, as in 1954, France had to be led by someone other than a colourless mediocrity and eyes turned once again to General de Gaulle as a possible saviour. He at least was strong-minded, decisive and could win the trust of patriots and soldiers. Yet when the General was invested as premier on 1 June 1958 he was not only given full power to deal with the political crisis but also authority to devise a new constitution. The Fourth Republic was at an end, and for a second time Charles de Gaulle was called upon to save his country from humiliation and self-destruction.

## De Gaulle's Republic, 1958–69

The Fifth Republic which de Gaulle created in 1958–9 was, in many ways, a reaction to the weak constitution and unstable governments of the Fourth. A strong President and government were intended to control parliament, the political parties, the civil servants and Army, to give France a better sense of direction and to improve her international status. Yet this was not to damn the Fourth Republic completely. The previous regime had succeeded in preserving liberal democracy in France through a difficult period, it had provided a basis for French economic expansion through the Monnet Plan, it re-forged relations with West Germany in the framework of European unity, and (thanks to a decision of the Mollet government) it put underway the programme for a French atomic bomb, which was exploded in 1960 and became a symbol of the country's new dynamism. Neither should it be forgotten that the Fifth Republic was born amidst uncertainty. De Gaulle was nearly 70, he had been recalled to power by the parties he despised, and he relied heavily on Socialist support. No one was really clear about what the General stood for regarding Algeria and even the Army did not necessarily trust him. Gaullists like Jacques Soustelle had been heavily involved in the events of 13 May which led the Army to seize control in Algiers, and some feared that de Gaulle would join with French Algerians and the political Right to form a neo-Fascist regime. Only gradually did the General himself seem to become clear on what he wanted in Algeria, pursuing an ambiguous policy in which he was ready to use the emotive term '*Algérie Française*', on a visit to Algiers, whilst re-establishing the authority of Paris and preparing the way for a cautious offer of self-government to the rebellious province in September 1959.

Meanwhile, progress was made in founding a new political system. A draft constitution was published on 4 September 1958 and approved by four-fifths of voters on the 28th. This was largely a vote of confidence in de Gaulle: the Constitution was vague in important respects and left much to be interpreted in practice. All the main parties except the Communists approved it, yet, in the general election which followed the Fourth Republican parties lost support to the hastily-formed 'Union for the New Republic' of Gaullists – many of whom were ex-RPF members – who received one-fifth of the vote. Other conservative groups attained about a quarter of voters' support whilst the Communists were reduced to 19 per cent, the Socialists to 16 per cent and the Christian Democrats left on 11 per cent. Thanks to a new electoral system, defined in mid-October, the change in the political balance of power was even more marked because, in an attempt to create greater party loyalty, and minimise the representation of small or extreme parties, a system of single-member constitutencies was introduced, with a party list of candidates, and a second ballot in which candidates could only stand if they had secured a certain percentage* of the vote in the first ballot. As a result the Communists were reduced in Metropolitan France to only 10 seats and the Poujadists were annihilated. The Socialists (40 seats) and Christian Democrats (55) were swamped by the Gaullists (196) and conservatives (127) and many old parliamentary figures disappeared, including Mendès-France. In January 1959 de Gaulle was formally chosen as President (by an electoral college of notables) with another large majority. A week later a Gaullist, Michel Debré, who had done much to frame the new constitution, became premier. The Socialists were excluded from office, as were most other leading Fourth Republic politicians and only half the ministers were drawn from parliament. The Cabinet included the writer André Malraux, as Minister of Cultural Affairs and government officials like Maurice Couve de Murville who became foreign minister. Thus de Gaulle underlined that the government would now control parliament rather than vice versa.

In 1958 de Gaulle had already made his presence felt on the international scene by demanding equality with America and Britain as a leader of NATO, and in the economic field by introducing, in December, the 'New Franc' – valued at 100 old francs and intended to boost financial confidence. The main problem, however, remained Algeria, and this took four years to resolve. De Gaulle paved the way for Algerian independence through his policies in sub-Saharan Africa. No anti-colonialist guerrilla movements had emerged to challenge the French here, but the British had granted independence to Ghana in 1957 and, even before the General returned to office, French policy had changed its focus from trying to hold onto its colonies, to attempting to install friendly local leaders in power who would help to protect French interests in future. In September 1958 the French constitutional referendum included a vote in the African colonies too, in which they could opt either for full independence or for membership of a new 'French Community'. The Community, which replaced the 1946 French Union, would give natives self-government but leave Paris in control of their foreign and defence policies. In the vote only Guinea, influenced by the strongly anti-imperialist Sekou Touré, opted for full independence. Other countries wanted to retain French financial support. Then, in 1960, de Gaulle shifted ground again and gave all the Black African colonies full independence. It was a bold decision, which encouraged the British and Belgians (though not the Portuguese) to quicken their withdrawal from Africa. Like these other powers, de Gaulle still hoped to maintain French influence in the ex-colonies (and access to such materials as Gabonese uranium) through military and economic assistance, as well as linguistic-cultural links and diplomatic support. The General and his successors maintained quite a generous overseas aid programme compared to other Western countries, boosted by money from the European Community (EC).

* 5 per cent in 1958, raised to 10 per cent in 1966 and 12.5 per cent in 1976.

The abandonment of sub-Saharan Africa made it inevitable that Algeria would win independence too, but when de Gaulle first raised the possibility of Algerian autonomy in September 1959 he shocked conservative opinion. Nonetheless, the Algerian war was now absorbing a tenth of the budget and half a million troops, and the Assembly supported the General. In January 1960, during the 'week of the barricades', when rioters seized government offices in Algiers, de Gaulle stood firm and the bulk of the Army proved loyal to him. In January 1961 he was able to gain support, in a referendum on the offer of self-government to Algeria. There was another dangerous crisis three months later when an assassination attempt on the General coincided with a rebellion of some troops in Algiers. Premier Debré even feared an invasion of France from Algeria but de Gaulle again stood firm and the revolt fizzled out. Other attempts, by the right-wing Secret Army Organisation (OAS) to assassinate de Gaulle, failed to prevent a cease-fire being reached in March 1962 which led to the Evian agreements on French withdrawal and Algerian independence. By then the war had cost 17500 French dead and over 200000 Muslims. The Evian accords were approved, amidst great violence, by a referendum in July, and de Gaulle stood triumphant. His tortuous but careful policy had won through, the trials of decolonisation were at an end and France could now address other difficulties at home and in Europe.

Between 1958 and 1962 de Gaulle had acted 'above' party politics, as was traditional with French Presidents. He refused to identify with the Gaullist political party and took charge of foreign, defence and imperial affairs, whilst Debré handled domestic affairs. The Gaullist Jacques Chaban-Delmas even talked of the President having 'reserved authority' only in international affairs and defence. Certainly the 1958 constitution did not intend to create an omnipotent Presidency, though it gave wide powers to the President and restricted the rights of parliament. The President was elected for seven years, could be re-elected, was able to choose a premier without parliamentary approval, had the right to adopt certain emergency powers and could call a general election. The upper house, the Senate, chosen by an electoral college of notables, lacked effective power. The constitution defined the areas in which parliament could legislate, put the government in control of the parliamentary timetable and restricted the ability of elected representatives to bring the government down. All this of course marked a reaction to the practices of the Fourth Republic. The National Assembly, however, could still cause difficulties for a government. The fact that Assembly elections had to be called at least every five years increased the danger of a parliament being elected which was hostile to the President, who was unable to call more than one election in any twelve month period. The President could not veto legislation and he needed a majority in the Assembly to legislate effectively.

In 1962, however, freed from the Algerian imbroglio de Gaulle began to assert Presidential authority on a greater scale in domestic affairs. In April he sacked the loyal Debré and replaced him with the even more loyal Georges Pompidou, formerly the General's executive secretary, who had little standing in the Assembly. The MRP, already alienated by the controls on parliament and the lack of social reform, and by de Gaulle's policy towards the European Common Market, now left the government. The General, undismayed, then proceeded with a plan to change the constitution by referendum so that he could be elected, not by the electoral college, but by popular vote, a move calculated to increase his popular standing. It was a potentially dangerous step, however, because the Algerian settlement which had freed the General to act as he did, also made parliamentarians more confident about standing up to him: he had now, after all, resolved the principal problem they had called him to power to deal with in 1958 and might suffer a similar fate to Mendès-France in 1954. Under the constitution referenda could be called (by the premier or the Assembly) to decide on constitutional matters, but the Assembly had to approve them. Yet in 1962 de Gaulle effectively called the referendum on an elected Presidency himself, ignoring parliament, and raising the danger of an 'elective dictatorship'. In October the Assembly appeared to have its revenge when it voted, for the first time under the Fifth Republic, to depose the prime minister. But once again de Gaulle proved able to ride out a crisis. He simply reappointed Pompidou as premier and called a general election. Fortuitously this came at the time of the Cuban missile crisis, which naturally made people vote for stability. De Gaulle won the 28 October constitution referendum with 62 per cent of the vote and in the November elections openly identified himself with Gaullist candidates, who then won 35.5 per cent of the vote. Together with Valéry Giscard d'Estaing's Independent Republicans the Gaullists controlled 256 seats in the new Assembly. The second largest party the Socialists had only 65 seats, the Communists 40, and the MRP even less than that. Thus were the main parties of the Fourth Republic humbled.

At the start of 1963 de Gaulle seemed securely in power. He was able to appeal to the French people in carefully-timed television appearances, and sought to unite the country by an active cultural policy, economic growth and a strong international stance. He was helped enormously by the removal of underlying problems which had dogged French policy-makers for years. Of the '3 Cs' only class divisions still seemed important. Falling church attendances, the decline of the MRP and the tendency of Catholics to support Gaullism, meant that clerical differences no longer seemed important and the 'Debré Law' of 1959, which increased state aid to church schools provoked surprisingly little controversy. As to constitutional differences the Fifth Republic alienated those who feared an authoritarian Presidency, but it seemed far more successful than the Third and Fourth Republics. De Gaulle had also reduced the division brought about by the other two 'Cs' which had emerged since 1945. Algeria was the last serious problem brought by colonial issues; and the impact of Cold War divisions lessened as de Gaulle opened relations up with Russia, China and Eastern Europe, asserted French independence from NATO and developed the *'Force de Frappe'*, an independent nuclear deterrent which helped compensate the armed forces for the loss of Empire. Even class divisions appeared less pressing as the Gaullists established their electoral predominance in the country and the economy grew. Mollet's Socialists had been outmanoeuvred in 1958, they remained divided from the Communists and the latter – though they continued to win about a fifth of the popular votes – had few Assembly seats. Individuals like Mendès-France and François Mitterrand, hoped for a new left-wing alliance to match Gaullism but were clearly a long way from success.

Salaries, employment and social reform were still important political issues but de Gaulle's ability to deal with them seemed to be helped by the healthy economic base inherited from the Fourth Republic, and the continuation of growth. In part this growth was fuelled by demographic change. In 1945 the population still numbered 40 million but by 1970 it was 51 million. A large number of immigrant workers were also absorbed from North Africa and Southern Europe. There was a corresponding growth in the urban population: in 1946 22 French towns had over 100000 people; by 1968 there were ten more, Paris was growing at an enormous rate and much of rural France, especially the south-west, had become depopulated. The share of agricultural production in French GNP also fell, from 15 per cent in 1950 to 7 per cent in 1970, and economic development continued to be guided by national plans, successors to the original Monnet Plan of 1947–52. The aims of the Plans changed over time. The third plan (1958–61), for example, tried to improve France's balance of trade to cope with entry to the Common Market whilst the fifth (1966–70) stimulated regional development. EEC entry and the loss of colonial markets forced French industry to become more competitive, with a tendency for firms to become larger. Despite its tradition of being a protectionist, low-export country France now proved extremely successful at competing in world markets. Over half its trade went to the Common Market in 1970, compared to about a fifth 20 years earlier. Between 1949 and 1969 imports and exports both grew five and a half times over, steel output increased two and a half times and automobile output by ten times.

Despite the economic successes, and the appearance of stability in France between 1962 and 1968, there were signs of problems to come. An austerity programme in 1963, partly designed to build up gold reserves, led to slower growth. There were often trade imbalances, inflation (a problem since wartime) continued, and many were on low wages or pensions. As early as April 1963 public sympathy for striking miners forced government concessions. Anti-strike measures were introduced, including a 'cooling-off' period between a strike being called and its being put into effect, but these caused resentment. Questions were also raised about rural decline and how wealth was shared in society. In the December 1965 Presidential election, despite government attempts to stimulate the economy and de Gaulle's active foreign policy, a second ballot was needed before the General triumphed over François Mitterrand, around whom the Communists, Socialists and other leftists had proved ready to unite.

standing for national unity, a strong state, economic modernisation and an independent foreign policy. Jacques Chaban-Delmas was soon made premier and talked of creating a 'New Society' in which social security would be improved, the minimum wage increased and share ownership extended. Giscard d'Estaing was back as finance minister and the decision was soon taken to do what de Gaulle had refused to do: devalue the franc. 1969 and 1970 continued to see strikes, student militancy and protests from such groups as farmers and shopkeepers who felt threatened by economic change. But a loan from the International Monetary Fund, government spending cuts and other deflationary measures helped to ensure that, by the time General de Gaulle died in November 1970, France was recovering strongly from the effects of 1968. Industrial production was expanding, exports increasing and reserves were being built up again.

Pompidou's success continued in 1971–3 when he proved a strong President, taking an interest in domestic as well as foreign policy issues. Like de Gaulle he pursued détente with Moscow. He also visited China in September 1973 after the US has restored links to that country. At home he presided over continuing strong growth in 1971 and 1972, when France became the fourth largest trading nation in the world after America, Japan and West Germany. In 1971 the IMF loan was repaid and Pompidou's supporters emerged triumphant from the municipal elections of that year, when the Gaullists renamed themselves the Union for the Defence of the Republic. In July 1972, to please hard-line Gaullists, Pompidou replaced Chaban-Delmas as premier with Pierre Messmer, and preparations began for the 1973 general election. Meanwhile the Left were also active in trying to restore their fortunes. In July 1969 the old Socialist party* and other groups joined to form a new Socialist Party (PS). At the Epinay Congress in June 1971 the party was enlarged and François Mitterrand became leader. Then, in June 1972, the PS and the Communists reached agreement on a common programme (including a reduction of Presidential powers) and an electoral pact. Further evidence of the growth of a Left–Right division in Politics was that, when the centre parties regrouped to form the 'Reformist Movement' they allied with the Gaullists in an electoral pact. As a result of the Leftist alliance the Socialists were able to win 89 seats in the March 1973 election and the Communists 73, but they were still easily outnumbered by the alliance of Gaullists (175), Independent Republicans (54) and Reformists (30).

Despite their triumph in the election, the Gaullists had experienced their first decline in votes cast since the Fourth Republic, losing over two million of them. Their support had tended to consolidate amongst Roman Catholics, rural voters and the old. The Gaullists remained the best-organised party by far on the Centre–Right, but in retrospect 1971 marked the revival of Socialist fortunes, and they increasingly emerged as a threat to the Gaullists. Pompidou's fortunes also declined after the election. Inflation was already a danger and the international financial situation

---

* Called by the long title 'French Section of the Workers' International'.

97

uncertain when, in October 1973, the West had to come to terms with a four-fold increase in oil prices, sparked by an Arab–Israeli war. France had followed a pro-Arab policy under de Gaulle and Pompidou and, unlike Holland, did not face a cut in oil supplies, but in November measures were necessary to conserve energy. The boom of 1970–3 was brought to an end, the balance of trade suddenly became a pressing problem and the franc was again threatened. Pompidou's health was also in decline. Unknown to his people he was locked in a battle against cancer, and on 2 April 1974, shortly after returning from a visit to Moscow, he died. Like West Germany, Britain and America in the same year France underwent an important change of leadership in an atmosphere of great international economic uncertainty.

The Presidential election which followed Pompidou's death found the Right divided. Chaban-Delmas declared himself as the Gaullist candidate, but not even all the Gaullists wanted this. Many preferred the candidature of Giscard d'Estaing, who had the support of Centrists and who emerged well ahead of Chaban in the first ballot on 5 May. Giscard was still 10 per cent behind Mitterrand, who had won the support of all the Left, but on the second ballot the Gaullists all rallied to him. He won the Presidency by the slimmest of majorities, with 50.6 per cent of the vote. Giscard came to his new position as an experienced Minister of Finance under both de Gaulle and Pompidou, though he was not yet 50. He stood for financial stability but cultivated a young, reformist image; he had criticised the growth of Presidential power in the 1960s but he himself adopted an active, 'monarchical' role as President. His refusal to reduce the President's powers, his tendency to rely on the staff at the Elysée Palace and his liberal attitudes led his government to be described as 'Orleanist' after the liberal nineteenth-century monarchy. He hoped to reduce class divisions, to create a more equal society and to provide better opportunities for the individual, but without high government spending. Thus his reforms were cheap and populist. They included such measures as the appointment of a minister for woman's affairs, the legalisation of abortion in November 1974, the lowering of the voting age to 18, the reduction of government control of broadcasting and the introduction of comprehensive education. His governments also increased old age pensions and introduced a capital gains tax, but there was no major redistribution of wealth, women's wages remained low, and workers took little interest in the government's share ownership schemes.

A major difficulty for Giscard was that he continued to rely heavily on the Gaullists in parliament even if his government was more centrist in make-up than previous Fifth Republic cabinets. The Gaullist Jacques Chirac had become premier in May 1974 but the reforms carried out by the government divided the coalition. Even Independent Republicans were doubtful about the legalisation of abortion for example, and this reform had to be carried through with the parliamentary support of the Socialists and Communists. The depression brought by the oil crisis also inevitably affected the government. Profits were reduced, the trade deficit lingered and Chirac's attempt at an expansionist policy in 1975–6 only added to inflation – a similar result to that faced in Britain and Italy. The departmental elections of March 1976, in which most votes went to the Left, were a warning that the next general election, due in 1978, could be difficult for the government. The weakness and the divisions amongst the Gaullists, the mainstay of the Right, was particularly worrying and in August 1976, facing criticism from his own party and experiencing personal differences with the President, Chirac resigned as premier. He evidently did not wish to risk his popular standing further with unpalatable economic measures.

The new cabinet, under Raymond Barre, was more Centrist in make-up and the prime minister himself was determined to tackle unemployment, inflation and the trade deficit, hoping to bring new stability within three years. The seventh economic plan, the 'Barre Plan' of 1976–80, aimed at limited economic growth with concentration of investment in certain new industries, such as electronics, as the best investment for the future. By 1978 the policy seemed to have some success. The year saw the first French trade surplus since the oil crisis. Politically, however, the scene was uncertain. In December 1976 the Gaullists had tried to breathe new life into themselves by renaming their party yet again as the 'Rally for the Republic' (RPR) with Chirac as leader. The Gaullists were often critical of Barre, but parliamentary arithmetic forced the prime minister to bring more of them into his cabinet in March 1977 and the reforms of the early Giscard Presidency then came to a halt. (Ironically reforms became more difficult under Barre than they had been under Chirac.) Chirac strengthened his own hand in the country meanwhile by successfully campaigning to become Mayor of Paris. It was to resist domination by the Gaullists that the Independent Republicans and Centrists united in February 1978 to form the 'Union for French Democracy' (UDF), loyal to Giscard. But the RPR and UDF still fought the April 1978 general election as allies and emerged victorious. They were saved from defeat by the fact that their left-wing opponents proved even more divided. In 1977 the alliance between the PS and the Communists, which had fought the 1973 election, broke up. The Communists feared being overwhelmed by the Socialists and tried to reassert their own identity by supporting Soviet policy and claiming to be the only 'true' socialist party. In the election all four main parties won slightly more than a fifth of the vote but the Gaullists (141 seats) and UDF (125) easily outstripped the PS (102) and Communists (86) under the Republic's electoral system.

The strong showing of the UDF in the election allowed Giscard to retain Barre as premier and to rely more on Centrist policies after 1978. The President could still claim to lead a country which had performed better than most of the West during the 1970s in terms of inflation, social security payments and growth (which fell below 3 per cent per annum but still outpaced countries like Britain and Italy). France's indirect taxes still fell mostly on the poor, however, and improvements in living standards had undeniably slowed down over the decade. In 1979 came another major blow with further oil price increases and renewed depression. Barre's hopes of economic stability were ruined and even sizeable budget deficits could not cushion the French people. Unemployment doubled and social discontent grew. As elsewhere traditional heavy industries, like steel and coal, particularly suffered and resentment was directed against immigrants who had arrived during the years of expansion. 1981 saw a return to the years of large trade deficits and even foreign and defence policies turned sour on the President. The 1970s had seen major improvements in France's nuclear arsenal, but the defence budget proved a major burden. In the European Community Giscard allied with Helmut Schmidt and tried to develop a European policy on the Middle East problem. However, the Community proved unable to develop a common foreign policy and France itself continued to defend national interests by bending Community rules to protect its farmers from imports of Italian wine and British lamb. Like de Gaulle and Pompidou, Giscard followed an active Third World policy, but his links to the tyrannical 'Emperor' Bokassa of Central Africa (who was overthrown in 1979) became a scandal. Giscard maintained the traditional *Gaulliste* line of détente with Russia, but his attempts to maintain this détente in 1980, when he met Leonid Brezhnev after the Soviet invasion of Afghanistan, also provoked controversy.

In the May 1981 Presidential election, Giscard won 28 per cent of the vote in the first ballot and easily outmatched Chirac, who had stood against him. But the division with the Gaullists proved costly and Giscard was held by many to have carried out too little reform since 1974. Neither could the deep economic depression do other than cause him harm. Once again the Left appeared divided and it seemed this would help Giscard. The Communist leader Georges Marchais, who had taken a pro-Soviet line on Afghanistan, attacked the Socialist candidate Mitterrand bitterly. Marchais did so badly at the first ballot however that the Communists decided to back Mitterrand at the second, and Mitterrand emerged triumphant by 51.75 per cent – almost as narrow a margin as Giscard's seven years before. Crowds filled the streets in celebration, many expecting radical reforms, even though Mitterrand, who had only joined the Socialists after a long political career on the Centre–Left, had deliberately fought the election on a moderate programme. Mitterrand was experienced as a minister under the Fourth Republic, a man of strong principles (not least as a critic of colonialism in the 1950s) and a liberal, but he was not a Marxist, he did not reduce the length of the Presidential term as he had promised to do, and he was interested in social reform and the reduction of unemployment, rather than any fundamental transformation of society. Many indeed criticised him as opportunist. He was determined to be the leading figure in government, he decided many issues which divided the Cabinet and like previous Presidents he took the main role in foreign policy-making, personally ordering, for example, that French troops be sent to deal with problems in Chad in 1982 and the Lebanon in 1983.

On becoming President Mitterrand quickly appointed Pierre Mauroy, a moderate with a trades union background, as prime minister of a cabinet which embraced all elements of the PS. It was essential however, if the

President was to do anything constructive, to get a majority in the Assembly, and so he seized on the groundswell of support evident in his own victory and called a general election. The decision paid off handsomely. In June the Gaullists and Giscardians remained united but, demoralised, could win only 88 seats and 62 seats respectively, each with about a fifth of the vote. The PS on the other hand took numerous votes from the Communists and moderate voters, emerging with 37.5 per cent of the votes and 285 seats. The PS victory came ten years after the turn in their fortunes, when Mitterrand had become the leader of the new party. With sound leadership, an improved organisation and an attractive programme the Socialists had gradually extended their membership and support in society. In 1978 they had obtained more votes in an election than the Communists, something unseen since 1936. This time they had left the Communists standing and there was some surprise when Mauroy brought four Communist ministers into his government, for the first time since 1947. The question now was whether the Left could use the institutions of the Fifth Republic as successfully as the Right in fulfilling its political programme.

There were warnings in 1981 that the time was not right for Socialist-style reforms. In a situation of depression and inflation most Western governments were adopting policies of retrenchment and Barre's governments had already shown the difficulties of achieving high growth. Mauroy, however, was committed to reform and chose a policy of expansion to build up domestic demand and so reduce unemployment. Wages were improved, social security payments were increased, the government itself took on more employees and industry was encouraged to modernise. To strengthen its control of the economy, Mauroy's government rapidly carried through a large-scale nationalisation programme, which included most of France's largest industries in such diverse fields as banking, telecommunications and chemicals. The share of state control over industry doubled to almost a third of the total. Mitterrand himself favoured full nationalisation over the alternative policy of majority government shareholdings and the policy had some success in that French GDP did increase. By 1983 nonetheless, it was clear the costs were enormous. A major reduction in employment had not occurred but the government had spent huge sums on compensation to those who lost businesses in the nationalisation programme, so that the budget deficit grew and taxes had to be increased. The expansion within France had brought rising imports, but, since other countries had chosen retrenchment, there was no compensating increase in French exports and so the trade deficit grew. The fall in the value of the franc also threatened to upset co-operation with Germany in the EC's European Monetary System.

The Socialists adhered to their policies for as long as they could, but in 1982 attempts began to moderate wage demands and in March 1983 came cuts in social security and other austerity measures. Neither did the government carry out all the social reforms it had wanted. Working hours, for example, were cut in 1982 to 39 hours instead of the promised 35, and so did little to reduce unemployment. Mitterrand and Mauroy discovered that the control of state power was not enough to bring radical change, and that France could not isolate itself from international conditions. In June 1984 the Socialists received another shock when one million people demonstrated in Paris against a proposed education reform which would have brought church schools under fuller state control. The reform provoked popular concern over educational standards, rekindled the old clerical divisions in society and provided the Gaullists with the ideal issue to browbeat the government. The same month, in elections to the European parliament, more than one voter in ten supported the extreme right-wing National Front party of Jean-Marie Le Pen. Le Pen exploited concerns over immigration, law and order, and economic decline, offering simple, authoritarian solutions. In early June Mitterrand, concerned at the disorder in Paris, withdrew the controversial education bill. This led to the resignation not only of the education minister, Alain Savary, but also of Mauroy.

The new prime minister was Laurent Fabius who was young, technocratic and more likely to embrace austerity and economic liberalism. The Communists however, already disaffected at government policy, refused to join his cabinet. In 1984–6 there were attempts to cut government expenditure and to concentrate aid only on growth industries but, despite a fall in inflation and some improvement in trade, the budget was still in deficit, growth was low and unemployment remained above 10 per cent. Meanwhile, to protect his own position, Mitterrand withdrew from interference in domestic policy-making. He now cultivated the image of a President 'above' party politics and distanced himself from the economic and political failures of the government. For good measure however, in June 1985, with his eyes on the next general election, he also changed the electoral system to one of proportional representation in multi-member constituencies, similar to that under the Fourth Republic. This reform, condemned as an act of blatant opportunism, was calculated to aid the Left whilst dividing his opponents: a Rightist majority seemed almost inevitable in 1986, especially since Chirac had restructured and strengthened the Gaullists, but there was rivalry between the Rightist leaders, Chirac, Giscard and Barre, and by holding a single-ballot election Mitterrand could hope that they would harm themselves in the competition for seats. Some analysts predicted that the reform would encourage smaller parties, reverse the bipolarisation of politics and so bring a return of the political confusion of the Fourth Republic.

In the March 1986 election bi-polarity actually survived, but Mitterrand's supporters lost. The Gaullists and UDF offered joint lists in the elections, winning 41 per cent of the vote and 277 seats. The Socialists and other leftists did the same, winning 35 per cent of the vote and 216 seats. The main change was the emergence of Le Pen's followers who won 10 per cent of the vote and 35 seats, exactly the same as the Communists whose vote thus continued to decline. Mitterrand could take some satisfaction from

Le Pen's success, since this was embarrassing to the legitimate Right. There was little alternative, however, than to ask Chirac to become prime minister, thus beginning a period of 'cohabitation' between a President and a premier from different sides of the political divide for the first time under the Fifth Republic. There were those who believed that 'cohabitation' could be beneficial, but the relationship between Mitterrand and Chirac proved difficult. The 1986 election seemed to mark a rejection of Socialist policies, Barre for one believed the President should have resigned and Chirac had ambitions of becoming President in 1988. Mitterrand still had considerable powers, he controlled defence policy and Chirac could not differ with him too much because this might alienate the electorate, who wanted effective government. An early decision taken by the new cabinet was to change the electoral system back to that which existed before 1985. Chirac held meetings of ministers without the President. Mitterrand hit back by refusing to approve certain government measures, including the return of industries to private ownership, and criticised such actions as the attempt to restrict French nationality. In December 1986 he also had the satisfaction of seeing Chirac's government withdraw a new education reform after student protests. This seemed fitting revenge for the events of 1984.

By 1988 the French people had decided that cohabitation was no longer desirable and in May they re-elected Mitterrand President, with a clear majority (54 per cent) over Chirac. Chirac had insisted on pressing his candidature despite the evidence that Raymond Barre would have attracted more Centrist votes. Even strong-arm tactics against anti-colonialist rebels in New Caledonia* failed to save Chirac. Mitterrand's attempts to portray himself as the representative of the national interest 'above' politics had succeeded, and he repeated his action of 1981: after appointing Michel Rocard as premier, a general election was called for June. This did not bring quite the same results as in 1981 but the Socialists and their allies won 275 seats compared to 130 Gaullists, 131 Giscardians and their allies, 27 Communists and only 1 National Front. The Socialist majority was slim, but the Right were divided after their defeat, which many blamed on Chirac and some Centrists were tempted to co-operate with the Rocard government. Unemployment, the decline of the coal and steel industries in the North-East and the breakdown of old political loyalties had destroyed the Communists as the main force on the Left and the future for Mitterrand's party seemed secure.

In 1989 France celebrated the bicentenary of the Revolution. Mitterrand presided over grand celebrations, welcomed foreign leaders to Paris and opened various prestigious building projects in the capital, designed to portray France as a modern, prosperous, advancing nation. The Fifth Republic had not succeeded in resolving all the country's problems. France was vulnerable to international tension and economic changes; there had long been concern over the 'Americanisation' of culture; the

* A French territory in the Pacific.

events of 1968 and the demonstrations of 1984 had shown the inability of government to forestall discontent; and there were new concerns arising over racialism, drugs and the environment. Numerous forces were at work in society to limit government action – business and agricultural interests, bureaucratic intertia, regional problems. Yet the Republic had survived the passing of de Gaulle, the rise to power of the Socialists and even the trials of 'cohabitation'. The Fifth Republic certainly proved better able than the Fourth to provide France with stable institutions to cope with the economic and social change of the post-war world, and to give her an influential voice in the world.

# 5
# Great Britain

## The Attlee Governments, 1945–51

Britain was the only major European power not to suffer defeat in either of the two World Wars. In May 1945 she stood as one of the 'Big Three' victorious powers, the most powerful Western European state in economic and military terms, and the possessor of the largest Empire the world had ever known. Britain's unwritten constitution was far more resilient than constitutions drawn up on the Continent, her governments were generally based on strong parliamentary majorities and she had developed a 'Commonwealth' relationship with her most important colonies which allowed them a wide degree of independence whilst maintaining their loyalty in war. In 1940–1 the country had successfully stood alone against the Nazis, and many Europeans looked to London for leadership in the future. Over the course of the next four decades, however, British economic strength relative to her European neighbours declined, her Empire was lost, her share of world trade fell off rapidly, she failed to develop a leading role in the emerging European Community and even her much-admired constitutional stability seemed undermined by poor industrial relations, political fragmentation and ineffectual government in the 1970s. Britain's military strength, underpinned by nuclear weapons, was greater than ever in absolute terms, but far behind America and Russia; Britain's economy had expanded, but not as remarkably as West Germany and Japan. The mid-1980s saw something of an economic upturn, yet this was in an atmosphere very different to that of 1945 when the British people had hoped to build a brave new world of egalitarianism, welfare and social justice.

The end of the war in Europe was followed by a shock in British politics when the wartime leader, Winston Churchill, was defeated in the July general election. To many at home and abroad it seemed like the betrayal of a statesman who had been the personification of national resistance to Hitler. In fact, given the evidence of opinion polls and wartime by-elections, a Labour victory was not unexpected, but the size of the victory *was* surprising. Labour, with only 154 seats in the 1935 election, now had 393 seats and 48 per cent of the vote. The Conservatives were reduced to 213 seats and the Liberals to only 12. The two previous Labour governments had both been minority administrations, and it was the 1945 election which really brought about a two-party, Conservative–Labour system to British politics. Some of the reasons for the Conservative defeat could actually be blamed on Churchill. The party relied heavily on his reputation as a war leader, but he did not necessarily appeal as a peacetime premier. He had a reputation for being anti-working class, was blamed for economic problems in the 1920s and had spent the 1930s in the political wilderness. Neither did it help that he condemned his 'Socialist' opponents for wanting a 'totalitarian' form of government during the election campaign. The Conservative party itself also had a poor reputation, inherited from the inter-war years when they had presided over the years of Depression and had failed to stand up to Hitler's expansionism.

Labour's victory in 1945 also had much to do with their own strengths. Labour leaders like Clement Attlee, Ernest Bevin and Herbert Morrison had all served in the coalition government under Churchill in wartime, and established reputations themselves as competent ministers. Attlee, the party leader since 1935, seemed a cold, solitary, modest man but he was also sensible and persistent, a good chairman of committees who proved adept at controlling the various groups that made up the party. Labour had produced many proposals for post-war reform, based on ideas of greater state intervention and welfare provision. Although many people probably had a limited understanding of the nationalisation measures, the National Health Service and welfare state promised in the party's election manifesto ('Let Us Face the Future'), Labour undoubtedly caught the 'climate of opinion' at the end of the war. There was a strong desire for fairness, a better deal for the working class, a sharing of burdens, an end to profiteering, the provision of jobs and housing, and the avoidance of any new Depression. Thanks to the 'social levelling' brought about by the common experience of wartime sufferings, many middle-class (and especially young) voters were now ready to support Labour. Wartime propaganda about the need to build a better world, the success of the Soviet Union with its planned economy and the approval by the coalition government of the 'Beveridge Report' on social welfare, all helped Labour too.

Despite their sizeable election win and the achievement of victory over Japan in August 1945, the Attlee government faced a daunting task. Most Labour MPs had no experience of government and this helped the rise of such young men as Harold Wilson, appointed to the Cabinet in 1947 when aged only 31. The new government had to address complex problems regarding Britain's world role, the future of the Empire, the need to restore economic normalcy and the fulfilment of election promises on reform. The war had cost Britain most of its gold and foreign currency reserves, a quarter of its merchant navy and (though this was far less than other states) 326 000 lives. Living standards were lowered, half the country's industrial production was geared to war needs, inflation was a menace and commercial markets had been lost. Trading rivals like Germany and Japan had been defeated, but the power of the United States was overwhelming and the economic health of Britain was quite poor. To make matters worse extra commitments were taken at the end of the war, such as the occupation zone in Germany. The maintenance of substantial armed forces was necessary, however, because of the emergence of the Cold War and pressures within the Empire for independence.

The British hoped for a substantial US loan to help them achieve economic stability. The Americans were well aware of Britain's importance to world trade – half of which was in sterling – and the economist Lord Keynes negotiated a loan in December 1945 for $3700 million from America. Nevertheless, Britain would have to pay interest on this and also had to promise to make sterling convertible into dollars. The loan, though apparently generous, was therefore much criticised for 'mortgaging the British Empire'. Furthermore, when in Summer 1947 the British did introduce convertibility it merely led people to sell sterling and buy dollars. The Americans agreed to suspend convertibility but Britain's economic weakness was cruelly underlined. The winter of early 1947 had already seen food and coal shortages and, although America's Marshall aid programme brought some succour after 1947, Labour faced another blow in September 1949 when the pound was devalued from $4.03 to $2.80. The devaluation was blamed on a depression in the USA, but since the depression was only short-lasting it appeared that the government had panicked, and the scale of the devaluation seemed particularly unnecessary.

For all the criticisms, Labour did have some remarkable successes. Wartime controls and planning had made Keynesian economic practices acceptable, and the government was able to establish a policy of full employment after 1947 without causing high inflation. An export drive was also successful in boosting Britain's trade position in 1948–50 and demobilisation was successfully carried out. Yet these policies necessitated such austerity measures as high taxes, import restrictions and the continuation of rationing. Arguably Labour's failure was not so much its short-term management of the economy as the inability of its plans for greater state intervention to revolutionise British industry and reverse the long-term signs of decline relative to her major rivals. Britain, the world's first industrial economy, had been challenged increasingly by countries like America, Germany and Japan since the late nineteenth century. (Many would date the beginning of national decline in the 1870s.) Labour had promised nationalisation since at least 1918. Public control already existed on a limited scale before 1939 over such institutions as the BBC, the airlines and London transport, the last set up by Herbert Morrison who, as deputy premier under Attlee after 1945, had overall control over Labour's domestic programme. The Attlee government's nationalisations included the Bank of England and coal in 1946, the railways, road services and electricity in 1947, gas in 1948 and, amidst some controversy, iron and steel in 1949. The policy was designed to achieve many aims: for the workers it would improve working conditions, reduce unemployment and bring a sharing of profits; for the industries themselves it would improve investment and create better industrial relations; for the country as a whole it would shift economic power from a few powerful businessmen and create a 'mixed economy' in which the government could take control of key industries and shape a more rational economic future. Nationalisation, however, brought no great revolution. Many nationalised industries were already loss-making concerns and their owners were sometimes more than ready to take the compensation offered them for nationalisation. The management remained the same however; trades unions had to continue to fight for improvements in wages and conditions; profit-sharing schemes and worker-managers were not introduced. Furthermore, by guaranteeing state financial assistance in future, nationalisation bred complacency. Neither were the nationalised industries co-ordinated in any rational planning system. Instead, Chancellors of the Exchequer continued to manage the economy by changes in taxes, interest rates and credit controls. And the various power industries and transport industries continued to compete with each other.

Labour *was* able to improve living standards in the late 1940s through its social reform programme. In 1946 the Minister of Health, Aneurin Bevan, an energetic, ex-coal miner, successfully introduced the National Health Service (NHS). Seen as Labour's greatest achievement, the NHS did not destroy private medicine but it created a comprehensive system of free health care, with good standards. The principle of 'universal' provision of welfare, regardless of actual need, was also seen in the 1946 National Insurance Act which consolidated and expanded existing legislation to provide unemployment and sickness benefit, an extension of old age pensions, maternity and widow allowances. 'Universality' was criticised because it did not direct support at those who were genuinely poor, but Labour wished to end the humiliations of the 'means test' in the 1930s, when individuals had to prove they needed assistance. In any case the 1946 Act did *not* provide completely free assistance. It was paid for by National Insurance contributions from workers and employers, and in many cases assistance was only provided for a fixed period to those who had paid sufficient Insurance contributions. Other Labour reforms included the repeal of the 1927 Trades Union Act, which had restricted union finances, and raising the school leaving age to 15. (A major education reform had already been carried out in 1944.)

In foreign affairs Labour's strong man was Ernest Bevin, a former trades union leader. Bevin was criticised by the Labour left in 1946 for his arguments with the Soviet Union, and for his failure to settle the problem of Jewish–Arab tensions in the mandate of Palestine, from which Britain was forced to withdraw in 1948. Bevin himself had hopes of maintaining a strong British influence in the world, by making London the leader not only of the Empire–Commonwealth but also of Western European states. In 1947–9, however, the Soviet menace became too pressing, and Western Europe remained too weak, for a 'third force' to be created between Moscow and Washington. Instead Bevin played a leading role in Europe in accepting US economic aid, via the Marshall Plan, and an American military guarantee, through NATO. By 1950 his policy was based on Commonwealth co-operation and the 'special relationship' with Washington and, to maintain Britain's independence, he avoided membership of supranational bodies created in Western Europe, like the Schuman Plan. To further strengthen Britain, Bevin and Attlee also secretly developed an atomic bomb.

In the imperial sphere the Labour government is best remembered for its decision to give independence to the Indian Empire at an early date, despite the fact that India was large, wealthy and the strategic centre of Britain's world position. There were many reasons why the British were able to avoid the problems faced by those powers who tried to resist Asian nationalism after 1945, the Dutch in Indonesia and the French in Indochina. Self-government for India had been a major political issue between the wars and many Labour politicians, foremost among them Attlee, already agreed with independence in principle. It seemed practically impossible for Britain to hold a country of hundreds of millions of people in submission, nationalist leaders like Mahatma Gandhi had pursued a skilful but non-violent campaign for independence, and British defeats at the hands of the Japanese in 1941–2 had weakened Indian respect for the *Raj*. The British Army, unlike the French Army in Indochina (or later Algeria), proved loyal to its government during withdrawal and, despite Churchill's doubts, there was no major domestic opposition to the transfer of power in August 1947. The major problems were not concerned with British withdrawal but with the insistence of Indian Muslims on forming an independent state, Pakistan. Ceylon and Burma (1948) were also given independence and all except Burma agreed to join the Commonwealth. The existence of the Commonwealth was an important aid to independence, for the British, far from 'surrendering' their power, had high hopes of maintaining effective co-operation with their former colonies in a new Commonwealth relationship, similar to that which existed with the old 'White Dominions' like Australia, Canada and New Zealand. Such hopes were reinforced by the success of the 1950 Colombo Conference on development in Asia. But it should not be assumed that Indian independence would automatically lead to the complete unravelling of Britain's global position. In the late 1940s it was still expected, for example, that colonial rule in Africa would survive for decades.

Labour fared badly in the February 1950 general election. They fell back to 315 seats, whilst the Conservatives recovered to 298 and the Liberals gained only 9 (whilst retaining 9 per cent of the vote). There was a high turn-out but the austerity programme, the continuation of rationing, and devaluation all harmed Labour. Amidst a general disenchantment with government controls, many middle-class voters returned to the Conservative fold. The Conservatives had, since the shock of 1945, improved their party organisation. Younger party members like Enoch

Powell and Reginald Maudling, as well as established figures like R.A. Butler, were drawn into a revived 'Conservative Research Department' and produced such policy papers as the 'Industrial Charter' which was designed to prove the party was not anti-working class, and accepted the idea of a mixed economy. Lord Woolton as party manager after 1946 helped restore morale by improving fund-raising, encouraging the Young Conservatives and greatly increasing membership.

With an overall majority of only six, the Attlee government of 1950–1 proved far less confident than its predecessor. Sick MPs had to be brought to the Commons to vote in order to keep Labour in office. Attlee and Bevin were ill. In April 1951 Hugh Gaitskell, the Chancellor of the Exchequer, became embroiled in an argument with Bevan which led the latter, along with Harold Wilson, to resign. The occasion for the resignation was Gaitskell's proposal to introduce certain health service charges to cope with the economic problems brought about by increased imports and defence spending following the outbreak of the Korean War. The amount of the proposed charges was small, but for Bevan the principle of a *free* health service was fundamental. The government was also humiliated in the Middle East in 1951, when the nationalisation of British oil concerns was carried out by the nationalist government of Dr Mossadeq in Iran. Despite all these problems Labour managed to increase its vote when Attlee called an election in October and to emerge first in terms of votes (49 per cent to the Conservatives' 48 per cent). But Britain's first-past-the-post electoral system, based on individual constituencies, ensured that the Conservatives, with 321 seats, pulled ahead of Labour, who had only 295. The Liberals, with 6 seats, had lost many votes (their share was now only 2.5 per cent) compared to 1950 and many had evidently swung over to the Conservatives.

Labour since 1945 had largely fulfilled its electoral promises. The introduction of universal welfare, the creation of the National Health Service and the pursuit of Keynesian economic policies aimed at full employment were important developments. To some extent these reforms marked a continuation of previous social reform programmes, they built on the social cohesion and acceptance of economic planning created during the war, and some would argue that, if anything, they did not go far enough: there was no worker participation in industry, no major reform of the British education system and no major redistribution of wealth. Yet the Attlee governments proved better able to carry out a major reform programme than did later Labour governments, they had largely restored the country to normalcy, and in retrospect – and not without some exaggeration about the ease of the process – 1945–51 (along with the wartime coalition) was seen to have created a 'consensus' in British politics. The consensus was based around the US alliance, anti-communism and decolonisation abroad and, at home, around Keynesianism, full employment, the recognition of trades union power, and the welfare state. This was a major contrast to the depression, unemployment, social distress and international weakness of the 1930s and gave Britain the most advanced social welfare system in Europe.

## The Conservative Ascendancy, 1951–64

When Winston Churchill returned to 10 Downing Street in October 1951 he was 76-years-old and the average age of his Cabinet was 60. Anthony Eden, widely seen as Churchill's chosen successor, was back as Foreign Secretary, a post he had previously held before Munich and during the war. Eden was anxious to succeed to the premiership but Churchill, despite his age and a stroke in June 1953, clung onto office. With his reputation as a great war leader secure, the Prime Minister particularly sought a role as a peacemaker between East and West after the death of Stalin and only the onset of a general election finally induced him to retire in 1955. It was partly because of Churchill's age and because of the government's low majority that only limited attempts were made to reverse the previous government's reforms. The iron and steel industries were 'de-nationalised', as was road haulage, and in 1954 the Independent Television Authority was established to rival the state-owned British Broadcasting Corporation. But otherwise the nationalisation programme and welfare state survived intact. There were other reasons for caution: Labour's reforms had not been too radical; there were many Conservatives, such as Housing minister Harold Macmillan, who were interested in social reform; and there was the need to hold onto moderate support in the country.

Despite the lack of major legislation Churchill's government proved quite successful. In international affairs Britain faced decolonisation pressures in the Empire and in 1954 the government, despite a backbench revolt, even agreed to leave the vital Suez Canal military base under Egyptian nationalist pressure. But Churchill's international reputation still counted for something and Eden's diplomatic skills helped to resolve various international problems in 1954, when he acted as co-chairman of the Geneva conference on Indochina, and played a leading role in bringing West Germany into NATO. For the moment the full impact of British decline in the world was also masked by such technological successes as the explosion of an atom bomb in 1952 and the development of the world's first jet airliner, the Comet. The succession of Elizabeth II to the throne in 1952 led to talk of a 'New Elizabethan Age'. Meanwhile, the Conservatives were able to establish their identity as the party which stood for freedom, by bringing an end to rationing in 1954. Furthermore, Macmillan, by relying on private firms, seemed to succeed (where Labour had failed) in building over 300000 houses per year. The housing programme, especially when added to high defence spending, took money away from industrial investment but it fulfilled an important electoral commitment, allowed the Conservatives to become advocates of a 'property-owning democracy' and greatly helped Macmillan's political career.

Churchill's Chancellor of the Exchequer, R.A. Butler, also seemed to

111

succeed in overcoming the economic problems inherited from Labour. Butler, who like Macmillan was one of the new generation of Conservative leaders, had initially taken strong measures to deal with the problems for trade, prices and currency stability created by the Korean War. Butler raised interest rates from the first time since 1932, and acted to restrict credit, imports and spending abroad. In fact these measures may not have been necessary: the Korean War, as well as increasing new material prices, also served to stimulate demand in the Western economies. Britain's trade recovery was also aided by the 1949 devaluation. However in 1952–4 industrial output and wages rose, trade was healthy, and Butler was praised for his achievement. In 1955, despite signs that the 'boom' was running out of control the Chancellor cut income tax to help win the forthcoming election. Churchill finally retired in April and his successor, Eden, quickly decided to call an election to take advantage of Butler's budget and the weakness of the Labour party, whose left-wing 'Bevanites' opposed Attlee on such questions as German rearmament and nuclear weapons. With the economy looking healthy, no unemployment, little inflation and signs that détente with Moscow was progressing, Eden's gamble could hardly fail. As it was, the Conservatives won nearly half the votes cast.

Anthony Eden had waited a long time to be Prime Minister. He hoped for a successful premiership and a high international profile, so as to emulate his mentor, Churchill. Yet Eden's ambition was marred by insecurity and irritability, his political experience lay almost entirely in foreign affairs, and he was prone to ill-health. In December 1955 the Labour party matched him with their own new leader, Hugh Gaitskell. Gaitskell was young, an experienced minister and a sincere social democrat. His middle-class background alienated the Left and his political moderation led some to believe that there was little ideological difference between the two major parties – hence the term 'Butskellism' (an amalgamation of the names Butler and Gaitskell) as a description of politics in the late 1950s. But Gaitskell impressed the moderate voters who soon grew disaffected with Eden, especially when it became clear that Butler's 1955 budget had not been the success it appeared. In October a supplementary budget was needed which restricted credit and increased purchase tax, and in December Butler was replaced as Chancellor by Macmillan. Macmillan, who evidently understood the economy no better than his predecessor, continued to restrict investment and credit in 1956. Britain then found itself thrust into a cycle of behaviour by Conservative Chancellors which became known as 'stop-go' economics, as periods of stimulation for the economy (especially before elections) were interspersed with attempts to deflate it.

Ironically, Eden's downfall came, not with domestic problems, but with disaster in his supposed field of expertise, foreign policy. It has already been seen that, for various reasons, after the war Britain avoided embroilment in colonial wars on the scale of France in Indochina and Algeria, or the Dutch in Indonesia. Nevertheless, withdrawal from the world's largest colonial Empire was neither easily nor rapidly achieved.

In sub-Saharan Africa it was generally agreed that it could take decades to prepare native peoples for independence; it was feared that hasty withdrawal from the Empire would open the way for Communist takeovers and Soviet penetration; and in certain countries the British became involved in bitter struggles with local resistance movements including, in the 1950s, Communists in Malaya and the 'Mau Maus' in Kenya. Particular difficulties were faced in the Middle East because this area was seen as a barrier to Soviet expansion, a source of oil and a mainstay of Britain's claim to great power status. Iran's humiliating nationalisation of British oil assets in 1951 had been avenged a few years later when the United States and British efforts helped topple the radical nationalist leader, Dr Mossadeq. After 1954 Eden also tried to compensate for the loss of the Suez base to Egypt by supporting the Baghdad Pact of pro-Western Middle East states including Turkey, Iran and Pakistan, but Arab nationalist resentment prevented the Baghdad Pact becoming a success. The only Arab state which became a member was Britain's client Iraq, and opposition was led by the radical government in Egypt under General Nasser.

In 1956 the Egyptian leader provoked more Western criticism when he accepted arms supplies from the Soviet bloc. The USA then cut off aid which they had promised to him to build a dam, at Aswan on the Nile. Nasser responded, however, by nationalising the Suez canal. This was a sure source of revenue, but was largely owned by Britain and France and came as a major affront to those powers. International pressure failed to get Nasser to reverse his decision. Indeed, he won sympathy among Third World and Eastern bloc states because of his resistance to the Western colonial powers, and he also tried to behave moderately, offering compensation to the canal owners and allowing shipping through the Suez canal unmolested. Frustrated by such tactics, the British and French – secretly linked to Egypt's enemy, Israel – decided to restore their authority by force. In late October the Israelis invaded Egypt and the British and French used this as justification to invade Egypt to 'protect' the canal. However, the invasion invited widespread condemnation, not only from predictable sources like the Soviet Union, but also from the Labour opposition, the Commonwealth and even the United States. The United States' alienation helped to cause a 'run' on sterling and on 5 November Britain and France brought their campaign to a halt.

The Suez fiasco was of great significance in British history for many reasons. It strengthened Nasser's position in the Middle East and helped destroy Britain's influence there, especially when a coup in Iraq in 1958 put an end to its pro-British monarchy. Britain's decision to end the operation upset the French, who now committed themselves in earnest to the European Common Market. The crisis had highlighted Britain's relative decline in the world and exposed her inability to dictate terms even to Third World nations. It also showed British reliance on the United States, divided the government and provoked a new economic crisis. And it helped to bring an early end to the premiership of Eden who, politically isolated and ill, left office in January 1957. His successor was Harold Macmillan.

The new premier had been a critic of Conservative policies in the 1930s, and had proved ruthless in abandoning Eden. Yet Macmillan also seemed personable, confident and energetic, the ideal leader to help the party recover from the Suez disaster. He quickly acted to restore the American alliance through meetings with his old friend Eisenhower, and he developed a 'new look' in defence policy in 1957 with greater reliance on hydrogen bombs and the reduction of costly conventional forces (allowing conscription to be ended after 1960). Credit controls were needed to cope with the economic aftermath of Suez and in 1957 Britain also had to get a loan from the International Monetary Fund. Growth slowed to a snail's pace but in January 1958 government plans to increase public spending led to the resignation of the Chancellor of the Exchequer, Peter Thorneycroft, who feared inflation would result. Macmillan's confidence in dealing with the resignation won widespread respect and Thorneycroft's successor, Derek Heathcoat-Amory, stimulated a new boom in 1959. This allowed Macmillan to win the 1959 election even more forcefully than Eden had won in 1955. The Conservatives now had 365 seats to Labour's 258. Labour's programme of reform had appeared to threaten tax increases and significantly many voters chose the Liberals (whose share of the vote had doubled since 1955) as the alternative to the Conservatives.

Macmillan's political recovery from Suez was remarkable and his personal position seemed unassailable as Labour – after their third consecutive defeat – became increasingly divided. Moderates around Hugh Gaitskell, rather like moderate elements in the German SPD, hoped in the late 1950s to turn Labour away from its working-class image and to reduce the emphasis on nationalisation policies. Some hoped to change clause four of the party's 1918 Constitution which committed it to the public control of the means of production, distribution and exchange on Marxist lines. Labour was also divided over the question of nuclear weapons. In February 1958, a Campaign for Nuclear Disarmament (CND) was formed which, in April, held its first successful march to the nuclear weapons research establishment at Aldermaston. Its members saw a British nuclear deterrent as immoral, dangerous (the argument went that it was 'better red than dead') or as based on an outmoded belief that the country was still a superpower. At the Labour party conference in 1960 the Left and the trades unions, on a narrow vote, carried a motion against both the British hydrogen bomb and US bases on British soil. The party Right responded by forming the 'Campaign for Democratic Socialism' but in 1961 Gaitskell could only get a partial reversal of the 1960 party decisions.

Despite his 1959 election success and the Labour divisions, Macmillan could not overcome the sense of national malaise which deepened after Suez. The Prime Minister insisted that 'most of our people have never had it so good' and there was much to support such a view. Keynesianism and consensus politics seemed fully vindicated as the 1950s saw wages rising faster than prices, better pensions, little unemployment, better education and diet, a shorter working week, more people taking holidays abroad, the continued reduction of slum housing, remarkable improvements in Britain's agricultural production, the development of new industries like electronics and cars, and considerable artistic and scientific creativity. Between 1951 and 1964 the proportion of people owning their own home rose from a quarter to a half, the number of cars grew from 2.5 million to 9 million, and the number of televisions from a million to over 12 million. Productivity was up, there were more women in work and many families could live on one salary. Except for 1960 the years 1957–62 saw a favourable trade balance and in the early 1960s hospital and university building was expanded. Yet affluence itself led to questioning of the *way* in which wealth was shared. Despite generally rising living standards, poverty and deprivation went on; some could make fortunes out of speculation on the stock exchange whilst the government attacked those on low wages who took strike action. An elite 'Establishment' was believed by many to control the country despite the development of democracy. The sense of social outrage was reflected in the rise of the 'New Left', the literary writings of the 'angry young men' and the production of 'kitchen sink' films in the cinema. Furthermore, despite all the signs of improvement it was clear that Britain was in economic decline relative to other countries. Living standards and industrial output were rising but not as fast as in America, Japan and much of Western Europe. Britain's share of world trade fell from a quarter in the late 1940s to less than a fifth a decade later.

The causes of British decline relative to other economies were hotly debated, and continue to be so. The 'stop-go' policies of Conservative Chancellors suggested a government which had little idea about how the economy worked and was reluctant to take harsh measures because this could lose it the next election. Macmillan himself was obsessed with fears of a return to the 1930s depression and was ready to tolerate high government spending and some inflation. Yet every time the Conservatives tried expansion, the trade situation worsened and deflation was necessary, which harmed investment and sapped confidence. This of course followed a Labour government which (in contrast to France) had failed to develop an effective system of economic planning for the long term. But 'stop-go' could not be blamed for the fundamental weakness of the economy. The government itself put much of the blame for Britain's failure on trades union activity, and certainly Britain had a trades union system which was marred by demarcation problems, 'unofficial' strikes and unrepresentative leaders. British workers appeared determined to be paid more than they had really earned and, around 1960, to go on a 'spending spree' for new consumer products, like refrigerators and washing machines, often bought from abroad. But industrial relations do not seem to have caused many more strikes than those experienced in other Western countries and many criticisms could also be levelled at British managers who, in contrast to their German counterparts, were frequently poorly trained, failed to complete vigorously abroad and give their employees little share in company decisions or profits. Some tried to put the blame for decline on the war, which had exhausted so many British assets. It was also argued that the destruction of industry in Germany and Japan during the war had allowed those countries to modernise more thoroughly.

Certainly Britain's declining share of world trade after the war was inevitable to an extent, because countries like Germany and Japan were bound to re-emerge as trading powers in due course. Yet such considerations could not explain why Britain consistently failed to keep up with her competitors into the 1960s, nor why she was unable to achieve sustained growth. A more convincing explanation of decline can be found by looking at longer-term problems, stretching back to the industrial revolution. The successes of the past bred the weaknesses of the present. Britain's class system, archaic trades union structure, unprofessional managers, old staple industries (textiles, shipbuilding and the like), large overseas commitments and complacency over its political structure had been ingrained over several decades and – partly because Britain avoided defeat in the Second World War – were not fundamentally called into question as they were on the Continent. Britain's Empire had arguably served to weaken the country by fostering such complacency. Imperial considerations ensured that British leaders sought a world role, kept defence spending high, tried to maintain sterling as a major trading currency (in the Sterling Area), and avoided membership of the European Community, whilst British companies concentrated on trade with the Commonwealth, invested outside Britain and failed to maintain their competitiveness in advanced industrial markets. Another legacy of the past was that, unlike France or Italy, Britain was already highly urbanised in 1945 and could not shift any more labourers from the land into industry as a source of growth. Britain also had the fundamental problem of being forced, as a densely-populated island, to export large amounts of goods in order to import food and raw materials. This became more difficult as new trading rivals emerged in the post-war world.

After 1961 it became clear that Macmillan's successes since 1957 had merely papered over the problems brought by British decline, economic sluggishness and increasing self-doubt. Despite the creation of a National Economic Development Council as a new economic planning body, growth was slow, trade poor and sterling insecure. Already in 1960–1, in order to recover from problems left by the pre-election 'give-away' budget, the government had introduced higher interest rates and a 'pay pause' to limit salary increases. Further attempts, by the new Chancellor of the Exchequer, Selwyn Lloyd, to control wages in 1962 led to a series of strikes. Yet when Macmillan in the 'Night of the Long Knives' in July, sacked Lloyd and several other ministers, it seemed more like an act of desperation than an assertion of authority. Reginald Maudling, Lloyd's successor, then engineered yet another spending 'boom' which simply increased imports and drove trade into deficit in 1963–4. Internationally the pace of decolonisation quickened after 1960, with most African colonies rapidly being given their independence as the French and Belgians also decided to quit the continent. Remarks by the former US Secretary of State, Dean Acheson, that Britain had lost its Empire but failed to find a new role, caused consternation. Yet the facts were that the Commonwealth had failed to become an effective vehicle for maintaining British influence in the world and the 'independent' nuclear deterrent relied on US missiles after 1962, whilst the attempt by Macmillan to enter the Common Market in 1961–3 was vetoed by General de Gaulle.

Macmillan's problems after 1961 were compounded by various developments. Racial tensions, resulting from West Indian and Asian immigration from the colonies led the government to restrict the inflow in 1962. The Liberal party revived as a major force in by-elections. The Vassall, Blake and Philby spy cases undermined faith in the security services. Cynicism about British government and society reached new heights when the Secretary of War, John Profumo, became involved in a sex scandal about which he lied to the House of Commons. Macmillan, ill and with his position increasingly untenable, resigned in October 1963. Some Conservatives then hoped for a younger leader to emerge; others felt that R.A. Butler was the best successor. Instead the party leaders turned to the Foreign Secretary, Lord Home.* However, some Conservatives refused to serve as ministers under Home, who seemed a safe, reliable but uninspiring 'stop-gap' Prime Minister. Meanwhile, Labour had become a more dangerous opposition since 1962 when Gaitskell had pleased the Left by opposing entry to the Common Market. Gaitskell died suddenly in January 1963, but his successor was Harold Wilson, a pragmatic politician who was popular with the Left, had Cabinet experience, was a good television performer and managed to portray himself as a dynamic leader who promised to modernise Britain and repair the damage of 'thirteen wasted years' under the Conservatives.

The October 1964 General Election was called at the last possible date by the government. Remarkably, Wilson did *not* succeed in overwhelming his opponents. Home had seemed competent as premier and even proved tough enough to end retail price maintenance, a price-fixing system among shopkeepers. Furthermore, the Liberal party had maintained its good showing since the 1950s and took many anti-Conservative votes (11 per cent in the election, although the party won only 9 seats). The Conservatives (303 seats) lost office, but denied Labour (317) a large working majority.

## The Labour Ascendancy, 1964–79

The 13 years of Conservative rule after 1951 were followed by 15 years in which Labour became, as Wilson put it, 'the natural party of government'. Wilson's victories in four general elections were interrupted only by the

---

* To become Prime Minister, Home gave up his title and entered the House of Commons as Alec Douglas-Home.

surprise Conservative win in June 1970 which was reversed less than four years later. Yet on only one occasion, in 1966, did Wilson succeed in winning a substantial parliamentary majority, the Labour party often appeared divided and Wilson's promises to modernise the economy, improve management and planning, and develop science and technology were largely unfulfilled. Britain in 1979 seemed much weaker than she had in 1964 – her economic strength relative to other Western powers had continued to decline, her political system was under challenge, and even her pretensions to a world role had ceased. Wilson himself proved remarkably conservative in his attitudes and sought to retain Labour's hold on office by relying in foreign affairs on the US alliance and in domestic affairs on 'consensus politics'.

Wilson came to office in 1964 with promises of a dynamic 'hundred days', the Left were satisfied with several leading posts in the government and Labour's determination to improve British economic planning was shown by the creation of a Department of Economic Affairs (which drew up a National Plan) under the moderate, George Brown, and a Ministry of Technology (to stimulate new industries like electronics and computing) under the trades union leader, Frank Cousins. Wilson, however, could not easily reverse the poor economic situation inherited from the Conservatives and problems began immediately for the new premier. His appointment of Patrick Gordon-Walker as Foreign Secretary soon backfired. Gordon-Walker had lost his parliamentary seat in the election and an attempt to return him to the Commons in a 'safe' by-election at Leyton ended in another defeat. Wilson's personal leadership style, with its reliance on a 'kitchen cabinet' of advisers and lack of ministerial discussion drew criticism. Controversy was also created by the government's decision to cancel the costly TSR-2 aircraft project, whilst continuing to develop the equally costly 'Concorde' airliner with France. Wilson's insistence on maintaining Britain's military presence in the Far East was criticised by the Left, as was his decision to continue the purchase of Polaris nuclear missiles from America. And in 1965 came a humiliating episode when the white-dominated government of Southern Rhodesia made a unilateral declaration of independence from Britain under Ian Smith, rather than accept black majority rule.

Wilson compensated for the disappointments by extending trades union rights, improving redundancy payments, keeping house rents low and introducing a Race Relations Act which outlawed incitement to racial hatred. The government also acted quickly to fulfil two election promises, an increase in old age pensions and the end of medical prescription charges. Such changes were, however, very costly. In an important early decision Wilson and his economic ministers ruled out a devaluation of sterling to cope with the budgetary situation. A devaluation could have resolved trade problems, but Labour leaders, with memories of 1949, were reluctant to become identified as the 'party of devaluation', especially since another election would soon be necessary. Instead of devaluation, therefore, the government introduced an import surcharge. This was criticised abroad, and rather than strengthening sterling, the air of crisis led to a 'run' on the currency. In November 1964 a package of measures was needed to tighten credit. More credit restrictions, government spending cuts and tax increases followed in 1965. And yet, despite all the problems, respect for Wilson rose in the country. The Conservatives (using an electoral system for the first time) chose a new, younger leader in 1965, Edward Heath, but he failed to match the Prime Minister in popular appeal and, despite improvements in their presentation of policy, the Conservatives continued to be blamed for the country's economic malaise. As a result Wilson was able to secure a firm majority in an election in March 1966, when the economic crisis seemed to be easing at last. Labour won 363 seats to the Conservatives' 253.

Labour won the election with more promises of economic growth, better national and regional planning and further social reforms. However, the government's performance over the next four years disappointed its supporters. True, a number of measures were carried out. Steel was renationalised in 1967, the government encouraged the creation of large companies (such as the car producer, British Leyland) to compete internationally, there were efforts to improve training and investment, local government spending was extended, the civil service was reformed, the introduction of decimal currency was agreed (it was introduced in 1971), an Ombudsman was appointed to investigate maladministration, comprehensive education was encouraged, and in 1969 the voting age was reduced to 18. Private Members' Bills in the House of Commons also helped to advance 'permissive' legislation: abortion and homosexuality were legalised, and divorce made easier. Opposition from the Left combined, however, with Conservative criticisms to prevent a promised reform of the House of Lords: the Conservatives wanted to preserve the hereditary principle, the Left saw a House of Lords in any form as undemocratic. In foreign affairs Wilson's reputation was not helped by his inability to resolve the Rhodesian situation, a vain bid to enter the European Community in 1967, nor his failed attempts to mediate in the Vietnam War. At home, the Prime Minister's 'Presidential' style of leadership led to the resignation from the government of George Brown. During 1968 Britain largely escaped the widespread student unrest seen in West Germany, France and elsewhere. Nonetheless, there were occupations of university buildings, anti-Vietnam war protests and even the beginnings of a terrorist movement in the 'Angry Brigade' (which was not destroyed until 1971). Of far greater long-term importance were civil rights marches by the minority Roman Catholic population in Northern Ireland, which had remained tied to Great Britain after the creation of Eire in 1922. The marches led to a backlash from the Protestant majority, who dominated the political and economic life of the province, and in 1969 the British government sent troops to maintain order.

One reason for increasing discontent was Labour's failure to achieve good rates of economic growth. Growth *did* continue during the 1960s, and living standards rose, but once again this was at a slower rate than Britain's competitors and, like the Conservatives, the government frequently seemed adrift in dealing with economic problems. In July 1966 Frank Cousins resigned in protest at the idea of a prices and incomes policy and was replaced at the Ministry of Technology by Tony Benn. The months May–July 1966 also saw a seamen's strike for higher pay. Wilson, determined to show that Labour was not at the mercy of the unions, resisted the demands but he upset Labour's working-class supporters, whilst the strike harmed trade figures and sterling. In July 1966 the government introduced credit limits, tax increases, cuts in investment and a six-month wage freeze. However, after a short-term improvement, trade in 1967 was again poor and growth low. Confidence was further undermined by the failure of the Common Market application and by the June Arab–Israeli war. In November, despite echoes of 1949, Wilson and the nation had to suffer the humiliation of a devaluation of sterling. The Chancellor of the Exchequer, James Callaghan, was then replaced by Roy Jenkins; medical prescription charges were reintroduced; cuts in the housing programme and, even, defence were accepted. Yet in 1968 sterling remained insecure and the continuing uncertainty, plus the cutbacks in government investment, helped destroy Labour's hopes for rational planning of economic growth. The country never achieved the 1965 National Plan's aim of 3.8 per cent growth per annum: average growth in 1964–70 was only 2.2 per cent. In 1969 the rising number of unofficial strikes led the government to introduce a Labour Relations Bill ('In Place of Strife') but this again upset an important group of government supporters, the trades unions, and had to be withdrawn.

By June 1970, for all Labour's troubles, trade was improving and wages were on the increase, thanks in part to the 1967 devaluation. Wilson was able to call a general election against a background of favourable opinion polls. Yet even the Prime Minister admitted his government had been 'blown off course', failing to introduce major reforms or to control the economy. Inflation had doubled to 6 per cent since 1964, fuelled by wage demands and government spending. The Conservatives, following their Selsdon Park Hotel conference in January, put forward a radical new policy, based on dissatisfcation which had grown over 'consensus politics' since the Macmillan years. The Conservatives who had themselves increased public spending and begun wage restraint under Macmillan, now wanted to reduce state intervention in the economy which had grown through nationalisation, state investment and prices and incomes policy. The Conservatives also wanted to restrict welfare provisions and to cut taxes. A market economy, preferably part of the European Common Market, would be more competitive in world markets, it was believed. To widespread surprise, by fighting on this programme, Edward Heath became Prime Minister with a comfortable majority of 330 seats to Labour's 287.

The Heath government introduced a number of major structural reforms. This included literally redrawing the map of Britain in local government reforms of 1972–3, which created a new system of county borders and redefined local government responsibilities. In 1973 the health service was also given a bureaucratic overhaul, though this did little to improve health statistics. A Central Policy Review Staff was formed to help long-term government planning. Elsewhere, however, the government was forced into policy changes. A 1971 Act restricted immigration, but the government had to accept the arrival of 30 000 Asians with British passports who were expelled by the Ugandan dictator, Idi Amin. In Northern Ireland the government introduced internment without trial in 1971 to try to deal with the rising tide of violence and especially the campaign by the Irish Republican Army (IRA) to end Britain's presence in Ireland. This step created its own problems, and in 1972, when 468 people were killed in 'the troubles', the government introduced direct rule over the province, putting an end to the local parliament at Stormont. The IRA campaign spread to the British mainland, the Protestant MPs from Northern Ireland broke with the Conservative party in the House of Commons and although the situation seemed to ease somewhat in 1973–4, an attempt to return to local rule through an Assembly proved a failure. Heath's greatest personal triumph was to take Britain into the European Community (EC) in 1973, though his methods of doing so caused controversy, mainly because he had not specifically stated in the 1970 manifesto that he would carry entry through to completion. The Labour party, divided after their election defeat, had decided to oppose Heath on EC entry in 1971 and agreed that the electorate should be given a choice to vote on the issue. Pro-EC Labour members nonetheless voted with Heath to push entry through in 1972. Public feeling about the EC was mixed, particularly when membership meant the introduction of a new Value-added Tax (VAT) on purchases, higher agricultural prices and further strains on old Commonwealth relationships.

The most vital area on which the government was judged was the economy, and here Heath, like Wilson, failed to live up to the promise of change in his party's manifesto. Heath's personal commitment to the Selsdon Park decisions was not strong. An intelligent, decent but secretive individual, he proved to be yet another defender of the post-war consensus and soon effected a 'U-turn' on the Conservative commitment to reduce state intervention. When Rolls-Royce ran into financial difficulties Heath provided assistance to the company, then nationalised it. Aid was also given to the Upper Clyde Shipbuilders and by 1972 the Conservatives' policy of state directed investment seemed similar to Labour's. In 1971 the government introduced an Industrial Relations Bill to reduce the number of strikes and force trades unions to obey a certain code of behaviour. However, this merely led to demonstrations, a breakdown in relations with the Unions, and greater strike activity in 1972–3, spearheaded by the National Union of Mineworkers who won a major pay increase in 1972. Yet again a government failed to achieve co-operation between itelf, the unions and businessmen. There was a similar failure to live up to earlier promises by the Chancellor of the Exchequer, Anthony Barber. He began with attempts to stimulate private enterprise through tax cuts and reductions in public spending. Health charges were increased, free school milk ended and council house subsidies cut. But these policies fuelled working-class discontent without winning any response from British businessmen, who seemed incapable of meeting Barber's challenge to expand. The international economic crisis of these years presented, in any case, formidable difficulties. Growth was low, in 1972 unemployment rose over a million, whilst inflation was high and trade slipped into deficit. The sterling crisis was now met by 'floating' the pound, but this led to increased import prices, as did a general rise in world commodity prices.

To try to control inflation the government abandoned its commitment to market forces and, in November 1972, introduced a pay and prices 'freeze'. Pay and price increases continued to be limited by legislation in 1973, yet inflation – fuelled by world factors, government spending and wage demands – remained high, strikes were widespread, interest rates rose over 10 per cent, and the trade deficit was made even worse by the oil price increases following the 1973 Middle East war. Britain was facing 'stagflation' and to make matters worse October also saw the mineworkers reject a new pay offer. In November the government was trying to carry out 'stage three' of its prices and incomes policy whilst simultaneously dealing with the oil crisis and a miners' overtime ban. Electricity workers added to the malaise by taking 'sympathy' action with the miners. As a result, cuts in electricity supplies were needed, interest rates rose to 13 per cent and finally, in January, the drastic decision was taken to begin a three-day week for industry, because of the lack of power supplies. When, in early February, the miners voted for an all-out strike Heath decided to call a general election. He hoped to portray the miners as representing a challenge to the elected government, and at first seemed in a strong position. The election campaign, however, went badly for him. Although many people believed that the power of the trades unions had grown too great, there was sympathy for the miners because of their low pay and dangerous working conditions. Amidst talk of Britain having become 'ungovernable', many blamed the Conservatives for mishandling the economy and industrial relations since 1970. The February 1974 trade deficit was the worst ever. Labour, on the other hand, was able to patch up its differences and Wilson talked of making a 'social contract' with the unions to ensure their co-operation. Another blow for Heath came when his old rival Enoch Powell, an opponent of the EC, advised the electorate to vote Labour. Even so, what finally defeated the Conservatives was the 'first past the post' electoral system, for with 38 per cent of the vote they won only 296 seats, whilst Labour's 37 per cent won them 301. As in the late 1950s and early 1960s many anti-Conservative votes went to the Liberals, who won a remarkable 19 per cent of the vote but only 14 seats. There were also 11 Ulster Unionists and 9 Scottish or Welsh nationalists.

Britain in February 1974 seemed anything but a United Kingdom. A state of emergency had been declared, industrial relations were in tatters, inflation seemed out of control, Northern Ireland was troubled, there were demands for 'devolution' in Scotland and Wales (encouraged by local economic conditions), doubts still existed over EC entry, the two-party system was endangered and Wilson became Prime Minister of a minority government, supported by little more than a third of voters. Wilson quickly acted to fulfil the 'social contract' by ending the miners' strike, repealing the 1971 Industrial Relations Act and abandoning compulsory wage restraint. In return the unions promised to use voluntary restraint in making annual wage demands. A full working week was soon restored, price controls remained and rents were frozen. Labour also began to renegotiate EC entry terms, speeded up comprehensive education and improved social security payments. Wilson hoped that such determination, along with promises of devolution in Scotland and Wales, would win him a secure majority in the election, which he called in October. However, the Chancellor of the Exchequer, Denis Healey, had introduced tough tax increases at first and many voters (25 per cent) continued to opt for the smaller parties. Labour, with 319 seats (39 per cent of the vote) won a majority of only three over the Conservatives (276 seats, 36 per cent of the vote) and others combined.

With the election over the Conservatives quickly acted in February 1975 to remove Heath as party leader. His successor was Margaret Thatcher, Minister of Education in 1970–4 who shared Heath's middle-class background, but was far more energetic and doctrinaire in her political policies. Wilson remained in office a year longer, resigning in March 1976 on grounds, he said, of his age. Sceptical observers looked in vain for an alternative reason for Wilson's surprising departure. He was succeeded by the older James Callaghan, who came from a working-class background and had little charisma but who was moderate, popular and had already filled the posts of Chancellor of the Exchequer, Home Secretary and Foreign Secretary. Callaghan proved quite adept over the following three years in clinging onto office, despite losing his Commons majority because of by-election defeats. In March 1977 he formed a voting pact in the House of Commons with the Liberal leader, David Steel. The Liberals had been rocked by the resignation in May 1976 of their own leader, Jeremy Thorpe, after an embarrassing court case and so were ready to keep Labour in power. By summer 1978 the 'Lib-Lab pact' even seemed to put Callaghan on course for an election victory, according to opinion polls but, like the Conservatives in 1964, he decided to delay the election until the government's fifth year. It was a fateful decision which left Labour with little room for electoral manoeuvre at the end of a very troubled government.

The Labour administration of 1974–9 had some notable successes. By April 1975 EC terms had been renegotiated an the Cabinet's differences on the issue were papered over when it was decided to hold a national referendum on the issue. Referenda were alien to British political life but the surrender of sovereignty to EC institutions seemed important enough to justify the decision. The June referendum resulted in a two-thirds vote in favour of EC membership, with the main opponents being nationalist right-wingers like Enoch Powell and left-wing socialists like Tony Benn. In 1975 the government also carried through an Act which made it illegal to discriminate against women in employment and other fields, setting up an Equal Opportunities Commission to monitor this. In 1976 a Commission for Racial Equality was also established. A Police Complaints Board was set up, comprehensive education was extended, and in 1975 a National Enterprise Board was established to handle government share-holdings and improve state planning. The car-maker British Leyland was nationalised; as were aerospace and shipbuilding concerns, and in 1975 Britain began to earn money from North Sea oil. The number of deaths in Northern Ireland was reduced, especially after the rise of the local 'Peace Movement' in 1976, although another attempt to hand over responsibility to local politicians failed in 1975–6.

Yet the experiences of 1974–9 further undermined beliefs in the mixed economy and welfare spending because Labour's attempts to control the economy through state intervention and co-operation with the unions failed once again. In 1974–5 productivity remained low and trade poor, but the unions continued to press for higher wages as inflation rose over 20 per cent. In July 1975, with the 'social contract' seriously questioned, Denis Healey introduced wage restrictions and higher taxes. In 1976 a new sterling crisis forced the government to request an IMF loan but, with 'stagflation' in Britain worse than that in most other Western countries, the IMF insisted on swinging cuts in public spending. These spending reductions helped bring inflation under control in 1977, when trade also returned to profit, but this was at the price of growing working-class dissatisfaction as improvements in living standards stagnated. In 1978 the government tried to compensate for its wage restraint policy with tax cuts but the early months of 1979 saw new depths of national pessimism as a wave of strikes affected road transport and the public services. The 'Winter of Discontent' destroyed pay guidelines, brought violence on picket lines and fuelled Conservative criticisms of the trades unions. The 'social contract' was in tatters. February 1979 also saw two referenda on Labour's schemes for limited devolution to Scottish and Welsh assemblies, although in neither vote did those in favour of devolution reach the level, of 40 per cent of the electorate, necessary to carry the measure through. The Scottish and Welsh nationalists, who had helped to keep Callaghan in office until the referenda were carried out, now turned against the Prime Minister, whose government seemed to stumble from crisis to crisis, unable to provide the prosperity and strong leadership which Britain desperately needed.

Finally, on 28 March, Margaret Thatcher won a vote of no confidence in the government by one vote, thus forcing an election. On 3 May she won a clear majority of 339 seats (44 per cent of the vote) to Labour's 268 (37 per cent) with the Liberals falling back to 11 (14 per cent) and the nationalists similarly suffering a dramatic decline. Traditional Conservative voters had returned to the fold after the difficulties of the Heath years and, more significantly, many more lower-middle and working-class voters were ready to put their faith in right-wing policies as the way to secure a better future.

## Ten years of 'Thatcherism', 1979–89

Margaret Thatcher, the first woman prime minister in the Western world, came to power in 1979 with promises to reduce trades union power, lower state spending, cut taxes, control inflation and, by making Britain more competitive and market-orientated, reverse the nation's decline. Britain suffered, the Conservatives argued, from a lack of enterprise owing to socialist reform, high taxes, trades unions who opposed modernisation, and the destructive effect of inflation, itself fuelled by state spending. Britain's share of world manufacturing exports was now less than a tenth; foreign manufacturers took up a quarter of the domestic market; profits, productivity and investment were all low compared to West Germany, France or Japan. The country had the reputation of being the divided and strike-ridden 'sick man of Europe'. To reverse this Thatcher wanted to end the post-war world of 'consensus politics' and replace it with a new era of 'conviction politics', and policies that became known (somewhat vaguely) as 'Thatcherism'. Many have seen 1979 in retrospect as a major turning-point in British history. There was much evidence of a break with the past, as Thatcher concentrated on reducing inflation, adopted policies of spending controls, favoured 'Monetarism' and the control of the money supply over Keynesian economics, abandoned any pretence of seeking full employment, initiated the 'privatisation' of state-owned industries and put her faith in the *laissez-faire*, Victorian values of self-help, hard work and individual initiative. She reinforced her position with populist appeals to traditional values and the need for law and order, in reaction to permissiveness. Her energy and toughness helped her to remove the members of her own party – contemptuously referred to as 'wets' – who defended the old consensus values.

The idea of 1979 as a turning-point in British history should not be exaggerated. Britain between 1945 and 1979 had *not* seen the constant predominance of 'consensus politics'. Many Conservatives had hoped to reverse Labour's welfare spending and state intervention in this period, as seen in the 1970 party manifesto, to which Thatcher's policies bore a striking resemblance. The difference in 1979 was that radical Tories had a leader who was ready to carry out the policies and determined to avoid the 'U-turns' of Heath. Then again, the 1979 Conservative manifesto was quite moderate in its intentions: the government later went much further, for example in its privatisation programme and spending cuts, than it originally promised. It must also be remembered that Britain in 1979 was still one of the seven wealthiest industrial states, with considerable military power and diplomatic influence despite its relative decline in the world. Inflation had already been lowered from its peak in the mid-1970s. The devolution votes in Scotland and Wales showed that the 'break-up of Britain' thesis had been overstated, there was general acceptance that the country must remain in the EC, North Sea oil had begun to flow, and the British people themselves now seemed ready, in contrast to 1974, to accept controls on trades unions and on state spending. Arguably the IMF-inspired spending cuts of 1976 had already marked a turning-point for the economy and full employment had effectively ended in the 1970s. It is possible to argue too that the real turning-point for British fortunes was not 1979 but 1981 or 1982. It was in 1981 that the economic depression, triggered by more oil price rises, reached its nadir, with high unemployment, riots in major British cities and a major reshuffle of the government. But 1982 saw the revival of Conservative and national self-confidence with the Falklands crisis.

The new government surprised observers, used to the politics of compromise, with its determination to carry out its policies. Geoffrey Howe, the Chancellor of the Exchequer, as part of the new faith in market forces, quickly acted to end wage controls despite the danger of inflation. He also cut taxes, promised spending reductions and shifted the burden of taxation from income tax to VAT. The last move added to inflation, which reached 22 per cent again in 1980 before falling off. North Sea oil supplies, by keeping the value of the pound high, proved a mixed blessing for trade. The Chancellor maintained high interest rates to control inflation, but these too kept sterling's value high. Alongside the world depression, government policies led unemployment to rocket, rising above three million in 1981. GNP fell consistently between 1979 and 1982, and by 1983 industrial output had been cut by a tenth. Only in 1988 would investment in manufacturing industry recover to its 1979 level. Traditional industries in the north, such as steel and shipbuilding, were especially hard hit, and unemployment was correspondingly worse, leading to fears of a 'North-South divide'. Difficulties in measuring the money supply, and therefore in carrying out Monetarist policies, led greater emphasis to be put on spending cuts as a weapon of economic policy. But this added to unemployment and harmed public services. Once again Britain seemed harder hit during a depression than other advanced nations, except perhaps the USA, and by 1981 there was considerable pressure on Thatcher to effect a 'U-turn' in the style of Heath. Bitter memories of 1974 and her own strength of character led the Prime Minister to persevere but her commitment to Monetarism was now diluted: in 1981–2 the value of sterling was more closely managed, public sector wages were controlled as a 'yardstick' for the economy as a whole, and government borrowing was allowed to increase. By 1983 trade was healthy, inflation was under 5 per cent and the government argued that there was 'no alternative' to high unemployment and the closure of 'lame duck' industries if Britain was to become profit-making again. Yet there could be no doubt that the economic record of the first Thatcher government had failed to live up to popular hopes. Increases in VAT and national insurance contributions meant that, except for the wealthy, taxes had actually increased since 1979;

thanks to the depression and unemployment payments, state spending had actually risen as a percentage of GNP; and inflation was still higher when compared with Britain's competitors. In 1983, with an election in the offing, Howe introduced a tax-cutting budget but the survival of the government after this date was probably due to successes in other fields, as well as the failures of Thatcher's opponents.

It was not simply in the economic field that the Conservatives proved resolute in pursuing a new political direction. Government sales of the profitable parts of nationalised industries and of its shareholdings (in oil, cable and wireless, and aerospace) served to provide revenue whilst reducing the state's role in the Economy. New chairmen were also employed to improve the efficiency of nationalised industries, ready for a more far-reaching privatisation programme after 1983. The government restrained education spending and sold off council houses. The last proved a popular move, helping to promote the Conservatives' long-standing ideal of a 'property-owning democracy'. As to the trades unions, they stood at the height of their strength, militancy and influence on government in May 1979 but were always destined to be a victim of Conservative attack. What was surprising here was that, having excluded Union leaders from policy-making, Thatcher's government developed its policy against trades union power cautiously. A 1980 act controlled 'secondary picketing'* and encouraged secret balloting in union elections; in 1982 secondary action was banned altogether and the definition of 'lawful disputes' was restricted. The decline in the influence of trades unions at this time, seen in falling membership and a reduced number of strikes, was probably as much due to the demoralisation brought by the events of 1979 and the subsequent high unemployment than it was to government action. Discontent against the government during the depth of the depression in 1981 was seen, not in trades union activities, but in the riots of spring and summer in London, Birmingham, Manchester, Liverpool and elsewhere. The riots could be blamed on a number of factors, from unemployment, inner-city deprivation and an uncaring government to poor policing, racial problems, and the disaffection of youth. There had been earlier disorders, in Bristol in 1980, and there would be further problems later, but 1981 was a disturbing, if short-lived, experience. The government responded by strengthening the police, giving aid to inner-city areas and attempting to improve race relations.

Margaret Thatcher was little known abroad in 1979 but her forthright style soon made an impact. Her right-wing beliefs in the Soviet menace, the 'special relationship' with America and a strong defence were well-suited to the new cold war of the early 1980s and made her a natural ally of US President Reagan. She had little faith in the Commonwealth but had an early success in 1979 when her Foreign Secretary, Lord Carrington, finally resolved the long-running Rhodesian problem. An agreement was made which led to black majority rule in 1981. Thatcher

---

* That is, picketing by workers away from their own workplace.

127

was also suspicious of the EC and successfully campaigned for a reduction in Britain's contribution to the Community budget. In 1980–1 she also resisted international pressure for concessions to IRA hunger strikers, ten of whom starved themselves to death. Thatcher's greatest success in world affairs, came, however, from a sudden and unexpected challenge in April 1982 when the Argentinian military dictator, General Galtieri, invaded the Falkland Islands, in the South Atlantic, one of Britain's few remaining colonies. Galtieri hoped to win popular support by enforcing an old Argentinian claim to the islands, and he had probably been encouraged by British defence cuts to believe that Thatcher would not respond. The invasion was, however, a major affront to British dignity and the Prime Minister acted accordingly. A 'war cabinet' was formed, a military task force hastily assembled and by mid-June the Falkland Islands were recaptured. Despite the loss of several ships and over 200 men, the crisis proved to be something of a 'Suez in reverse'. Britain had proved able to project its military power at a great distance, national pride received a major boost and Thatcher's own position – in stark contrast to Eden's in 1956 – was enormously strengthened.

Before the Falklands crisis the Conservatives had seemed in danger of being overwhelmed in a general election. As in previous periods of discontent with Conservatism the main danger came not from Labour but from the political centre. Labour had again become bitterly divided after their 1979 defeat, when they obtained their lowest share of the vote since 1931. The Left, led by Tony Benn, criticised the moderation of Wilson and Callaghan and put forward a third, radical alternative to both consensus politics and Thatcherism. At home Benn wanted greater state intervention, higher welfare spending and the destruction of such class-based elements in society as the House of Lords and private education. Abroad he favoured unilateral disarmament, détente and withdrawal from the EC. In October 1980 Callaghan resigned as party leader and the left-wing Michael Foot narrowly won the succession race over Denis Healey. Foot, a libertarian socialist, ex-Bevanite and EC opponent, had been in parliament since 1945 but won ministerial experience only after 1974. He was chosen just as the Left succeeded in having a special conference called, at Wembley in January 1981, which defined a new method of leadership election designed (along with other proposed changes) to make party leaders more responsive to the wishes of its members. The Wembley conference, Foot's triumph, the rise of the Trotskyite 'Militant Tendency' within the party and the revival too of the Campaign for Nuclear Disarmament, provoked disaffection among Labour moderates and in March 1981 a breakaway Social Democratic Party (SDP) was formed, led by the so-called 'Gang of Four': Shirley Williams, Bill Rogers, Roy Jenkins and the former Foreign Secretary, David Owen. The SDP stood, they claimed, for 'true' Labour values (in contrast to Benn) and consensus politics (in contrast to Thatcher). With Thatcher's government so unpopular in 1981, and with an electoral alliance between the Liberals and SDP, the new party soon began to score remarkable by-election victories. However, after the

Falklands crisis the SDP–Liberal position in the opinion polls declined almost as rapidly as it had grown, whilst Labour remained in disarray.

The June 1983 election showed how Thatcher could gain from the divisions among her supporters. World trade, profits and living standards were now recovering, the rise in unemployment had levelled off and the Falklands war was won. The Conservatives promised tax cuts, more controls on the trades unions and a strong defence whilst Labour stood for higher spending, nationalisation and the cancellation of Britain's new nuclear weapons system (again bought from America), Trident. Actually the Conservatives had a lower share of the vote (42 per cent) than in 1979, but Britain's 'first-past-the-post' electoral system accentuated the impact of opposition divisions and gave the Conservatives 397 seats. Labour, with 28 per cent of the vote, had 209 seats; the Liberal–SDP alliance, who predictably favoured the introduction of proportional representation, won only 23 seats despite getting over 25 per cent of the vote. After this setback Michael Foot soon resigned as Labour leader to be succeeded by the young, relatively inexperienced Neil Kinnock, of the moderate-left. Roy Jenkins also gave way as SDP leader to David Owen. Thatcher, for her part, strengthened her hold on the government and maintained the policies developed since 1979. Council house sales were maintained, health service charges were increased, and in 1986 a whole level of local government, the Metropolitan Councils, was abolished. These Councils were all expensive and Labour-dominated. Spending on 'infrastructure' (such as roads, railways and water supply) was cut back. Non-market elements of government policy which did remain, often survived because of their value to the middle classes: these included free hospital care, tax relief on mortgages and grants for university education. In 1984 another Trades Union Act enforced regular elections of officials and secret ballots before any strike action, and the government held firm during the twelve month miners' strike of 1984–5. High fuel stocks, tough police action and a split in the miners' union helped ensure a reversal of the events of 1974. The miners suffered a resounding defeat and in 1985 strikes were at their lowest level for 20 years.

The second Thatcher government experienced a number of problems which became known as 'banana skins': in 1986 there were criticisms of the Prime Minister for allowing US aircraft to bomb Libya from British bases; government prosecutions under the Official Secrets Act provoked concern about civil liberties; then, in January 1986, the Cabinet became divided on the sale of Westland Helicopters to a US company and two ministers resigned, including Michael Heseltine, widely seen as a possible successor to Thatcher, and an advocate of close co-operation with Europe. The government was able to compensate for such difficulties with what appeared to be a dramatic change in Britain's economic fortunes, as growth rates outstripped those of EC rivals. The 'sick man of Europe' now became a major success story, a centre of 'enterprise culture'. In retrospect, the growth and tax cuts of the mid-1980s can be seen to have relied on global recovery and three short-term factors: the natural pace of recovery from the depths of 1981, the flow of North Sea oil (which reached its peak in these years) and money earned from privatisation. In the financial year 1986–7 alone, £4.4 billion was earned from privatisation, with sales of British Telecom, British Airways and the gas industry proving particularly lucrative. Even unemployment, which peaked at over three million in July 1986, began to fall as Thatcher's second Chancellor, Nigel Lawson, reduced taxes and engineered a 'boom' in the British economy. Meanwhile Labour were divided between old-style Marxists, new groups such as feminists and CND campaigners, and moderates. The last group wanted to appeal to voters by accepting certain popular Thatcherite policies – such as council house sales, reliance on the market economy and restrictions on union power – whilst defending the welfare state and health service. However, the SDP–Liberal Alliance remained a viable alternative opposition and in the June 1987 election Labour was able to improve its public image but not its support. The Conservatives had 376 seats, Labour 229 and the Alliance 22.

Margaret Thatcher's third election victory in 1987 led to talk of a generation of Conservative governments. The Prime Minister herself soon afterwards became the longest continually serving premier since 1827. Home ownership rose to over two-thirds of the electorate, working-class voters consistently put their faith in Thatcherism, and Britain after 1979 had become something of a model for other countries who adopted spending cuts, market economics and lower state intervention. In 1987–8 the government continued its radical programme with more tax cuts and a new Employment Act which enforced secret ballots before strike action could be taken. Yet as the Conservatives prepared to celebrate ten years of Thatcherism doubts began to grow about the British 'miracle'. By the time British Water was sold off in 1989 criticism was growing about the privatisation programme. Nationalised industries appeared to be deliberately underfunded, to make them profitable, before being sold at prices below their real value. Firms like British Telecom were able to operate a virtual monopoly after privatisation. Meanwhile the most costly and inefficient industries, like coal and the railways, remained in public ownership. Government reforms of the health service and education system put cost-effectiveness and market economics before public well-being, they added to the burdens of staff and threatened to destroy the last vestiges of the egalitarian, universal welfare system. Rising health charges, and the planned introduction of student loans threatened even middle-class interests. Rent increases, restrictions on social security benefits and the introduction of a new local 'poll tax' (in 1988, in Scotland, in 1990 in England and Wales) fell particularly heavily on the poorer members of society whose living standards were hard hit. The government was crticised as being niggardly and uncaring, and to have fostered values of selfishness and greed. In 1989 Thatcherism seemed to lose some of its popular appeal. All the profitable nationalised industries, save electricity, had now been sold and North Sea oil was beginning to run out. Unemployment had fallen but was still over 1.5 million (with about

700000 additionally on 'job creation' schemes) and its reduction was in any case accompanied by a revival of strike action, especially in the public services where wages lagged behind the private sector. Disaffection was increased by evidence that Nigel Lawson, rather than laying the basis for sustained growth with his tax cuts in the mid-1980s, had fuelled a consumer boom reminiscent of the 'stop-go' era. In 1987–9 a massive trade deficit built up as British industry failed once more to meet domestic demand. The government, committed as it was to income tax reduction, chose to tackle the deficit with interest rate increases but these were slow to work, harmed investment and contributed to inflation. In 1989 the trade deficit was nearly £20 billion, inflation was over 7 per cent and growth fell below 3 per cent. Neither did Thatcher seem able to respond imaginatively to international developments: rather than break with traditional foreign policy, she had maintained high levels of defence spending relative to the rest of NATO and opposed membership of the EC's exchange rate mechanism. Arguments with the Prime Minister over the last issue finally led Lawson to resign as Chancellor, to be succeeded by a new Thatcher favourite, John Major.

Conservative popularity had also declined at times under Thatcher's earlier governments, but this time round there was also a marked revival of Labour's fortunes in the opinion polls. The party now accepted a nuclear defence policy and EC membership, and ceased its opposition to council house sales and privatisation. Labour's revival was also helped by divisions within the SDP–Liberal alliance. Following the 1987 election pressures to fuse the two parties were resisted by the SDP leader, David Owen. A new Social and Liberal Democratic (SLD) party was eventually formed, but amidst such acrimony that support for the political Centre was, for a time, decimated. In the May 1989 European elections 'protest' votes went to the hitherto insignificant Green Party. (Voters evidently had little understanding of the environmentalists' plans to overthrow the existing socio-economic system.)

After ten years of Thatcherism Britain in 1989 was more confident, wealthy and united than it was ten years before. Major constitutional change did not seem likely, even if many people, concerned by the power of government, favoured a Bill of Rights and a shift to proportional representation in elections. Yet many old problems were still apparent: a weak manufacturing base, balance of payments crises, an unstable currency, a reluctance to participate enthusiastically in Europe, inflation, poor union-employer relations, 'stop-go' economics, a failure to develop technical education, and the persistence of class divisions. It could not be said that Thatcher, any more than Macmillan, Wilson or Heath, had succeeded in reversing Britain's relative decline in world affairs.

# 6
# The Triumph of Democracy – Southern Europe

## Liberal-democracy and the problem of Southern Europe

The foundation and survival of liberal-democracy in Western Europe after 1945 was neither an easy nor an inevitable process. In the aftermath of the First World War various new liberal-democracies had sprung to birth only to be destroyed by economic problems, internal wrangles and international animosities, and by 1939 much of the Continent was under one form of authoritarian rule or other. Certainly there were many countries where democracy continued to flourish largely because it had been ingrained over a long period. Switzerland, Eire and Sweden were countries where democracy survived the war intact because these states managed to maintain their neutrality. Denmark, Norway and the Benelux states suffered occupation but, as in the case of France, democracy was re-established there quite promptly. Of course the resuscitation of democracy in 1944–5 owed much to the actions of the US and Britain, who fostered the process as they liberated Western Europe.

By the early 1950s liberal-democracy seemed secure in much of Western Europe. Switzerland, despite its linguistic divisions and lack of natural resources, remained a thriving democracy whose strong cultural identity helped it to combine a decentralised political system with social stability and economic strength. In Scandinavia, too, liberal-democracies seemed stable and prosperous, even if greater unity in the region proved elusive. Denmark, Norway and Iceland joined NATO, Sweden remained doggedly neutral under its progressive Social Democratic Governments, whilst Finland had now to steer a cautious policy towards its vast neighbour, the USSR. Denmark's geographical position and economic links to Germany and Britain made it natural to join the European Community in 1973, but Sweden, Norway and Iceland, mountainous, sparsely populated and insular, held aloof from the rest of the Continent. Commercial dependency on Britain did much to draw Eire, too, into the EEC in 1973, although the Republic had cut its political ties to the Commonwealth in 1949. Eire found the EC a forum wherein to limit British influence and find support for its relatively poor agricultural economy. In contrast the Benelux states, more industrial and urbanised, had joined the EC at the outset and found that, by acting together, they could have a major impact on the shape of post-war Europe. Both survived the traumas of decolonisation without major upheaval: Dutch resources were too limited to restore their authority in Indonesia in 1945–9; Belgium rapidly abandoned the Congo in 1960. At home Belgian democracy remained secure but was plagued by nationalist tensions between the Flemish majority of the population and the French-speaking Walloons, who for years dominated political and economic life. The Netherlands, despite Protestant–Roman Catholic differences and a plethora of political parties, managed to produce stable governments, at least until 1977 when months of political deadlock were combined with the same economic difficulties – inflation, unemployment and low growth – which had come to plague much of Western Europe.

The 'stagnation' of the 1970s put an end to the economic growth of the 1950s and 1960s. Yet it was in precisely this period that three European states – Greece, Portugal and Spain – saw the restoration of a liberal-democratic system after various periods under authoritarian rule. All these states had fallen under the umbrella of the Western Alliance after the war. Portugal and Greece had joined NATO, whilst Spain had military links with America since 1953. In all three cases Washington and other NATO states proved ready to tolerate dictatorial regimes for a time in Greece and Iberia so long as these were anti-communist. The resurgence of democracy in Southern Europe was all the more remarkable because it succeeded in the face of relative economic backwardness and the troubled economic scene of the mid-1970s. In the three countries very different forces were in play, yet in all a powerful factor in shaping events was the desire to end authoritarianism, to establish individual rights and social justice and to modernise themselves so as to enter the mainstream of European political life, not least by joining the European Community. Then again, the possiblity of establishing a lasting (if troubled) liberal-democracy in Southern Europe after decades of authoritarianism, had been shown long before the 1970s, in Italy.

## Italy

Italy had been united in the mid-nineteenth century as a nation-state with high hopes of matching the strength of established great powers, like Britain and France, and of emulating the success of Germany, another nation reunited after centuries of division. The Kingdom of Italy lacked the natural resources of Britain or Germany, however, and was unable to recreate the social stability of France. Although the Po Valley in the north had a rich agriculture and some industry, southern Italy was generally poor, populated mainly by landless labourers who worked on large estates. Many emigrated to the USA or South America, the government failed to introduce social reforms and a 1911 census revealed half the population to be illiterate. Italy's attempts to create a colonial empire led to a humiliating defeat by Abyssinian tribesmen in 1896. Papal opposition to the new kingdom (which had absorbed Papal lands by force) meant the alienation of the Catholic majority whilst unrepresentative government helped to fuel support for extreme brands of socialism and anarchism. The attempt to introduce a more representative democracy in the 1919 election brought the Socialists and *Popolare* (a Catholic party) into parliament as mass parties but the animosity between them helped paralyse the government in 1922, amidst strikes and inflation. Benito Mussolini came to power with a new political doctrine, 'Fascism'. He created a one-party dictatorship, rigidly divided into social groups, where trades unions were banned, civil liberties destroyed and political opponents imprisoned or murdered.

For a time the fascist regime seemed stable but by 1943 it was clear that Mussolini too had failed to modernise and strengthen Italy. Its entry into the Second World War on Hitler's side merely exposed Italy's industrial and technological backwardness. There was considerable social discontent, strikes began in the northern cities, and a united resistance movement was formed by Communists, Socialists and Christian Democrats. In July 1943 the powers of the *Duce* (leader) were shown to be less than total when his own 'Grand Council' united with King Victor Emmanuel III to overthrow him. Aided by the Germans, Mussolini escaped but was recaptured in April 1945 and shot. Meanwhile his former Chief of Staff, Marshal Pietro Badoglio, had formed a government which, in September 1943, made an armistice with the Allies. The following month Italy re-entered the war, but against Hitler. The anti-Fascist resistance forces were not impressed with Badoglio's credentials as the leader of a new Italy and in June 1944 he resigned. When the war ended Italy, like France, was governed by a multi-party government in which the Communists, Socialists and Christian Democrats were the major forces. Like much of Europe Italy faced the challenge of overcoming food and fuel shortages, reconstructing industry, and drafting a new constitution, as well as facing up to its economic backwardness and two decades of Fascist rule.

The three main parties had united under the 'Pact of Rome' of 1944, to create a single anti-Fascist front. As in France the Communists, though they emerged from the resistance as a determined and well-organised force, were limited in number and their leaders were ready to make an 'historic compromise' with the other parties. By working to control inflation to limit wage demands and to increase industrial production the Communists hoped to gain popular legitimacy and electoral support. In the first wave of post-Fascist idealism the Christian Democrats (DC) were interested in social reform, and there was talk (as elsewhere in Europe) of forging the Communist and Socialist parties to create a single working-class force. Elections for a Constituent Assembly were held in June 1946 and gave the DC 35 per cent of the vote, a clear lead over the Socialists (21 per cent) and Communists (19 per cent). At the same time a referendum decided that the new Italy should be a Republic. Victor Emmanuel III thus paid the price for his toleration of Mussolini before 1943. In international affairs Italians tried to emphasise their support for the allies after 1943 but in February 1947, in a peace treaty, they lost land to Yugoslavia, Austria and France, as well as all their colonies. It was only a few months after the peace treaty, however, that the breakdown of the victorious wartime alliance, and the beginnings of the Cold War, brought a similar breakdown in the 'historic compromise'. In May 1947, the same month that the Communists were expelled from the French Cabinet, Italy's DC premier Alcide de Gasperi broke with his Communist allies. To Italy's other problems was then added a deep and lasting political division. At the end of the year the Communists became the political force behind an outbreak of strikes, which caused further economic distress.

The expulsion of the Communists left the DC as the dominant party in government, a position they were to retain down to 1989 and beyond. It was an important factor in Italy's later political stability, however, that the Constitution which came into force on January 1948 was drafted by all three major parties, and reflected much of the idealism and unity of the Resistance, not least in its first article which declared the country to be a 'democratic republic founded on labour'. As well as protecting individual rights the Constitution enshrined such socialist ideals as the 'right to work' – although it later became clear* that this did not guarantee full employment. In reaction to the Mussolini period the Fascist party was banned. The President's position was weak, there was pressure for the decentralisation of government to the regions (though a regional system was not properly created until the 1970s) and the overriding political aim, as in the French Fourth Republic, was that Italy should be governed by the political parties, working through a parliament which was re-elected every five years. Not all Mussolini's acts were reversed; the 1929 Lateran Treaties with the Papacy, which made Catholicism the national religion, were retained. As in West Germany constitutional rights were protected by a special court, which was eventually established in 1956.

The electoral system, defined in a separate law, was a complex proportionally-based system but one which gave the advantage to parties fielding lists of candidates. The constitution and electoral system together gave national political parties a strong role in a very powerful parliament, which they exploited by developing systems of patronage throughout society known as '*clientelismo*'. Put simply, in Italian politics, people generally seek power not to carry out major legislation – which is rare – so much as to control government spending and patronage. Power is used to reward a party's supporters, who in return supply financial aid. Inevitably, scandals and corruption often result. The armed forces, which might be expected to challenge such an ineffective system elsewhere (as in France in 1958 or Greece in 1967) have no major role in Italian society. Spending on defence is low and officers are kept satisfied by rapid promotion – hence the fact that the Italian navy has more admirals than ships. The most successful party at exploiting the system, helped by its early dominant position, is the DC which represents an amalgam of conservative and Catholic groups

* As was formally stated in a 1965 decision by the Constitutional Court.

such as businessmen, shopkeepers, landowners, Catholic trades unionists and peasants. The varied make-up of the DC helps to explain why Italy should have one dominant political party, yet have numerous short-lived governments. Governments often fall not because of differences between coalition parties but between the factions of the DC, which range from extreme rightists to social democrats, some extremely conservative, others ready to accept quite radical reform.

Despite the DC's factional nature and short-lived governments, its predominance in Italian politics was laid under the leadership of one man, Alcide de Gasperi. De Gasperi remained prime minister through several changes of government between December 1945 and August 1953, highlighting the fact that Italy's rapid turnover of cabinets – there were 48 governments (and 18 different premiers) in 1945–89 – masks a good degree of continuity in their composition. Roughly half the ministers in one government can expect a role in the next. De Gasperi was able to make good use of American support, after breaking with the Communists, to tighten the DC's grip on power. In mid-1947 Italy eagerly welcomed the Marshall aid programme and soon became one of its biggest beneficiaries. In April 1948, when the first elections were held under the new constitution, the DC received the support of the Western Allies. Amongst other things the Americans, British and French promised de Gasperi the return of the port of Trieste, lost in the 1947 peace treaty. This helped give the DC over 48 per cent of the votes in the elections whereas the Communists and Socialists, fighting together, could only muster 31 per cent. The Socialists, though the oldest of the main parties (founded in 1892) and the runner-up in the 1946 election, had allowed themselves to be dominated by the Communists through fear of losing working-class support. Because of this, in 1949 many socialists left to form a new Social Democratic Party led by Giuseppe Saragat. From then the Communists, led by the experienced Palmiro Togliatti, and for the moment loyal to Moscow, became the main opposition party.

After 1948 the DC, ably led by de Gasperi, effectively created an anti-Communist state, leaving the Communists almost as a separate society. Although a Catholic party, de Gasperi did not allow the DC to be dominated by the Vatican. Although well disposed to capitalism, the DC sought to protect special interest groups like the shopkeepers and peasants who could become the victims of market forces. Thus the various elements which made up the DC were kept in balance. The party combined Catholic and anti-Communist beliefs with an ability to modernise Italy and wield state power, and the longer it remained in office the more the bureaucracy, armed forces, judiciary, banks and other institutions became loyal to it. The DC's position could be bolstered, when necessary, by coalitions with smaller parties. De Gasperi also tied the country closely to the Atlantic Alliance and into the development of Western European union. This pro-Western identification was not only significant at a diplomatic level, it also showed Italy's determination, despite its lack of raw materials and its economic underdevelopment, to compete with developed countries. Mussolini's government had been very protectionist and in 1945–7 Socialists and Communist ministers had tried to develop their own brand of state planning in Italy, but de Gasperi favoured the free-market policies of the Liberal party politician, Luigi Einaudi, who became Minister of the Budget in 1947 and who had the enthusiastic support of businessmen. The IRI (Institute for Industrial Reconstruction) a diverse group of industries which were taken into public ownership by Mussolini, continued to exist and to produce the bulk of Italy's steel and ship building production, amongst other items. The IRI became the largest single industrial group in Europe in the 1960s, but its role in 1950s Italy was secondary to that of private enterprise. Government generally acted only to create expensive items of economic infrastructure, such as railways and a motorway system, which business could exploit and there was no national economic plan.

Einaudi's efforts to control inflation, which had taken prices to five times their pre-war level, meant that there was virtual economic stagnation in 1947–50. But this laid the basis for future growth, which was also aided by other factors: Marshall aid brought US technology, the Korean War stimulated growth throughout Western Europe, the loss of the Italian colonial empire freed resources to use at home, population was growing and Italy's low wages and plentiful manpower attracted large-scale foreign investment. The average annual growth rates in 1950–8 were already over 5 per cent (better than Britain or France), then in 1958–63, came the 'economic miracle', when average growth rates of 6.6 per cent were better even than West Germany. As incomes rose so further growth was stimulated. Exports grew and new industries, for example, electrical goods, were created. Such success could only further strengthen the DC in power, especially since the party's opponents had continued to suffer reversals. Trades unionism was weakened by political divisions after 1947 and in 1955 a major strike at Fiat cars was defeated. In 1956 the Soviet invasion of Hungary shocked even Communist leaders and led the Socialists to draw away from the Communists.

Italy's emergence as an industrial, urbanised state in the years 1950–63 was not without its problems. Rapid growth inevitably brought uneven development and social inequalities. The DC government, fearing rural unemployment if agriculture were modernised, had continued to protect agriculture which remained inefficient. Companies like Fiat – which quadrupled production in the 1950s and began to have a major role in politics – became competitive on world markets, but others remained technologically underdeveloped. Italy began its expansion from a weak position and was still poor in terms of national wealth relative to most of Western Europe in 1963. Trade figures, helped by tourism, only moved into surplus in 1958 whilst unemployment remained above 7 per cent even at the end of the 1950s, and this despite almost two million Italians going to work abroad. The Italian bureaucracy also remained inefficient. The government was unable to raise taxes effectively, failed to provide decent, cheap housing and failed to create adequate health and education systems. Weak trade unions and low wages – Italians only achieved average European wage levels in the later 1960s – reflected the fact that many people did not share in the new wealth. Rising middle-class incomes might feed the demand for household appliances, but expansion also depended on the large pool of unemployed workers and Southern agricultural labourers who were absorbed into the factories. There was some attempt to develop the South through tourism, better communications, limited land redistribution and, finally, the 1961 'Green Plan'. But agriculture in the South remained backward, many small farms closed (especially as young males left for the North) and there was little industry. By 1962–3 the 'miracle' had run its course.

A series of strikes in 1962 showed that working-class passivity was coming to an end. Many Italians were now employed as skilled workers in the modern industries of the North, the unemployed labour pool had shrunk and trades unions were suddenly able to demand much higher wages. Inflation of 7.6 per cent, lower profits and a trade deficit were the inevitable results and in late 1963 the Bank of Italy – a conservative institution which controlled the monetary situation independent of government – introduced credit controls to cut imports and inflation. The strategy dealt a blow to the revival of the unions, but it also brought falling investment, the closure of smaller firms and rising unemployment in 1964–5, the worst effects of which were again felt in the South.

Even before 1963 there had been signs of a re-adjustment in Italian politics. Although the DC had remained the largest party in Italy since de Gasperi's day, its share of the vote fell in the 1953 and 1958 elections before reaching 38 per cent in 1963, a level at which it roughly remained for 20 years. The Communist vote meanwhile had risen to 25 per cent and the DC thus had to rely on the support of various smaller groups in parliament to form stable governments. This could prove a difficult exercise. In April 1960 differences with the Liberal party led a new DC premier, Fernando Tambroni, to rely on the support of right-wing groups, including the small Monarchist Party and the Neo-fascist MSI (Italian Social Movement). This provoked widespread dismay and even some popular disturbances, and led to Tambroni's replacement in July by Amintore Fanfani, who allied with the Socialists. The Socialists (who attracted about 14 per cent of the votes in 1958 and 1963) had broken with the Communists in the vote on Italian entry to the EC in 1958. They could provide the basis for an improved social reform policy, greater economic planning and an attack on the North–South problem. It was partly to please the Socialists that the DC nationalised electricity in 1962. Despite opposition from left-wing Socialists (who formed their own independent party in 1964-72), and conservative doubts in the DC about an 'opening to the left', a formal coalition with Pietro Nenni's Socialists was eventually formed in December 1963 under another DC moderate, Aldo Moro. The liberal attitudes of Pope John XXIII (1958–66) helped this re-adjustment. Social Democrats and Republicans also joined in centre-left coalitions under Moro in the mid-1960s, and he remained premier until 1968.

Like the West Germans the Italian government now hoped to demonstrate that all society could share in the growing wealth. However, many DC politicians simply wanted to use the 'opening to the left' to control dissent, and the falling growth rates of 1964–5 limited the options for reform. The Moro coalitions in fact had limited successes with state planning and redistribution of wealth. The European Community's common agricultural policy did little to help the small, inefficient farms of Southern Italy and the Italian government, through the 'Second Green Plan' of 1966, tended to aid larger, profitable farms. Industrial projects in the South became 'cathedrals in a desert', benefiting only local areas, and the poor of the South – many of them old men, women and children who could not find work in the North – had to be supported by a costly programme of social welfare. At national level the first economic plan, the Pieraccini Plan of 1966–70, reflected the government's new desire to use state intervention and deficit spending to achieve increased incomes, stable prices, better trade and improved North–South balance, but it was vague on details, and was not approved until 1967. Its execution was undermined by the survival of the 1950s liberal economic outlook in the Bank of Italy and by the continued inefficiency of the Italian bureaucracy.

By 1969 Italy was one of the top seven industrial nations with 5 per cent of the world's manufacturing exports. Whatever the problems of the South, 1967–8 had seen a new boom and full employment, helped by state spending, healthy global trade, wage moderation, more overtime working and the rationalisation of Italian industry (as small firms were taken over by larger concerns). In 1968 however, there was student unrest and strike activity. Then, in 1969, pent-up frustrations burst out in the 'hot autumn' of discontent. Overcrowded cities, the demands of overtime work, poor public services, lack of social reform, high rents, the government's reliance on indirect taxes (which fell most heavily on the poor), resentment over business profits – all these caused resentment amongst Italy's new working classes, who wanted a better quality of life and who often felt, especially in the South, that the established parties (even the Communists) and trades unions no longer represented their interests. 1969 saw the worst strike-wave since 1947, with far graver results than the events of 1962–3, and discontent continued well into the 1970s. Large wage rises were achieved, overtime was reduced, the working week shortened, and the government granted workers a charter in 1970 to protect their bargaining position. Such troubles of course were not uncommon in the Western world and Italy also shared in the perils brought by the 1973 oil price rise, the radicalisation of the middle-class groups, the decline of religion, and at the extreme, the creation of urban terrorist groups, most notably the 'Red Brigades'. The economic costs of the 'hot autumn' and its aftermath were enormous, and affected Italy far more than the problems in France, West Germany or even Britain in the 1970s. Industrial production actually fell by 2.7 per cent in 1971 and inflation rose from under 5 per cent that year to 19 per cent in 1974. Italy's trials were at their worst in 1974–6 but inflation was still nearly 19 per cent in 1981. Italian businessmen invested what money they had overseas, and industry was now threatened by cheap Third World competition in areas like textile and shoe manufacture. The value of the lire against the dollar, which had been held stable beteen 1949–71, fell constantly.

The DC-led coalitions seemed at a loss what to do in the new situation, which completely destroyed the confidence and growth of the post-1950 period. A sane wages policy was rendered unworkable by worker militancy, protectionism was impossible because of Italy's reliance on world trade, deflation (such as West Germany pursued in the 1970s) would have led to large-scale unemployment in an economy which was still, at root, dogged by poor technology, scarce raw materials and the North–South divide. The best governments could do was to survive from day-to-day, to attempt credit squeezes, alter the taxation system (in 1973–4) and try to answer some of the demands for social reform. But such reforms as the liberalisation of divorce (1970), a sex discrimination act (1977) and the legalisation of abortion (1978) divided the DC without fully satisfying radical opinion which remained alienated by the corruption of many in government. In 1978 even President Giovanni Leone was forced to resign over alleged involvement in a bribes scandal. In 1977 the 'Autonomia' movement sprang up among young workers and students, who protested against traditional values by holding demonstrations, looting supermarkets and 'squatting' in empty property. Meanwhile the Mafia crime syndicates, always an important force in the South, extended their activities to kidnapping and drug trafficking. Italian democracy sometimes seemed on the verge of revolution or anarchy, as parliament was reduced to irrelevancy, the DC became more factionalised, and coalition partners proved more difficult to find. The Socialists, having failed either to reunite with the Social Democrats (despite an attempt in 1968) or to satisfy radical demands for reform, won less than 10 per cent of the vote in the 1972 election and became less eager to share office with the DC. The Socialists took no part in government in 1972–3 or 1974–80, though they did support some governments in parliamentary votes. Neither could the DC find a really outstanding leader like de Gasperi to tackle Italy's crisis: the veteran Amintore Fanfani, DC secretary in the mid-1970s, was energetic and clever, but his impulsive and arrogant personal style was out of place in a political system which abhorred authoritarianism; the tenacious Aldo Moro, who took on the premiership again in 1974–6, championed the idea of working with the Communists and trades unions to achieve stable government, but his very moderation led to his being kidnapped and murdered by the Red Brigade terrorists in 1978; Giulio Andreotti actually persuaded the Communists to support his DC government in parliamentary votes in 1976, and drew up a common programme with them in 1977, but could not transform this example of 'national unity' into a full coalition.

The new 'historic compromise' between the DC and Communists of July 1976 ahd followed an election in which the latter won over 34 per cent of the vote, only 4 per cent behind the DC. Co-operation between the two arch rivals in the Italian political system might seem odd, but it came at a time when the DC was desperate to control dissent, when a policy of reflation seemed a possible solution to Italy's economic difficulties, when working-class co-operation was vital to restore the economy to health, when the Socialists refused to take on the responsibility of office, and when the Communist Party – which had gradually distanced itself from Moscow – was portraying itself as a moderate, 'Eurocommunist' force. Under Enrico Berlinguer, the Communists even accepted in 1975 that Italy must remain part of NATO and the EC, a decision which did nothing to please the radical left who felt betrayed by Berlinguer. Though excluded from office since 1948 the Communists had, by the mid-1970s, become very much part of the decision-making 'system'. They had easily remained the second largest party in parliament, dominated local government in many areas (especially the 'Red Belt' of North-central Italy), accepted membership of various government bodies and had an interest in certain reforms of the 1970s, including better workers' rights, sexual equality, and the creation after 1970, of a new level of regional government. The 'historic compromise' was criticised by many in the DC, broke down in 1978 and arguably cost the Communists support in the 1979 election when their share of the vote fell, for the first time since 1948 (to 30 per cent). But their support for the DC had helped to ensure the survival of democracy.

Various other factors combined to preserve Italian unity in the difficult 1970s by releasing social tensions whilst preserving parliamentary government: trades unions restored their position of representing the working classes, but remained too divided among themselves to threaten the government; regional administrations answered a long-standing demand for decentralisation but Rome kept considerable decision-making powers and financial control; reforms proved that pressure groups which had grown to challenge the power of political parties, could obtain reforms against the doubts of the DC even if the results (as with the sex discrimination law) were modest; referenda (called for by petitions) placed some important decisions, including abortion and divorce, in the hands of the whole electorate; the Moro murder brought a strong reaction against the radical left and justified repressive measures (and stimulated a backlash from terrorists who killed 85 people in the 1980 Bologna station bombing); the DC itself – despite criticisms of its inefficiency and high spending by businessmen – succeeded in using government measures to placate a wide body of opinion; and at root, Italians and their political leaders had no wish to re-create authoritarian government in any form.

After 1979 the Communists hoped to achieve a non-DC coalition at last, but the DC moved to re-establish links with the Socialists and the Socialists, trying to restore their political fortunes, decided to seek centrist support by supporting DC-led coalitions once more. In the 1980s Italy continued to mirror changes seen elsewhere in Western Europe. The years after 1979 witnessed a renewed depression, with 1983 seeing inflation at 15 per cent and unemployment at over 10 per cent. 20000 workers were made redundant by Fiat in 1980. But the 'Pandolfi Plan' of 1979 reflected the new belief that rising wages and increased public spending were *not* the ways to solve such problems. The welfare state was vital to many Italians, especially in the South, and could not be cut back on the British scale, but the government hoped to reduce public spending overall as a percentage of GDP. Parts of the IRI were privatised and spending on education remained low compared to Northern Europe. To stay competitive in Europe, Italy joined the EC's exchange rate mechanism and after 1981 recovery was helped by the growing American trade deficit, with the most successful achievers being small firms producing jewellery, ceramics and textiles. The DC was shocked in 1983 by a fall in its share of the vote (a decline most marked in urban areas) from 38 per cent to 33 per cent, with the Communists only 3 per cent behind. Then in the 1984 Euro-elections, the Communists narrowly came ahead of the DC with a third of the vote. But the DC showed its continuing ability to respond to circumstances. Already, in 1981–2 Giovanni Spadolini, a Republican, had become the first non-DC premier since 1945, with a coalition supported by the DC, Socialists, Republicans, Social Democrats and Liberals – a five-party alliance which was the backbone of the 1980s' governments. Then in August 1983 the long-serving Socialist leader Bettino Craxi, became premier, supported by the same five parties and his government proved the longest lasting in post-war history. Despite a major crisis in 1985 over the release of an Arab terrorist, Craxi eventually served until June 1986. He soon returned to lead a further government and in the 1987 election helped the Socialist party to achieve a level of support (14 per cent) not seen since the 1960s. The DC's predominance seemed secure once more (34 per cent) and the Communists easily retained second place (27 per cent). The five-party coalition survived afterwards under DC premiers.

Part of the reason why Craxi was so important was that his governments had seen considerable economic success. As in France and Spain, a 'Social-ist' political label did not prevent Italian Socialists from relying on middle-class support, risking trades union opposition, tolerating unemployment (12 per cent in 1987), reducing wage indexation and concentrating on the struggle against inflation (5 per cent in 1987) to achieve growth rates of about 3 per cent in the late 1980s. Italy in 1989 remained a country divided between North and South, periodically rocked by scandals and criminal outrages and with generally short-lived governments, made up of various political parties and led by unremarkable politicians who lacked political idealism. But since the war Italians had become much wealthier, educated and better fed. Their standard of living was comparable to Britain's, though behind West Germany or France. They had rejected political extremism, despite the upheavals of the 1970s and a Fascist past, and kept one political party as the backbone of government for over 40 years.

# Greece

In 1945 Greece, like Italy, was a country whose heroic age had long since passed. In the fifteenth century the Greeks had fallen under Ottoman Turkish rule and it was not until the 1820s that, aided by Ottoman decline, a new, independent 'Kingdom of the Hellenes' was founded. Originally covering only a small area, it gradually expanded northwards into the Balkans and out across the Aegean sea, its last major territorial gain being the Dodecanese islands, including Rhodes, from Italy in 1947. Greek politics was troubled in the early twentieth century by rivalry between conservative elements, represented by King Constantine I, and the Liberals and Republicans, championed by premier Eleutherios Venizelos. In 1924, after a war with Turkey had ended in disaster, a Republic was established in Greece but it proved politically weak and in 1935 the monarchy was restored under George II. The following year the military dictatorship of General Joannis Metaxas took power. Tolerated by the King, Metaxas made some attempts to modernise the Greek army and administration, but he died early in January 1941, soon after Greece had been attacked by Mussolini's Italy. Greece had rid itself of the dictatorship, and at first resisted Mussolini's invasion, but within a few months was conquered by Italy's ally Germany. The country thus faced many problems similar to Italy's in the mid-twentieth century. Hopes of restoring former greatness had been dissipated, the country was economically underdeveloped – with a poor population, lack of natural resources and little industry – as well as politically unstable. In the 1940s it faced the dangers, first, of foreign conquest and, second, of Communist domination.

As elsewhere in Europe, the most successful resistance to the German occupation was led by the Communists, who headed both the National Liberation Front (EAM) and its military offshoot, the People's Liberation Army (ELAS). A pro-royalist resistance group, (EDES), also existed but was largely restricted to Epirus, in north-eastern Greece. The EAM/ELAS not only led the struggle against the Germans, but also hoped for a social and political revolution similar to that carried out in neighbouring Yugoslavia and Albania against monarchs who, like George II, had presided over authoritarian regimes before the war. EAM authority was extended over most of the Greek countryside in 1944 as the German forces withdrew. Several factors, however, were at work to prevent a Communist take-over. George II's government-in-exile in Cairo was backed by the British, who were determined to keep Greece out of Communist hands because of its strategic importance to the Middle East, an area of British predominance. In October 1944 two significant events occurred. First, British troops arrived in Athens under General Ronald Scobie to restore royal authority and these succeeded in keeping the major cities out of Communist hands. Secondly, Josef Stalin, eager to ensure control over other areas of eastern Europe, proved ready to make a deal by which Britain would have primary influence in Greece, whilst

Russia had primary influence in Bulgaria and Romania. Soviet pressure was put on EAM leaders to enter a coalition government under George Papandreou, a moderate and pre-war Venizelist minister, who the King had appointed premier. After complex negotiations the EAM agreed.

The compromise between Communists and Royalists soon broke down. In November 1944 the Greek army's Third Brigade returned to Greece. Some elements in the army had earlier wanted to work closely with the EAM, but the Third Brigade was entirely loyal to George II. General Scobie wanted to make it the base for a new Greek army and he wanted the resistance organisations to be disbanded. The Communists, however, did not relish the idea of putting the monopoly of military force in Royalist hands and EAM ministers decided to leave the government. In December violence broke out in Athens and the British – though widely criticised for aiding a right-wing regime against former resistance fighters – succeeded in matching the Communist challenge. In January, a truce was possible, after George II declared that he would not return to Greece yet. Archbishop Damaskinos, head of the Orthodox church, became regent. Then in February the 'Varzika Agreement' provided the basis for a compromise political settlement: the ELAS would disband, but the police force would also be purged of right-wing elements; a new conscript army would be formed from all elements in Greek society, although the foundation stone would be the Third Brigade; reforms were promised, there was an amnesty for political crimes and a plebiscite would be held to decide the future of the monarchy.

The Varzika Agreement seemed to provide many concessions to the EAM, which continued to control much of rural Greece. But the Royalists remained in control of Athens, with a series of right-wing prime ministers, and they soon launched an anti-Communist backlash. There was none of the promised social and economic reform and the plebiscite on the monarchy was delayed. In protest the EAM boycotted the first post-war elections in March 1946 and by the time the plebiscite on the monarchy was finally held, six months later, Greece presented a very troubled spectacle. Underlying economic weaknesses had been compounded by the wartime destruction and the inflation which followed. Food shortages, incompetent administration and a lack of welfare provisions did nothing to relieve social distress. There had been no parliamentary government for ten years, and in any case, the country was deeply politically divided. Indeed, when the September plebiscite resulted narrowly in a vote to restore George II, the Communists decided again to turn to armed struggle. From October 1946 General Markos Vatiades, aided by the Communist regimes in neighbouring Yugoslavia, Albania and Bulgaria, led a guerrilla war against the government. It was in these circumstances in March 1947, with the British unable to maintain past levels of support for the Royalists, that American aid to Greece was promised under the Truman Doctrine. Over the following months US military and economic aid began to flow into Greece, which also joined the Marshall aid programme. The Greek civil war had become an important element in the Cold War –

altnough how far the Soviet Union itself was involved in supporting the Greek Communists was debatable.

Despite American assistance it took three years to end the renewed civil war. In October 1948 there was still martial law across Greece, but the Tito–Stalin split* at that time led to a decline in support for the Communists from Yugoslavia. the Greek Communists alienated people by using terrorism to control the countryside and adopted poor tactics by trying to defend towns against the conventional armed forces of Marshal Alexander Papagos. By the time a cease-fire was called in October 1949 over 25 000 people had been killed in the struggle and there was inevitably a bitter legacy of political divisions. Meanwhile the US and the army had become important forces in Greek politics and Greece became tied to Western organisations such as the OEEC, Council of Europe and (in 1952) NATO. There was some economic improvement under Marshall aid, although regrettably not in the field of industrialisation. Political instability had also continued. In 1947 George II had been succeeded by his brother, Paul, and there was a whole series of Populist-Liberal premiers after the 1946 election. Further elections in 1950 and 1951 failed to break the political deadlock, but under American pressure a new election was held in October 1952, with a simplified electoral system. This led to the victory of a new political force, the 'Greek Rally'. Formed by Marshal Papagos, the victor of the civil war and widely compared to de Gaulle's RPF party in France, the Rally finally provided Greece with political stability. Indeed Papagos was succeeded in 1955 by one of his ministers, Constantine Karamanlis, who continued in office for a continuous period of eight years, longer than any Greek premier before. As leader of a new 'Radical National Union' Karamanlis won the elections of 1958 and 1961.

The period of conservative rule in 1952–63 did not bring national reconciliation between the Communists and the Right. Spending cuts, increased taxes and devaluation, to bring inflation down, provoked an attempt at a General Strike in 1953 and there was renewed social discontent in the early 1960s. Some manufacturing industry was built up, including ship building and oil refining, but often this was in foreign hands and the major export remained tobacco, much of which was sent to West Germany in the 1950s. Greece's reliance on tourism and the export of cheap labour underlined the fact that it remained essentially underdeveloped, and this meant that Karamanlis's attempts to enter the European Economic Community resulted only in the offer of associate status in 1962. The loyalty of the army was maintained but at the cost of devoting one-third of the budget to its needs. US assistance continued but after 1955 even relations with America and Britain became troubled, partly because of resentment over US influence in Greece but also because of the Cyprus problem.

Cyprus was a British colony in the eastern Mediterranean with a

* See pp 203–4.

population that was 80 per cent Greek and 20 per cent Turkish. The Greek population wanted self-determination and '*enosis* (union) with Greece, and in 1955 the EOKA movement led by Colonel George Grivas, began a terrorist campaign to achieve this. The Athens government naturally felt sympathy for the Greek Cypriots but this provoked tensions with her NATO allies, Britain (faced by the EOKA campaign) and Turkey (concerned for the fate of Turkish Cypriots), it also caused grave concern in Washington especially when Karamanlis tried to improve relations with Eastern bloc states as a way to win international support. In 1959 a compromise settlement was reached in which Cyprus gained independence from Britain under its religious leader, Archbishop Makarios III, but without *enosis*. Grivas saw this as a betrayal and there were renewed Greek–Turkish tensions over Cyprus in 1964 which led UN forces to be sent to the island. King Paul remained well-disposed to Britain through these events, partly due to the close links between the two royal families, but this added to popular criticisms of the monarchy. It was the King's insistence on visiting London in 1963 that led Karamanlis to resign in protest.

Conservative rule had brought political stability to Greece and ended the Communist threat. But chronic trade and economic problems, resentment at spending on the army and royal family, and the lack of social reform, all contributed to the victory of left-wing parties in the November 1963 election. It required another election in February 1964 before a single party, the Greek Union, obtained a clear majority under its leader George Papandreou, the old Venizelist leader who had been premier in 1944–5. The succession to the throne of the young Constantine II that same year added to the impression that Greece was about to experience a new era of reconciliation and reform. But it was not to be. There were many reasons for the growth of instability. The new government cut defence spending and improved social services, but this triggered off inflation and – importantly – alienated the army. Papandreou was seen as a spendthrift, too forgiving to the Communists, and over-influenced by his radical son, Andreas, who in May 1965 was accused of having been involved in a plot to overthrow the earlier conservative government. The prime minister also began to bicker with King Constantine, thus reviving the old division between Monarchists and Republicans. In July 1965 an argument with the King over ministerial appointments led Papandreou to resign and Constantine, showing questionable judgement, appointed the former deputy premier, Stephanos Stephanopoulos, in Papandreou's place. This simply led the Greek Union to split, making effective government very difficult, and heralding a series of strikes and demonstrations in support of Papandreou, who seemed destined to win the next general election.

It was on 21 April 1967, with a general election due the following month, that a group of army Colonels seized power in Athens. They claimed to have forestalled a Communist plot, but the main aim was clearly to forestall an electoral victory by Papandreou. The Colonels enforced martial law, suspended parliamentary government and democratic freedoms, and arrested opposition leaders including, for a time, Papandreou. The former premier died in 1968 and his son Andreas went into exile. Meanwhile the still active Karamanlis refused to associate with the Colonels' regime. As to King Constantine, he accepted the new government on condition that it worked for an early restoration of democracy, but continued to show political incompetence when on 13 December he vainly launched his own attempt to take over government. His failure was followed by exile. The King's departure allowed the Colonels to tighten control on Greece, and at first they seemed secure. Many Greeks had become cynical about the political scene, and the Colonels combined the use of censorship, secret police and imprisonment of opponents with some popular acts such as pension increases and price controls. Western governments condemned the regime at first and the use of torture led to Greece's eventual expulsion from the Council of Europe. However, in 1968, the Colonels increasingly won international recognition, they remained part of NATO and in November they introduced their own constitution, which was approved in a rigged referendum. The most important figure under the new constitution was that of the prime minister, George Papadopoulos. In June 1973 after accusing the exiled Constantine of again seeking to overthrow them, the Colonels abolished the monarchy and Papadopoulos then became President.

Papadopoulos's increasing personal power added to the mounting sense of concern about the Colonel's regime. From the start the regime had shown administrative incompetence, its attempts at economic growth in 1970–3 led to inflation of over 30 per cent, and it was ridiculed abroad. The moralising intolerance of its leaders led it to take such ridiculous actions as banning the wearing of mini-skirts. Talk of a 'guided democracy' and the appointment of a 'parliament' (merely with advisory powers) in 1970, did nothing to forestall growing opposition from liberals, intellectuals and labour leaders, nor were people impressed by Papadopoulos's promise that elections would be held in 1974. In November 1973 unrest among Athens students was put down so harshly that certain military elements themselves decided to overthrow Papadopoulos. The Presidency was handed to General Gizikis but real power lay with the man who engineered the coup, Brigadier Ionnidis. The Colonel's regime did not long outlast Papadopoulos. In 1974 it crumbled because of its failure to deal with a new crisis in Cyprus. In July Greek Cypriot extremists tried to overthrow Archbishop Makarios. *Enosis* between Greece and Cyprus could have boosted the Colonels' regime enormously but instead the coup was botched – Makarios was able to escape – and then ended in disaster. Cyprus slipped into anarchy, Turkish troops invaded the island to protect the Turkish Cypriot community, and once again Greece's NATO allies, America and Britain, did nothing to help her. Alone the Colonels could do nothing to match Turkey. Cyprus became partitioned effectively between the Greek and Turkish communities, *enosis* was as far away as ever and the Greek people were aghast at the Colonels' incompetence. On 24 July President Gizikis asked the veteran conservative Karamanlis to return from self-exile in Paris to lead a new civilian government. The Colonels' regime was at an end. Fortunately its collapse, like its foundation, did not see widespread violence.

On his return to office Karamanlis restored the 1952 constitution, ended martial law and even legalised the Communist party, which had been banned since 1947. To show displeasure over Western inaction in the Cyprus affair he also took Greece out of NATO's military command structure. Various members of the Colonels' regime were arrested and later put on trial. In 1975 Papadopoulos was condemned to death but the sentence was commuted to life imprisonment. Elections in November 1974 unsurprisingly resulted in a victory for the prime minister's conservative 'New Democracy' party, yet a referendum the following month resulted in a decision to abolish the monarchy, which was a blow to many conservatives. It reflected understandable ill-feeling against King Constantine and it at least removed an old source of division in Greek national politics. Criticised by the left, the new republican constitution, finalised in June 1975, created a strong President who would be elected every five years. Constantine Tsatsos was the first President, but he was closely allied to Karamanlis and was widely expected to hand over to the latter in due course. In November 1977 Karamanlis was re-elected premier with a reduced majority and Andreas Papandreou emerged as the main opposition leader, heading the Socialist party, PASOK. Karamanlis hoped for a more stable democracy with less bitterness between the major parties. To placate the opposition he introduced tentative social reforms and nationalised certain industries, whilst abroad he visited Moscow and Peking in 1979 and distanced himself from the US. In 1979 he was also finally able to achieve his old aim of taking Greece, despite its economic backwardness, into the EC. This last action, like many other of his policies however, was bitterly condemned by Andreas Papandreou and PASOK, and political enmities continued to run deep.

In May 1980 Karamanlis finally became President, appointing George Rallis prime minister. In October they took Greece back into NATO's military command. Once again this pro-Western move was criticised by Papandreou and it was the latter who won the general election the following year. PASOK's victory showed that a smooth handover of power from right to left was possible in Greek politics and there was no military coup this time, although there were rumours that one was being planned early in 1983. The Socialists came to office with promises to help the underprivileged and leave both NATO and EC, echoing the policies of 'hard left' socialists in Britain and West Germany and provoking exaggerated fears of a Marxist state. Yet in actual fact there was no break with the Western alliance and nationalisation measures were limited. EC membership and higher spending on social services brought inflation but this was tackled by such orthodox steps as devaluation, credit controls and wage limits. Measures to strengthen worker participation in industry were countered by restrictions on the right to take industrial action. Many reforms seemed unremarkable in the Europe of the 1980s: in

1981 the voting age was lowered to 18 and in 1982 civil marriage was introduced. The continuation of deep divisions between PASOK and the New Democracy party was seen in March 1985 when the former refused to support Karamanlis's re-election as President and in protest the latter resigned. Three months later however, despite all the problems, it was again PASOK who won the election.

Papandreou ultimately survived as premier for eight years, matching Karamanlis's success in 1955–63, but PASOK's second period in office was marred by even greater economic difficulties. In 1985–7 inflation, trade problems and high public spending led to a number of austerity measures, including a wage and salary freeze, which in turn sparked widespread protests and strikes. Unemployment was high, investment low and inflation remained well over 10 per cent. This was at a time when other West European states were emerging from the post-1979 depression. Meanwhile Papandreou's domineering political style, his nationalist and populist declarations, and acrimonious dealings with the opposition, all invited criticism. In 1988 the prime minister spent two months outside Greece (having heart surgery in London), he divorced his wife to marry a young air hostess and he was accused of being implicated in a banking scandal. In March 1989 there was a general strike and in June PASOK unsurprisingly lost the general election to the New Democracy party. Yet, since the balance of power in parliament was held by a coalition of left-wing parties (including the Communists), Greece did not find an end to its troubles. A caretaker government was installed until new elections were held. By including New Democracy and the left-wing parties it seemed to symbolise the final reconciliation between those groups in Greek society who had fought each other in the civil war and who had fallen out again so disastrously in the mid-1960s. A further election in November was also inconclusive. Greek democracy had survived the Communist challenge in the 1940s and re-emerged from authoritarian rule in the 1970s, the monarchy issue seemed resolved and a two-party system existed between PASOK and New Democracy. However, in 1989 Greece's economy was still weak, living standards were well below most of the EC and the political deadlock was similar to that seen in 1950–2 and 1963–4. Politics relied heavily on personalities like Papandreou and Karamanlis, many of whom had been active since before the Colonels.

## Portugal

Three months before the fall of the Colonels in Greece, a much longer-lasting authoritarian regime had been overthrown in Portugal. Here too, as in Greece in the early twentieth century, a struggle between conservatives and progressives had led to the replacement of the monarchy by the First Republic (1910–1926), but the republic had failed to provide strong government and was overthrown by the military. They, in 1932, handed power to one of the few capable figures in government, Dr Antonio de Oliveira Salazar. Fascist ideas had already found fertile ground in Portugal and Salazar emulated Mussolini in Italy by setting up a one-party government, banning trades unions and establishing a corporate state. The regime was very different to Nazi Germany however: Portugal was tolerant of other races in its colonial Empire, the Roman Catholic church was protected and trust was placed entirely in the values of a stable, landed society rather than industrial strength. Like Spain, Portugal remained neutral in World War II. After the defeat of the Axis powers in 1945, Salazar seemed troubled by international criticism and pressures to democratise. He succeeded, however, in defeating a wave of strikes, and survived a half-hearted attempt at a military rising in 1947. Salazar's opponents, already divided among themselves, were then imprisoned or exiled, and rigid censorship was enforced. In 1949 the development of the Cold War in Europe came to Salazar's assistance when he was invited to become a founder member of NATO.

Throughout the 1950s educated Portuguese recognised their country's backwardness compared to the rest of NATO, yet all opposition continued to be crushed. In 1958 General Humberto Delgado challenged Salazar's Presidential candidate but, with an electorate restricted to property owners, the result could easily be rigged. Delgado lost the election, was exiled and later murdered. In 1958 even the Bishop of Oporto was exiled for criticising Salazar and the following year an attempted military coup again failed. Social and economic difficulties under the dictatorship were, however, immense. In 1974 about 31 per cent of workers still earned their living from the land. Northern Portugal was farmed by smallholders who lived at subsistence level but remained politically conservative. In contrast, in the Alentejo region of the South, labourers were employed on a part-time basis on large estates, were very poor and became sympathetic to Communism. Illiteracy was widespread and Salazar's extremely orthodox financial policies prevented the growth of industry and commerce until the late 1950s. By 1974 36 per cent of workers were in industry, but the vast majority of these were in small workshops of less than ten employees, whilst larger firms were controlled by foreign multi-nationals or a few rich families loyal to the regime. Despite some attempts to improve the economic infrastructure, Portugal was characterised by an inefficient administration, inadequate health provisions and, in Lisbon, the growth of slum housing. Unsurprisingly over one million Portuguese, mainly young, left the country between 1960 and 1974 to seek a better life in north-west Europe or the Americas. Money sent home by these emigrants became, along with tourism, a major source of Portuguese earnings. In 1968 Salazar suffered a stroke and handed power to Marcello Caetano, who talked of creating a new 'social state' but failed to bring any real liberalism. Urban guerilla groups emerged to challenge the regime at this time and new opposition parties were formed among exile groups, most notably the Socialist Party of Mario Soares, which was re-founded in 1973. When the end of the regime came in 1974, however, it was not due to civilian opposition but because of resentments built up in the army through years of colonial wars in Africa.

For Portugal there was no easy retreat from Empire. After 1958, Charles de Gaulle was able to withdraw from Africa and compensate for France's lost prestige by pursuing an independent foreign policy backed by nuclear weapons. But for the Portuguese there seemed no way to maintain their country's international standing without possession of Angola, Mozambique and Portuguese Guinea, which in the 1960s were left as the world's largest colonial Empire. The desire to retain the Empire was reinforced in 1961 when, following Salazar's refusal to negotiate on the issue, India seized control of the Portuguese enclave of Goa on the Indian coast. In the 1950s Salazar made the hitherto underdeveloped colonies trade at a profit. They provided a source of cheap labour for coffee and cotton plantations, and contained such mineral resources as iron ore and diamonds. Portuguese industrialisation in the 1960s was partly built on the processing of colonial products. Furthermore, between 1945 and 1974, the white population of Angola was increased from less than 50000 to about 350000. Many of these were poor farmers who, like French settlers in Algeria, were determined to hold onto their land. Apart from the desire for economic gain and a settlement colony, Portugal (like other powers) believed it had a 'civilising mission' in the colonies or, as they became known in 1951, 'Portugal overseas'.

In 1961 native resentments led Holden Roberto's liberation movement to begin its struggle to end Portuguese rule in Angola. Certain leading army officers warned Salazar that the Empire would be indefensible in the long term but the dictator simply removed these critics from office. In fact in Angola the nationalist guerrilla movement became divided on tribal lines into three elements by 1968 – Roberto's FNLA, Agostino Neto's Marxist MPLA and Jonas Savimbi's UNITA – who began to fight each other. Meanwhile, in 1964 the FRELIMO movement had begun a guerrilla war against Portugal in Mozambique, whilst in 1963–7 a campaign by Amilcar Cabral's PAIGC movement won control of much of Portuguese Guinea. The cost of these conflicts to a poor country like Portugal was crippling. The African wars soon took up 40 per cent of the national budget and the army mushroomed to 220000 men (2 per cent of the population) by 1973. The value of exports to the colonies fell from 43 per cent of the total in 1960 to only 10 per cent in 1973. Many Portuguese simply tried to forget the unrelenting African wars and this helped increase disillusion in the army: officers already faced low pay, slow promotion and poor leadership from generals who were chosen for their loyalty to Salazar rather than military competence; conscripts were drafted for four years after 1967 and faced long periods of service in an unhealthy climate, far from their families. Draft-dodging became widespread. Between 1968 and 1973 the liberal General Antonio de Spinola was able to restore army morale in Portuguese Guinea and introduced reforms there to win native sympathy, but even Spinola believed that the colonial war could only be resolved by negotiation, not military victory. In February 1974 Spinola, supported by the Chief of Staff, General Costa Gomes, published *Portugal and the Future*, criticising the Lisbon government and calling for greater autonomy in the colonies. Yet Caetano, like Salazar before him, resolutely refused to negotiate with the guerrillas. Instead, in March, he sacked both Spinola and Costa Gomes.

Despite the rising discontent with the regime, world opinion was stunned on 25–26 April 1974 by the sudden overthrow of the oldest right-wing dictatorship in Europe and its replacement by a Junta. The coup was led by middle-ranking officers under Major Otelo de Carvalho who, in September, had formed the Armed Forces Movement (MFA). The MFA was a disparate group in the armed forces. Some were professionals who wanted to restore the military's self-respect, and who particularly resented the June 1973 'Rebelo Decrees' (named after the defence minister) which made it easier for conscript officers to turn professional. Others had absorbed left-wing ideas (sometimes from their Marxist opponents in Africa) and hoped for a modernised non-colonial Portugal. They knew that they would need a sympathetic high-ranking officer to lead them and naturally turned to Spinola as a provisional President. As a liberal and a national hero he could be expected to unite progressive and conservative elements in Portuguese society, and he immediately promised elections and the restoration of basic freedoms. Despite the peaceful nature of the Revolution and – in contrast to most military juntas – the determination of Portugal's new rulers to carry out reform, the transformation of the country was by no means simple. At times over the next two years Portugal seemed ready to slip into anarchy.

The change of regime unleashed much pent-up discontent. The coup on 25 April immediately brought crowds onto the streets crying for 'Liberty' and passing red carnations to each other as the symbols of a peaceful revolution. May Day 1974 saw large-scale demonstrations; private houses in Lisbon were forcibly occupied; and there were demands for social reforms and higher living standards. On 16 May a cabinet was formed mainly of civilians, including two Communists. The Communists were well-organised and had already seized control of much of local government. But most politicians were as politically inexperienced as the army. Party leaders like the Socialist Soares, who now became foreign minister, returned from years in exile with little real knowledge of Portuguese problems. The new premier was a University academic, Palma Carlos, whose cabinet soon granted wage increases, improved family allowances, and froze both rents and prices. However, since the Carnation Revolution had come at a time of world recession, and led to a decline in tourism and a reduction of foreign investment, the economic outlook was bleak. Resources were stretched even further by the return of settlers from the African colonies.

The first six months of the new Republic were marked by the continuing importance of the army and a growing power struggle between Spinola and left-wing officers who became dominant in the MFA, which remained as a vital element in the political equation. The MFA soon criticised the

President's actions, not least his decision to exile Caetano rather than to put him on trial. Spinola's position seemed strong after 31 May when a Council of State, superior to the cabinet, was formed and on which his supporters appeared to have a majority. In July, however, the Council itself baulked at governmental reforms, including an early Presidential election which would have strengthened Spinola's position. Neither the MFA nor the political parties relished the idea of giving substantial authority to one man. Instead, after intense debate, the MFA's role on the Council of State was increased and a new cabinet was formed headed by Colonel Vasco Gonçalves, an MFA left-winger who was a close political ally of the Communist party leader Alvaro Cunhal. This was a major defeat for Spinola and opened the way to a potential Communist–MFA alliance which could take over the government, although for the moment the Communists and MFA wished to retain the support of other political parties and the middle classes. Meanwhile Otelo de Carvalho, architect of the April coup was made head of a new organisation, COPCON, which was able to by-pass the established military authorities and had the job of preventing civil disorder. There was little doubt that COPCON would act to protect the interests of the MFA, who now pressed for such radical ideas as the destruction of capitalism, the creation of a socialist state and immediate decolonisation. It was the last issue, the fate of the colonies, which ironically proved Spinola's undoing. The President did not interfere with the grant of independence to Guinea and Mozambique, but he was determined that Angola must not fall under the control of the pro-Soviet MPLA. In September he therefore ignored the MFA and the cabinet, and secretly negotiated an agreement on Angolan independence with other nationalist groups there. When this was discovered, the MFA and the political parties were outraged. Spinola appealed to the 'silent majority' of Portuguese to support him, and hastily called a rally in Lisbon for 30 September. But his opponents feared that the General aimed at dictatorship and barricades were raised in Lisbon against the planned rally, which he was then forced to cancel. On 30 September Spinola, his power shattered, resigned, to be succeeded as President by his former ally Costa Gomes.

Spinola's resignation speech warned of the abuse of democracy by the left but his downfall could only strengthen the left still further. The MFA and Communists now controlled the media, could mobilise workers against any 'counter-revolutionary' tendencies in the capital and also seemed to have won control of the army, navy and air force, which they sought to politicise by creating military assemblies which undermined the traditional authority of the officers. In January 1975 the government negotiated a new agreement on Angolan independence, which eventually led the MPLA to take power and in February various reforms were promised including fairer taxes, health insurance and unemployment benefits. On 11 March 1975 pro-Spinola officers, shocked by the decline of discipline in the army and the power of the Communists, tried to overthrow the government. But the coup was launched prematurely and became a fiasco. Spinola, his political failure complete, was now forced into exile, and both the Junta and the Council of State were replaced by a 'Revolutionary Council' which took over the leading role in government.

The MFA and the Communists were now in a strong position, but they knew that defeating Spinola was only part of the battle for power and that they had a major rival in Soares and the Socialists. In January 1975 attempts by the Communists to take control of the trades union movement, by creating a single union in each industry, had been criticised by Soares. He had previously allied closely with the Communists behind the revolution and had opposed Spinola. But now the Socialists feared a left-wing dictatorship. Soares condemned the idea of a one-party state and was rewarded with demonstrations of popular support. Soares's party greatly strengthened their position when they came first in elections for a Constituent Assembly which were held on 25 April. They attained 38 per cent of support, and the liberal-centrist Popular Democrats received 26 per cent, compared to only 12.5 per cent for the Communists. This was a major blow to Communist standing, and showed a strong popular rejection of political extremism either on the left or the right. Two weeks before the elections however – and as the price of letting them go ahead – the MFA had forced the political parties to accept a 'pact' which guaranteed the future political role of the Revolutionary Council in any constitution that was drawn up. MFA leaders saw themselves as the pre-eminent revolutionary force which, like a 'liberation movement' in a Third World state, should guide Portugal to a socialist future. The MFA and the Revolutionary Council thus remained a major threat to the position of the political parties despite the election.

Portugal in April 1975 was a sea of confusion. Yet the political divisions, the strikes and demonstrations, and the economic malaise all seemed to grow worse in the 'Hot Summer' that followed. The MFA, the Communists and the democratic political parties were only the main elements in a complex web of political events. In July the decision to put the influential *Republica* newspaper under workers' control led the Socialists and Popular Democrats to leave the Cabinet. Street demonstrations followed, some in favour of the government and some in favour of the Socialists as fears were raised of a revolutionary 'Triumvirate' being formed by president Costa Gomes, premier Gonçalves and COPCON's Otelo de Carvalho. The Roman Catholic Church now openly opposed the left, the 'Mario de Fonte' movement began to bomb Communist party headquarters in northern Portugal and civil war seemed possible. However, the 'Triumvirate' itself soon began to fall apart. Costa Gomes was the most conservative of the three and worried by the deep divisions in society, Gonçalves continued to advocate strong central control of the country on Soviet lines, but Carvalho favoured a radically different course – the decentralisation of government to 'people's committees'. Meanwhile moderately-minded officers in the army, appalled at military indiscipline, were beginning to organise themselves and on 6 August their leaders issued the 'Document of the Nine' which condemned Gonçalves for using totalitarian methods.

In the wake of this Gonçalves began to lose influence and was replaced as premier in September by Admiral Pinheiro de Azevedo, in a government which brought the Socialists and Popular Democrats back into office. Despite this the political scene remained incredibly confused. Lisbon was virtually ungovernable, it seemed likely that conservative northerners could march against the radical capital and in early November COPCON did nothing to prevent striking construction workers from laying siege to parliament. On 18 November, to bring Portugal to its senses the cabinet took Soares's advice and itself went 'on strike'! – demanding that the Revolutionary Council guarantee its safety. The cabinet 'strike' seemed farcical, the last act in Portugal's decline into anarchy. Yet it fulfilled Soares's purpose: it forced the country to address the problem of order. The need to restore Portugal's international standing, and especially to rebuild trade with Western Europe was also a positive force for order and the US used its influence against the far left. Moderate officers on the Revolutionary Council now decided to assert their authority. The result on 25 November, following new disorders among left-wing paratroops, was that the moderate officers seized power in Lisbon themselves. Leftists were arrested, COPCON was disbanded, the media were freed from political control, and a new army commander, General Ranalho Eanes, set about restoring military discipline.

Ultimately the army itself had turned against the MFA, whose Marxist tendencies had already alienated the Church, centrist politicians, the northern peasantry and most of the electorate. The MFA had destroyed the cohesion of the army but failed to provide strong leadership in the country. From now on, although the Revolutionary Council remained an important force and violence persisted for a time, the politicians would have the decisive hand in shaping Portugal's future. Earlier agrarian reforms were now restricted in extent, the stock market (closed since 1974) was reopened in January 1976 and a constitution was finally published on 2 April. It included many elements born of the earlier reformist fervour, such as an elected President, a commitment to socialist-style economics and a role for the Revolutionary Council in defending 'The principles of the Revolution'. Elections on 25 April confirmed the popularity of the Socialists (35 per cent of the vote) and Popular Democrats (24 per cent). The Communists and their allies remained on the defensive (15 per cent), even falling behind the conservative Social and Democratic Centre (16 per cent). General Eanes easily emerged as victor in the first Presidential election on 27 June and called on Soares to form a government.

Mario Soares's attempts to reunite Portuguese society after the turmoil of 1974–5 were aided by the evidence, dramatically shown in the 1975–6 elections, that the people were committed to democracy. He was faced, however, by a difficult economic situation in which a quarter of industry had just been nationalised, inflation of over 20 per cent had wiped out the effect of wage increases since 1974, unemployment had risen, the tourist industry had collapsed and trade was in deficit. Soares also headed a minority government. Austerity measures, including tax increases and higher interest rates were introduced in 1976–7, foreign loans were negotiated and talks began on entering the EC. In January 1978 Soares re-formed his government and was forced to rely on the Social and Democratic Centre (CDS) for support in parliament, but further unpleasant economic measures put strains on this relationship and in July the government collapsed. A difficult period followed for Portugal's nascent democracy when no two parties proved ready to join in coalition. In late August President Eanes tried to install his own nominee, Nobre de Costa, in power but this experiment soon collapsed, and another government, with conservative-centrist support survived only until June 1979. Eanes then reluctantly decided that early elections must be held.

In October 1976 the Popular Democrats, whilst remaining a liberal, middle-class party, had renamed themselves the Social Democrats and, led by Sá Carneiro, they allied with the CDS and monarchists to fight the December 1979 election as a single 'Democratic Alliance'. Sá Carneiro hoped to control parliament with the Alliance even if outnumbered by the Socialists and Communists, since the last two parties would never be able to co-operate following the events of 1974–6. The Alliance groups could then introduce a market economy in Portugal: as elsewhere in Europe there were now strong conservative hopes of reversing the nationalisation and high social spending of the mid-1970s and creating a more competitive economy which could take advantage of EC membership. Sá Carneiro fulfilled the first part of this plan when the Alliance won over 40 per cent of the vote in the December 1979 elections. However, President Eanes, who was re-elected in 1980, and the Revolutionary Council opposed many of the Alliance's economic measures as 'unconstitutional', and the Alliance could not get the two-thirds majority required for constitutional changes in parliament. This was an unpleasant reminder of the fact that, in 1974–6, the left and the army had managed to place limits on the behaviour of future governments. A further blow struck in December 1980 when Sá Carneiro was killed in an air crash. The Alliance of Social Democrats and conservatives became more divided under his successor, Francisco Pinto Balsemao. 1981 saw a wave of strikes and the beginning of terrorist activity by the FP-25 group. In August 1982 certain constitutional amendments proved possible which finally brought the army back under civilian control and replaced the Revolutionary Council with a new Council of State. Economic problems however remained daunting. In early 1983 inflation was over 20 per cent, and unemployment over 10 per cent. Illiteracy still affected a quarter of the population.

Elections in April 1983 were followed by a new government experiment in which the 'Central Block' of Socialists (with 36 per cent of the vote) and Social Democrats (27 per cent) brought Soares back to the premiership. But further austerity measures took their toll on the government, the legalisation of abortion in 1984 alienated conservatives and Roman Catholics, and another election was needed in October 1985. The election saw the Socialists sink to 21 per cent of the vote, paying the price for their failures in government, but the Social Democrats (30 per cent) distanced themselves from the policies of the coalition and ironically emerged as the strongest party under a new leader, Anibal Cavaço Silva. There was some compensation for Soares when he was elected President in January 1986 but the Social Democrats again emerged triumphant in the general election of July 1987, when they obtained a remarkable 50 per cent of the vote. The Social Democrats had clearly emerged as the major party on the centre and right just as the Socialists were the major force on the left. Cavaço Silva's governments were able to decrease state intervention in the economy, to reduce unemployment and, finally, in June 1989 – with Socialist support – to remove Marxist elements from the 1976 Constitution, paving the way for such measures as privatisation. Following the reassertion of civilian control over the army in 1982 and the passing of the Eanes Presidency, such constitutional amendments could be seen as ending the undesirable restrictions placed on democratically elected governments in the mid-1970s. Portugal, though the poorest member of the EC, had taken its place in the mainstream of Western European development, with a democratic government, EC membership and now a market-orientated economy with the privatisation of industry. Then again, not everyone saw the moves away from nationalisation and socialist-style reforms as progress. In March 1988 changes in the law for dismissing labour had provoked the biggest strike in Portuguese history, and showed the workers' desire to protect the gains *they* had made in the wake of the Carnation Revolution. Cavaço Silva's government received a further blow in the municipal elections of December 1989 which showed widespread discontent over the austerity measures of the late 1980s.

## Spain

Events in Portugal and Spain in the mid-1970s inevitably had an impact on one another. The overthrow of the Salazar regime added to the pressures facing General Franco's dictatorship and Franco's death in November 1975 gave increased hope to the reformers in Portugal. The Spanish experience was already similar to Portugal's in the early twentieth century. Clashes between conservative and reformist forces brought political upheaval, the dictatorship of Primo de Rivera (1923–30), the deposition of King Alfonso XIII in 1931 and then the establishment of the Second Republic. Spain too was an agricultural society, where the Catholic Church was a major force and there were impossible hopes of recreating the glories of the 'Golden' sixteenth century. Spanish politics, however, were also different to Portugal's in many respects, untroubled by colonial issues (almost all the Empire had been lost in the nineteenth century) but more violent and deeply affected by regional differences. The Second Republic alienated conservative elements such as the church, landlords and the monarchists, and in 1936 the army sought to overthrow it. Unlike Portugal in 1926 or 1974, the Spanish army's attempt to topple the regime was resisted. For three years Spain suffered a bloody civil war before the Nationalist forces, led by General Franco and aided by Mussolini and Hitler, established an authoritarian regime. More than half a million people were killed in the conflict and over 300000 Republicans fled into exile afterwards. The war left Spain facing daunting problems of reconstruction in the short term and the challenge of national re-conciliation in the long-term. It also meant that most Spaniards had no wish to turn to political violence again. This fact alone made it easy to tolerate the Franco dictatorship.

Many elements of the dictatorship existed before the civil war was over. In 1937 Franco had become head of state, head of government and head of the army. In 1938 he introduced strict censorship and reversed many Republican laws, including civil marriage and the right to divorce. He also banned trades unions and replaced them with government-controlled 'syndicates'. In 1939 he outlawed anyone who had actively opposed the Nationalist cause and so made national re-conciliation very difficult. Many saw Franco as a Fascist. He himself talked of organising Spain 'into a fully totalitarian concept'; he favoured a corporate state of rigid social divisions, on the Italian model, which rejected both capitalist and communist methods; and he set up a one-party government under the *Falange Espanola*, later known as the National Movement, the main element of which was the Spanish Fascist party. He was therefore anti-liberal, anti-socialist and strongly nationalist with no toleration of minority groups. He even adopted the title '*Caudillo*' – similar to Hitler's *Fuhrer* or Mussolini's *Duce*. Yet much about the dictatorship was far from totalitarian. Franco gave an important role to the Catholic Church in society, particularly in education and moral matters, he claimed to rule 'by the Grace of God', he stood for traditional values like the family or law and order rather than any revolutionary doctrines, and he often seemed to act not as an all-powerful dictator but as an arbiter between the traditional conservative groups who supported him – the church, monarchists, army, landowners and Nationalist Movement. He also avoided direct involvement in the Second World War.

In 1945 Franco, like Salazar, faced considerable criticism from the victor powers, who fought to destroy Fascism, and in 1946 the Allies withdrew their ambassadors from Madrid. Franco made little attempt to impress his critics. He had set up a Cortes (parliament) in 1942, but it was effectively appointed by him; he published a Charter of citizens' rights in 1945, but these could be suspended at any time; in 1945 too he introduced a Referendum Law, but he was the one who decided when referenda were called. In 1947 a referendum *was* held to approve a new law, on the succession, by which power would return to the monarchy on Franco's death. This move was not surprising. Monarchists had supported Franco since the civil war, he himself claimed that the monarchy had never ceased to exist and support for the Bourbons could be used to give his regime legitimacy. Franco did not yet say which of the Bourbons would succeed him. Meanwhile, Franco's opponents in exile were divided between the various elements – socialists, communists, anarchists – who had fought him in the civil war. In 1944 they tried to revive a guerrilla war against him but this was called off in 1950, after which only the Basque region in the north – with its strong desire for independence – remained troubled. By then the international scene too was becoming more favourable especially since the Americans, faced by the Soviet menace in Europe, looked to Spain for support. In 1953 the US gave financial and military assistance to Franco in return for bases. By the mid-1950s, therefore, the Franco regime seemed repressive but secure. Fear of renewed civil war, support from conservative groups, the appeal to traditional values, a divided opposition and international recognition all helped to underpin the regime.

By the late 1950s Franco faced growing pressures to modernise Spain and provide better living standards for his people. The influx of US money and military personnel, and the development of the tourist industry, made Spaniards aware of their backwardness compared to most of the Western world. Traditionally Spain had been an autarchic state, trying to protect the markets of landowners and businessmen behind trade barriers. With little industry, few natural resources and no attempt at expansion, the economy stagnated. Franco had merely tried to run this system more ornately, influenced by Fascist notions of state intervention. Rationing and price fixing were used to share out goods, Spain was cut off from the world economy in a bid for self-sufficiency, and a state-controlled National Industrial Institute (INI), based on Mussolini's IRI, was established in 1941 to provide items which the market could not. There were attempts to exploit agricultural resources more fully and the INI eventually became active in producing aircraft, cars and chemicals, but in the 1950s Spain was left standing by the post-war recovery of north-western Europe. Almost half the people lived off the land. As in Portugal, many were illiterate and in 1950–75 about one and a half million left to find work abroad. The INI became a refuge for loss-making firms and, thanks to the lack of skilled labour or high technology, could not compete in world markets. It was in this situation that in 1957, Franco brought new, technocratic ministers into his cabinet. These were young, educated individuals, many of them members of the *Opus Dei* movement, a Roman Catholic lay organisation. In contrast to the leaders of the National Movement they believed in using capitalist methods, reducing state intervention and abandoning the corporate state in favour of a more dynamic society.

In 1958 Franco re-stated the pre-eminence of the National Movement in the political organisation of Spanish society. Nevertheless, the rise of the technocrats showed that even the *Caudillo* recognised the need for change. A new generation had emerged which knew nothing of the civil war and adopted fresh means of opposition to the regime. 1958 saw the formation of the first secret 'Workers' Commissions' which, under Communist influence, began to penetrate the official syndicates in the 1960s. Strike action increased from about 1957, students and young workers were more ready to question the regime and in 1959 a new Basque independence movement, ETA, was founded which used terrorist methods. It was in 1959 that, under the influence of the technocrats, the government introduced a Stabilisation Plan which, whilst keeping many state controls in place, began to reduce protectionism in the economy. Tariffs were lowered, price controls removed, support for inefficient industry was cut and foreign investment encouraged. The technocrats modelled their action on the French system of 'indicative planning', setting targets for industrial growth and building co-operation between the INI and private industry. In the short term there were bankrupticies and a rise in unemployment but in 1961–4 Spain saw an 'economic miracle' as impressive as Italy's. As previously untapped resources were released and foreign investors exploited Spain's low wages, GNP grew at well over 10 per cent per annum, better than anywhere else in the world except Japan. That this could be achieved in an authoritarian state seemed doubly remarkable, and helped both to strengthen and to threaten the Franco regime. Growth remained good throughout the 1960s, living standards rose, consumer products such as televisions and cars multiplied, and Spain underwent a rapid urbanisation which continued until, by 1980, less than a fifth of Spaniards lived off the land. But the new middle-class groups which emerged also wanted greater freedom, justice and political representation. Franco's problems were further increased by the liberalisation of the Catholic Church in the 1960s.

In the late 1960s, as well as providing greater affluence, Franco tried to stave off political discontent by a certain amount of liberalisation. In 1966 censorship was eased, in 1967 the Cortes was made directly electable by the heads of families, legal discrimination was ended against non-Catholics, and in 1969 the *Caudillo* announced that his successor would be the young prince Juan Carlos. However, Spain remained a country without social welfare reforms or the redistribution of wealth, its applications to enter the European Community (in 1962, 1966 and 1970) were refused because of the lack of democracy, and many of its laws were still repressive. Alleged terrorists, for example, were tried by closed military tribunals and executed. In 1973 the ageing Franco finally shared some of his personal authority when he handed the premiership to Admiral Luis Carrero Blanco. The Admiral, however, was entirely loyal to the regime and in December he was assassinated by ETA, in its most dramatic action so far. In the Admiral's place Franco appointed Carlos Arias Navarro, who promised new political freedom, but 1974 and 1975 were marked by a gathering sense of crisis, reinforced by events in Portugal. In 1973–5 in the aftermath of Carrero Blanco's assassination, over 5,000 Basques were arrested, anti-terrorist laws tightened and several terrorists from ETA and other groups were executed. Meanwhile, opposition groups called for a complete 'rupture' with the Franco regime after his passing. As the *Caudillo* became increasingly unwell in 1975, even cabinet ministers joined in the criticisms. By the time the General died on 20 November 1975 his regime was already faced by a daunting array of opposition and calls for reforms which it was incapable of providing.

The death of Franco did not necessarily mean the end of his regime.

The new King, Juan Carlos, had some loyalty to Franco's political system, inherited the *Caudillo*'s powers and retained Arias Navarro as premier. Few knew much about Juan Carlos, but he had always seemed loyal to Franco and, despite the release of some political prisoners, he appeared to aim at continuity with Franco's policies. In June 1976 certain political associations were legalised but not political parties and not any Communist or separatist groups. In July Arias Navarro was replaced as premier by Adolfo Suarez, but this did not impress the opposition since Suarez was the Secretary-General of the National Movement. Nevertheless, it gradually became clear that Juan Carlos and Suarez *were* committed to major change. Juan Carlos was determined not to suffer the fate of his fellow-monarch Constantine II of Greece, and he proved far more able than the latter in facing the challenge of political change. He and Suarez aimed to create a democratic constitutional monarchy in Spain. To do this peacefully, without the complete rupture favoured by much of the opposition was difficult, but they were helped by various factors: their control of state power; the King's strong position as Franco's chosen successor, the heir of the Bourbons and army commander; the common desire to avoid a new civil war; the wish of the middle classes for peaceful change; and the timeliness of their reforms. It was a very different picture to the anarchy of Portuguese politics.

When change did come to Spain it was quite rapid. Suarez met opposition leaders in October 1976, and the following month a law was introduced which ended the dictatorship and promised a Constituent Assembly elected by universal suffrage. This was approved in a referendum in December by 94 per cent, a vote which revealed the overwhelming desire for democracy and modernisation which had built up under Franco. In December too Juan Carlos tried to placate separatist groups by announcing that Basques and Catalans could use their own languages and that terrorist cases would be tried by ordinary courts. In February 1977 certain political parties were legalised, including the Socialists, led by Felipe Gonzalez. In March the right to strike and form trades unions was restored, and in April the Communist party was legalised. The legalisation of the Communists was a major step, given that Franco's regime had been founded on anti-communism, but it was a vital move for demonstrating that democracy could work in Spain. Some groups, particularly ETA, continued to use terrorist methods to undermine the government, but on 15 June 1977 most opposition groups chose to fight the first free elections since 1936. The result confirmed the importance of the Socialists (29 per cent) and revealed that the power of the Communists (9 per cent) had been greatly exaggerated. Conservative groups too, united in the 'Popular Alliance' and led by one of Franco's former ministers, Manuel Fraga Iribarne, fared badly in this first election (8 per cent). The most powerful group (35 per cent) was the Democratic Centre Union (UCD), an amalgam of social democratic, liberal and Christian democratic parties, whose main asset was that Suarez had chosen to lead them. The pattern of voting suggested that whilst most Spanish people wanted a more open, egalitarian society they also wanted order and political moderation. Suarez remained premier, with UCD support.

Most of the politicians elected in June 1977 had little political experience, and certainly not experience of democratic government, but the inconclusive election result forced them to work together in drafting a constitution. It was an important point in forging a new Spain, that no group would be able to force its wishes on the others. Even the Communists, pursuing a moderate line, proved ready to accept the monarchy and in October all the main parties agreed on the 'Moncloa Pacts', designed to guide the government's social and economic policy whilst a constitution was drafted. The Pacts promised such diverse measures as wage and price controls, reform of the police, the legalisation of abortion and the decriminalisation of adultery, but they did so within a framework of peaceful change and the maintenance of capitalism. In Spring 1978 there were complaints when UCD and Socialist leaders met without the other parties to achieve a compromise on major constitutional issues, but a constitution was finally published in October 1978 and approved by 90 per cent of voters in a referendum in December. It was the ninth constitution to go into effect since 1812. It combined traditional liberal concerns about individual freedoms with a new recognition of socio-economic issues. This, like the Italian constitution, included commitments to health provision, the right to work and the need for a fair distribution of income, although these would be interpreted according to circumstance. In reaction to Franco there was no state church and no strong executive. Elections were required every four years, the monarchy was reduced to a mainly honorific role and the regions were promised 'the right to self-government'.

The first elections under the new constitution were held in March 1979 and confirmed the strength of the UCD (35.5 per cent) and Socialists (31 per cent). The UCD remained a loose coalition of interests, rather like the Italian Christian Democrats, united mainly by its fear of political extremism. But since the extremists – Francoist or Communist – were evidently not a threat in Spain the UCD gradually became divided and Suarez, who had previously relied on his alliance with the King as a source of authority, lacked the political skills to hold it together. In 1980 the UCD fared badly in regional elections and in January 1981 Suarez resigned as premier. It was whilst his successor was being chosen that, on 23–24 February, the new democracy faced its gravest crisis so far. On the 23rd Lieutenant-Colonel Antonio Tejero Molina burst into the lower house of parliament with a group of Civil Guardsmen and took its members hostage. Others involved in the plot tried to win over Juan Carlos. It was the King, however, who saved the situation by contacting loyal army officers and making a public appeal in support of the constitution. The coup failed, Tejero and others were eventually imprisoned and even die-hard Republicans were impressed by the King's behaviour. The foundations of the constitutional monarchy were strengthened enormously. The exact extent of the plot remained unclear, but UCD politicians quickly chose Leopoldo Calvo Sotelo as a new premier.

Calva Sotelo's triumph did not last long. A political conservative, ambitious but indecisive, he too proved unable to unite the UCD. A referendum on divorce in July 1981 bitterly divided Social Democrats and Christian Democrats within the UCD, and increasingly after November 1981 its politicians began to leave to form smaller parties. These included a Democratic and Social Centre party, led by Suarez. Without a stable majority in parliament the King decided to call new elections and at the polls in October 1982 the UCD received only 7 per cent of the vote. Felipe Gonzalez's Socialists on the other hand, promising evolutionary reform, rose to 46 per cent, giving them a safe majority under the Spanish electoral system. The UCD's decline marked an astonishing reversal of fortunes and showed the fragility of the new political parties. Yet the willingness of the electorate to shift allegiance from a centre-right party to one of the centre-left, and the ability of the political system to withstand the change were also positive points. (Some elements in the army were not so understanding: in October plans for a military coup were uncovered.) As has already been seen in the case of Greece and Portugal, a peaceful transition of power between conservative and Socialist parties is an important sign of democratic maturity and a great contrast to past experience, when a particular regime was often identified with a certain political group. Furthermore, the triumph of the Socialists did not make opposition impossible. The Popular Alliance had now won respect as a well-led party, and gained 25 per cent of the vote making it a strong conservative opposition, and providing the basis for a two-party system.

Gonzalez became premier in a difficult economic situation. As Spain had modernised under Franco, so it was no longer able to insulate itself from changes in the world economy. In 1973–4, after years of high inflation, came the oil price increase and poor trade figures, whilst the years 1974–80 saw unemployment rise from 3 per cent to 12 per cent of the working population. Spain's problems were made particularly difficult by its reliance on imported oil, its low levels of investment from domestic sources and the return of emigrés from abroad in the 1970s. Thanks to economic growth in the 1960s and the peaceful transition to democracy in 1975–8, the country was far wealthier than Portugal, and illiteracy had been cut to below 10 per cent of the population. Yet there was still the need to import high technology goods from abroad, rural deprivation was widespread and tourism an indispensable source of income. In 1982 Gonzalez promised to create 800 000 jobs but he was soon saying – in exactly the same terms as Britain's Margaret Thatcher – that there was 'no alternative' to high unemployment if Spain was to compete in world markets. To show his 'reliability' to foreign investors, Gonzalez used such policies as devaluation, a wage freeze and public spending cuts to tackle inflation whilst unemployment rose above one-in-five of the workforce. Inefficient areas of the INI were shut down and some profitable areas, like Seat cars, were privatised. Entry to the EC in 1986, after seven years of talks, opened Spain up to

European competition which in the short term gravely increased economic difficulties.

Like the French Socialists after 1983, or the Greek PASOK government in the same period, Gonzalez's policies seemed very different to his original commitments and disappointed many of his supporters. In March 1986 Gonzalez also came out in favour of NATO membership in a referendum. The referendum had originally been promised by the Socialists in 1982, when the UCD government entered NATO amidst some controversy. Many Spaniards did not see the Warsaw Pact as a threat, were critical of US policy in Latin America and associated the presence of US bases with Franco's government. Gonzalez's new-found support for NATO nonetheless ensured a 'yes' vote in the referendum. He was then able to use his success to call an election in June, in which he again won a clear victory – 44 per cent to the Popular Alliance's 26 per cent. Gonzalez's conservative economic policies and support for the Western Alliance had stolen much of the appeal of the centre-right and the Spanish people still resolutely refused to turn to Communism. During 1987–9 there were widespread strikes, ETA terrorism continued and new concerns – common to all Western Europe – about crime rates, drugs, youth disaffection and the environment. In the next general election, called in October 1989, Gonzalez still obtained 40 per cent of the vote but the Communists (9 per cent) finally drew off some disaffected left-wing voters, and the Socialists lost their overall majority in parliament, though they remained well ahead of the runner-up Popular Party (as the Popular Alliance had become) which stood at 26 per cent. The division of the opposition between conservative, communist and separatist groups allowed Gonzalez to form his third consecutive administration. A decade of political practice in Spain by then had shown that a stable democracy could be founded after decades of dictatorship and in the face of daunting economic problems.

# 7
# The Soviet Union

## The Stalinist System and Reconstruction, 1945–53

Whilst most of continental Europe fell under the control of right-wing regimes between the wars, the former Russian Empire was ruled by an authoritarian government of the left. The Bolsheviks came to power in 1917 on the basis of Marxist doctrine as interpreted by their leader Vladimir Ilyich Ulyanov, known as Lenin. It was a triumph surrounded by contradictions. Marxism was an ideology based on a large industrial working class, the proletariat, yet Russia was still very much a peasant society. The Bolsheviks claimed to represent the people, but the party leadership effectively interpreted what policy should be in their new society. Marxists had expected to see the 'withering' of the state after capitalism was overthrown, but the Bolsheviks retained a strong centralised bureaucracy, along with a political police force to keep control of the vast Empire they had inherited. Abroad, Lenin hoped that a socialist revolution would spread around the world, but instead the new 'Union of Soviet Socialist Republics' found itself treated as a pariah in international society. Allied nations for a time helped the Bolsheviks' opponents in a civil war which threatened to strangle the Soviet Union at birth. Whether Lenin would have become a more genuine democratic leader once the civil war was won is a subject of intense historical debate. But in 1924 after months of illness he died, and by 1929 the Soviet leadership was dominated by Josef Stalin, who created a highly centralised and brutal dictatorship.

Stalin – the man of steel – had been born Josef Djugashvili, the son of a peasant. He rose in the Communist leadership largely because, in contrast to the intellectuals around him, he was ready to take on administrative duties. He had also developed a ruthless, secretive character which made him a formidable opponent in the power struggle which followed Lenin's death. After 1929 Stalin allowed no independent centres of power in the Soviet Union and sought to create a proletarian society by the swiftest means possible. Millions died, and millions were put into forced labour camps in the 1930s as the secret police destroyed the independent peasantry and liquidated anyone else (including government officials, army officers and members of other elite groups) who aroused suspicion. The terror generated by 'the Purges' was at its height in 1936–8 and served not so much to end real opposition as to solidify Stalinist rule.

The denunciation of Stalin's victims as 'capitalist agents' was unfounded but reflected a fear of outsiders which the Communist leader was able to exploit. Despite the isolation of his regime internationally, Stalin did not abandon Marxism but instead chose to build 'socialism in one country'. His vehicles for controlling society were the use of police terror and the creation of a one-party state, similar to the Fascist systems of Hitler and Mussolini. The 'All-Union Communist Party' developed an organisation which reached to all levels of society, including a youth movement (the KOMSOMOL), women's groups and leisure activities. Every factory and every level of government had party officials to provide 'guidance' to its decisions; indeed the main levels of party organisation – from the local village to the national level – were a mirror image of the government bureaucracy. Instead of responding to the needs of the electorate however, the Communist party existed to achieve certain ideological goals and to dictate policy to the people. There was no room for 'public opinion' or pressure groups as had developed in Western pluralist societies. Soviet elections were a farce, with no choice between candidates. The party claimed to represent the 'general will', but in fact it was the means by which the decisions of the leadership were made known. Millions joined the party but this did not necessarily reflect genuine enthusiasm for Marxist doctrine so much as a desire to 'get on' in society. For, under the system known as '*nomenklatura*', many positions in the government, army, education system, industry and even the arts, could only be filled with party approval. With the destruction of the aristocracy, the independent peasantry and many of the middle classes, the party eventually became a 'new class' in the supposed egalitarian, working-class society. Party officials and party appointees were not landowners, nor could they pass their offices directly to their children, but they undoubtedly held a privileged position.

Yet in the 1930s the process of forming a 'new class' was in its early stages and, however important the party was in holding together the country, under Stalin it was subjected to terrorism along with the rest of society. In the purges after 1934 Stalin wiped out nearly all the surviving leaders of the 1917 Revolution, he executed or imprisoned many of the party's paid full-time officials, and his victims included members of the army and secret police. He ruled 'above' the party and even gave up the title of General Secretary (party leader) in 1934, governing instead as Chairman of the Council of Ministers (or prime minister). Stalin was like a new, but more efficient Tsar – autocratic, withdrawn from the people whom he called his 'children', and using a centralised bureaucracy and a secret police to carry out his personal decisions. In this some have seen the triumph of Russia's autocratic history over whatever idealism originally inspired the Bolsheviks. Others, however, see Stalinism as a perversion of both Russian history and democratic values, in which Stalin – again like Hitler and Mussolini – created a system of personal rule based on totalitarian ideology, posed as a 'man of the people' and was known by the title *Vozhd* (leader).

Even in a totalitarian system a leader must deal with society's problems, prove an effective decision-maker and demonstrate some results. What Stalin offered most of all to the USSR after 1929 was economic growth. To build 'socialism in one country' he relied on the mobilisation of Russia's vast resources to create heavy industries, particularly coal and steel, which were the main measures of national strength in the world, and also the way to create a proletarian society on which Communism could securely be built. Lenin had been ready to co-operate with the peasants using capitalist, market-based elements in his 'New Economic Policy' of the early 1920s. But this had limited results and in the 1930s Stalin developed a much more radical policy which became the basis for Soviet industrial growth over the following decades. The independent peasantry was destroyed so that land could be 'collectivised' under state control, just as industry was nationalised. Agriculture and industry became part of a national planning system, based around five year plans, directed by the central agency GOSPLAN and carried out by a complex system of ministries at national and regional level. The purges, added to a system of incentive payments and the 'work ethic' which the Communists developed, encouraged people to fulfil the planning demands.

Stalin's system was built on 'extensive' growth which meant that all available resources were devoted virtually regardless of cost, to the creation of heavy industry. (This is in contrast to 'intensive' growth seen in post-war Western economies, where attention is focused on how efficiently resources are used, where existing methods of production are improved and where the cost of utilising labour and materials is of great importance.) In the Soviet Union in the 1930s 'extensive growth' meant that national income was invested heavily in coal mines and steel plants, and that labourers were drawn into these new industries from the countryside, from the unemployment queues and through the use of women workers. The result was similar in some respects to the pattern of industrialisation under capitalist systems, leading to urbanisation on an unprecedented scale, greater geographical mobility of the population, the growth of the industrial working class, the need for better education and training, the decline in importance of agriculture, and an initial reliance on labour-intensive industries. In the Soviet Union in the 1930s however, industrialisation was carried out at a remarkable pace and at a time when the capitalist world was in economic recession. Some in the West were very impressed by this feat and became sympathetic to Communism. But Soviet growth rates were possible only because of the failure to mobilise resources in the past, and also because the USSR – the largest country in the world – had raw materials and a substantial workforce which could be developed without the need for foreign investment or much overseas trade.

The Stalinist system performed well in its rapid early stage of industrialisation but it had many weaknesses which became obvious in later decades. The system relied, for example, on low levels of popular consumption, the limited provision of social welfare and the exploitation of agricultural resources, in order to achieve a large heavy industrial base. Low levels of popular consumption meant that there was limited material reward for the workers, even in such basic items as clothing and diet, and little development of consumer industries either. Added to the USSR's international isolation this also meant that there was no development of consumer exports, such as labour-saving products, radios, televisions or private automobiles, on which, say, Japanese expansion was built after 1945. Spending on social welfare was limited to the provision of industrial training and of kindergartens (freeing women to work) which directly helped industry, but relatively little was spent on housing or health. Thus despite high growth rates and the system's claim to represent working-class interests, living standards in the USSR were very low. There was no consumer society and no real welfare state. The agricultural sector suffered far worse than the rest of society because it was ruthlessly exploited in order to provide the food, labour, finance and many of the raw materials needed in industry. Peasants were forced to work for the state in fulfilling heavy production targets in an economic and social system which brought them little reward. As a result they lost their sense of pride and their desire to work.

The Stalinist system in fact suffered from numerous in-built inefficiencies. After all, as seen above, it was not created to be efficient in using resources but merely to mobilise resources as rapidly as possible behind heavy industry. The central planning system which was adopted did not work on a capitalist-type pricing system, nor take note of 'cost effectiveness' as part of production. There was no direct link between what the Soviet people wanted and what the economy provided for them. Instead, production targets were set under the central Five Year Plan and carried out according to this blueprint. It has already been seen that there was no consumer society in Stalin's Russia: instead of industry responding to the demands of the people as expressed through the market, Soviet industry responded to the dictates of the planners, who, under the Communist system, decided what was best for the people. Obviously, a currency had to exist, so that people could be paid and could buy goods. But again, it was the state which set wages and price levels, and prices of goods had no direct relationship to the actual costs of production. In carrying out the Five Year Plans the hierarchical planning system was overburdened with work, having to decide wage levels, workforce size and production targets across many thousands of farms and factories, as well as co-ordinating these units as a whole. The inevitable result was a high degree of waste. Some goods were produced which could not be used due to lack of demand whilst in other areas there were 'bottle-necks' in supply, owing to a shortage of necessary materials. Yet, in contrast to the burdens placed on the planners, this centralised system allowed little initiative at lower levels. This meant that factory and farm workers had no reason to fulfil any more than the basic demands made on them. Since raw materials, buildings and machinery were provided to managers 'free' of charge by the planners, all these items were used without regard to cost. No attention was paid to the quality of goods produced, and of course there was no competition in the system to force producers to innovate and out-match other factories. As a result the Soviet economy became characterised by shoddy workmanship, poor production levels and a complete inability to compete in world markets.

In due course Soviet economists would have to face up to the need for consumer goods, the need to improve quality and the need to take costs of production into account. For eventually it became clear that even the USSR's natural resources were not inexhaustible. There was a limit to population growth, a limit to how far agriculture could be exploited and a limit also to the cheap raw materials which the land could provide. In the 1930s, however, these problems lay in the future. Stalin largely succeeded, through ambitious targeting and the use of terror tactics, in his aim of creating an industrial state with a large proletariat and in 1941–5 his political system emerged triumphant from the ultimate test: world war.

In 1941–2, after Hitler's unexpected invasion, much of European Russia fell under German occupation, industrial centres were captured and some people, especially in the Ukraine, openly sympathised with the Nazis. In 1942–3 however, the Red Army, in the great battles of Stalingrad and Kursk, turned the German tide and became the liberators of Eastern Europe. Stalinism survived because of a number of factors. The sheer size of Russia made conquest difficult and the large population allowed vast armies to be raised. Industrial potential had been built up in the 1930s, and production was shifted after 1941 across the Ural mountains, far away from the Germans. Stalin's centralised government was more efficient than that of the Tsar in 1914–17. American 'lease-lend' aid was given. Hitler failed to appeal to the bulk of the Russian people for support, but Stalin was ready to abandon Marxist rhetoric and appeal to his people's patriotism, recalling the national heroes of the past, praising the sacrifices of the Red Army and even relying on the support of the Orthodox Church. However, the costs of the war were enormous. Between 1941 and 1945 steel, coal and agricultural output all fell and consumer goods were cut back even from their low level of production. Nearly five million houses were destroyed, much of the population was uprooted and millions were killed. Statistics on the population losses are hard to establish, but the USSR probably lost about 7–8 million soldiers killed and about 8–12 million civilians. Yet the war also left the country with substantial international gains. With Germany, Japan and Italy defeated, and France and Britain in decline, the Soviet Union had become the second most powerful state in the world. Eastern Europe was under Soviet domination, Stalin had a role equal to America and Britain in post-war peace-making, Fascism was destroyed and Communism vindicated. Whereas in 1918 the minor powers of Europe had looked to the Western democratic system as a model for future development, many emerging nations now hoped to emulate the Soviet system of development, which seemed to provide a rapid road to industrial and political strength. Now aged 65, Stalin was thus faced with the twin challenge of dealing with his country's reconstruction problems and exploiting his new-found international standing.

It was in one of his few public speeches, in February 1946, that Stalin declared that victory in the war meant 'that our Soviet social system has triumphed', but in the same speech he also summoned the Soviet people to new economic efforts. The fourth Five Year Plan for 1946–50, was designed to achieve recovery from the war and to renew the heavy industrial growth of the 1930s, and again it could be counted as a success. The plan got off to a slow start in 1946 due to a drought in the grain-growing region of the Ukraine and the problems of demobilisation. (The Red Army, though it remained the largest in the world, was cut from 11 million men in 1945 to less than 3 million in 1948.) But overall results by 1950 were good. Coal, steel and electrical production were all well above pre-war levels and agricultural and consumer goods were again produced in the volumes seen in 1940. This still meant that living standards for the Soviet people were just about where they had been in 1928, but it should be remembered that the scale of improvement in Western Europe was little better: French living standards in 1950 only just surpassed those of 1929, the year that the inter-war 'slump' began. Once again there was little spending on consumer goods, housing or welfare, and agriculture was harshly treated. Taxes were increased on the private plots which peasants had been allowed to keep to feed their families, and sometimes farmers were paid less by the state for their produce than could cover the cost of production. Even the Soviet economy could not escape the dangers of inflation due to the war and a currency reform in December 1947 effectively led to a fall in real wages. As in the West, much of the success in industrial growth after 1945 was simply because the USSR was making up for wartime losses. But the ever-higher production levels were impressive nonetheless and the Soviet system did indeed seem able to compete with the capitalist world.

In order to restore his control of the country after the trials of 1941–3 and to goad his people to accept the sacrifices necessary for industrial growth, Stalin still made full use of the secret police and the system of *gulags*, the forced labour camps, under the control of Lavrenti Beria. Yet there was no return to the widespread purges and show trials of the 1930s. In part no doubt this was because the Soviet people, having suffered under the excesses of war, accepted the need to work together for recovery. But Stalin was also able to develop a 'siege mentality' in the Soviet Union thanks to the Cold War. Tension with the West helped Stalin to re-assert Communist values following the appeal to nationalism and religion during the war. In particular those who had made Western or German contacts in 1941–5 were often imprisoned or executed. In 1947 over a quarter of Communist party district secretaries were removed, mainly in areas that had been under wartime German occupation. Travel abroad was closely restricted once more, minority groups were viewed with suspicion and millions were deported from their homes to other areas. The Volga Germans and Crimean Tartars, for example, were small enough in number to be deported *en masse* to Siberia. Anti-semitic policies were evident and in the Ukraine the secret police fought a civil war with local guerrillas until the early 1950s. Many Ukrainians were killed or deported. A harsh line was also taken against the local population in areas which had been re-absorbed into the USSR in 1945, having been lost after 1917: the Baltic states, Moldavia and Byellorussia. The enforcement of conformity extended to cultural matters: existentialist literature and cubist painting, for example, were banned. As in the 1930s even self-evidently loyal Russians could find themselves the victims of Stalin's suspicion and oppression. The Red Army was now put under close party control, through the appointment of Political Commissars, and leading generals were demoted. Russia's greatest wartime general, Marshall Zhukov, was moved to a minor command. The oppressive post-war policy of 1946–8 was particularly identified with Stalin's political favourite Andrei Zhdanov, head of the Leningrad Communists. Yet after Zhdanov's death in 1948 many of his followers and colleagues became the subject of a new, if restricted, purge. The exact reasons for this so-called 'Leningrad Affair', which resulted in several thousand Communist party members being executed or imprisoned in 1949–51, remain obscure. The most prominent victim was the young and intelligent Nikolai Voznesensky, who had been seen as a possible successor to Stalin. The man who gained from the struggle over 'Zhdanovism' was evidently Georgi Malenkov, who eventually did succeed Stalin.

In the late 1940s, faced by the problems of re-construction, the need to re-assert Communism, the atomic capacity of the United States and the revival of Western economies, Stalin may have felt genuinely vulnerable to capitalist pressures, but by 1950 he had laid the basis for post-war recovery, reaffirmed his totalitarian rule, secured control of Eastern Europe and (in 1949) exploded his own atomic bomb. The USSR was again treated as a pariah by the West, but was no longer isolated in the world. In October 1952 Stalin's 'personality cult' was at its zenith and he held a Communist party Congress, the first since 1939 (they were supposed to be held every four years) with 1200 delegates representing six million members, including party officials, the armed forces, the secret police, trades unions, the intelligentsia and local officials. East European leaders were in attendance, as was China's Mao Zedong. Yet Stalin, though heaped with praise for his achievements, said little at the Nineteenth Party Congress. No change in foreign policy was announced nor was there any major development in the economic system. If the Congress had a purpose it probably had something to do with the institutional changes in the party which were decided upon. The party's name was changed to the 'Communist Party of the Soviet Union'; the post of General Secretary was formally ended (it had been practically defunct since 1934); the leading body, the Politburo – which effectively acted as the Soviet cabinet – was renamed the Presidium and increased in size; and the size of other top-level bodies was expanded. These included the Central Committee (a body of several hundred members, elected by the party Congress to meet on a regular basis, whose duties included the election of the Politburo) and the Secretariat (responsible for implementing Politburo decisions). Stalin, whose favourite was now Georgi Malenkov, may have been trying, through these changes, to strengthen his position for a new power struggle, by bringing new people into the leadership who he could easily manipulate. Although depicted as a benevolent father-figure in his personality cult, Stalin actually remained a despot, obsessive and suspicious of all those around him, and he may have wished to replace some of his leading ministers. In January 1953 it was announced that a number of Kremlin doctors, several of them Jewish, had been arrested and implicated in the 'murder' of Zhdanov. The ex-foreign minister, Vyacheslav Molotov, had a Jewish wife who had been sent into internal exile in 1948 and seemed a possible victim of a new purge, as did the security chief, Beria.

Suddenly all fears of a new purge disappeared when, on 5 March, Stalin died from a stroke. His legacy haunted his successors thereafter. He had fused Marxist doctrine with oriental despotism, fostered industrial growth by creating a top-heavy economic planning system, made the USSR the second most powerful state in the world at the cost of isolating her from the capitalist West, and enforced Communist control by the use of police-state methods. The Soviet Union had been transformed under his rule at the cost of considerable hardship and many millions of lives. Yet his successors would find it very difficult to develop the positive elements in his policies – industrial growth, egalitarianism and political stability – without maintaining the centralised, one-party government and the threat of the labour camps. Ironically, in some of the troubled periods that followed, many Soviet people looked back on Stalin's years as a Golden Age of expansion, success and certainty. There was no coming to terms with the truth about the purges until a new generation had been raised after him.

## Khruschev and 'De-Stalinisation', 1953–64

In the aftermath of Stalin's death the most powerful political figure was Georgi Malenkov, a Politburo member since 1946. He was also the leading member of the party Secretariat, and inherited Stalin's position as Chairman of the Council of Ministers – the equivalent in Western terms of a prime minister. Despite a close alliance with the police chief, Lavrenti Beria, Malenkov never became the undisputed leader of the Soviet Union. His colleagues on the Presidium* insisted on forming a 'Collective Leadership' in reaction to Stalin's personality cult. They reduced the Presidium in size to nine members in reaction to the expansion of 1952, and in mid-March they also insisted that Malenkov should surrender either

---

* As the Politburo was known from 1952 to 1966.

his position as party leader or as head of government. Not surprisingly perhaps, Malenkov decided to retain the Chairmanship of the Council of Ministers, the position occupied by Stalin, and handed the leading party role to Nikita Khruschev. Khruschev and Malenkov had clashed in Stalin's last years over agricutural policy, so the former could be expected to emerge as a rival for power. But the party organisation, which Khruschev now headed had been treated with disdain by Stalin and Khruschev was not seen as being very able. Only over the following 18 months did it become clear that Khruschev – rather like Stalin in the 1920s – had been underestimated by the other leaders, could use the party organisation as a springboard to power, and was adept at exploiting other rivalries within the leadership, such as that between Malenkov and Vyacheslav Molotov. Molotov, now restored to his position of foreign minister, was seen in March 1953 as one of the three strongest figures in the leadership, along with Malenkov and Beria. The triumvirate broke up in late June 1953 when other ministers decided to oust Beria from the leadership. The Presidium members, with Khruschev foremost among them, evidently feared the powers of Beria's secret police and their actions in dealing with him were reminiscent of Stalin: Beria was suddenly arrested, secretly tried as a British spy and, in December, executed along with several of his political associates. Meanwhile, Khruschev had strengthened his position by adopting the title 'First Secretary' of the Communist party in September 1953.

The leadership struggle following Stalin's death was closely intertwined with an intense debate over policy changes. Although some Presidium members, notably Molotov, wished to maintain Stalinism virtually intact, others, including Malenkov, favoured economic reforms and some political liberalisation. In order to make the new leadership popular and to consolidate its hold on power certain measures were easily agreed upon. In April there were price reductions on certain basic consumer goods, such as food and clothes. April also saw the release of those implicated in the 'Doctors Plot' of Stalin's last months, thus ending fears of a new purge. Marshal Zhukov, the conqueror of Berlin, was recalled from obscurity and made deputy defence minister. In foreign affairs the new leaders put the accent on détente with the West. Another vital element in the political 'thaw' after March 1953 was that an amnesty was issued for some of those imprisoned under Stalin. The amnesty excluded violent criminals and most political prisoners but included, among others, Molotov's wife. The fall of Beria further aided the process of reducing and controlling the Soviet police state. This was a process which the Communist party and Soviet leaders could all support to some extent because, as much as anyone else in society, they had been victims of Stalin's despotism. Beria's trial provided an opportunity to criticise the secret police and was followed by the execution of some of Stalin's other henchmen. Mikhail Ryumin, held responsible for the 'Doctors Plot' accusations was executed in July 1954, and Victor Abymakov, who had taken charge of the 'Leningrad Affair' purges was executed the following December. It was apparently only during the Beria trial that some of Stalin's successors themselves discovered the full horror of the purges, including the mass murder of quite loyal Communists, from the files of the Ministry of Internal Affairs.

It was in order to prevent a return to the mass terror of the 1930s that, in 1954, control of the secret police was taken from the interior ministry and given to a new Committee of State Security (KGB), which was subordinated to political control. Authority over the labour camps was handed to the Ministry of Justice. The so-called 'Kirov Decrees' of 1934, which had allowed secret trials, without adequate judicial defence or appeal, were withdrawn. The KGB could now arrest but not try people. It is important to emphasise once again that this process of reducing secret police powers was *not* designed to bring about genuine political freedom, still less an independent judiciary. The reforms were actually carried out to prevent the use of terror tactics against the Communist party again. The secret police apparatus was reduced in size, but it still existed, along with a network of KGB informers. The judiciary and secret police, as well as the regular police forces and army, remained under Communist party control, ready to do its will. The 'Gulag Archipelago' also continued to thrive. Those released from the labour camps in 1953–5 numbered up to 15 000 but it often took time before they were fully 'rehabilitated'. 'Rehabilitation' was vital if those imprisoned and their families (including the families of those executed), were to be treated as loyal citizens, able to join the Communist party and exercise their rights to housing, an education and a job. Khruschev's support for the rapid rehabilitation of Stalin's victims helped strengthen his position with the people. He gained too from the controls put on the secret police (which reduced their importance in the equation of political power) and from the growing strength of the party *vis-a-vis* the state bureaucracy, which the legal reforms of 1953–4 had reflected. In the absence of mass terror, the Communist party became more significant in maintaining strong central rule under Khruschev's control.

The struggle for power between Malenkov, the head of government, and Khruschev, the head of the party, particularly centred around economic policy. In addition to abandoning Stalin's personality cult, controlling police coercion, and pursuing a mild foreign policy, the Soviet leaders sought a relaxation in economic policy. But there was considerable disagreement about how far this should go and what form it should take. Under the 'New Course' supported by Malenkov greater emphasis was to be placed on the production of consumer goods, light industrial manufacturers and housing. With post-war reconstruction achieved and heavy industry strong, it seemed that the leadership could at last offer the people better living standards and a share in the fruits of industrialisation. By the end of 1953 more consumer goods were being produced than at any time since the 1920s and real wages had risen markedly. The 'New Course' also improved agricultural output and reduced the burdens on the peasantry by easing agricultural taxes, paying higher prices for state procurements from farms and encouraging the peasants to grow food for the market on their private plots. Khruschev took a great interest in agricultural reform. It was Khruschev who, in September 1953, advocated higher prices for farm produce, a shift in investment to agriculture and increased production of livestock, corn (on which livestock could be fed) and fertilisers, all of which was very different to the crude exploitation of agriculture in Stalin's day. In January 1954, following a poor harvest, Khruschev also launched the 'Virgin Lands' campaign, designed to move farmers into previously uncultivated areas east of the Ural mountains, in Siberia and Kazakhstan. By 1956 the campaign had brought into cultivation an area equal to the Canadian wheat fields, with over 300 000 people working in 'Virgin Lands'. The campaign allowed the USSR to surpass 1914 levels of agricultural production for the first time and saved the country from famine in 1956. Yet the Virgin Lands effort demanded large amounts of investment, took spending away from agriculture in European Russia, and helped to intensify Khruschev's struggle with Malenkov, who would have preferred to concentrate resources on industrial reform. Khruschev indeed, though he later adopted much of the 'New Course' in industrial policy, became its leading critic in 1954. He argued that the shift of resources from heavy industry to consumer spending was going too far, that Soviet growth rates must be safeguarded and, of course, that money should be invested first in the Virgin Lands.

Although there was little evidence that Malenkov's reforms really threatened heavy industry, military spending or agricultural improvements, most of the Presidium shared Khruschev's doubts about the 'New Course' by late 1954. A sure sign of Khruschev's rising power, and the rising strength of the Communist party *vis-a-vis* the government machine was that, after August, policy decrees were issued in the name of the party first, and the government second, a change to previous practice. In December Malenkov evidently agreed to resign as Chairman of the Council of Ministers, although this was only formally announced in February 1955. He had lost the struggle for dominance with Khruschev. From February 1955 until the Gorbachev years the most significant post in the Soviet leadership was to be that of party leader, and party institutions were to be dominant over the government. As yet, however, Khruschev too remained less than secure in power. Malenkov was still on the Presidium, as was Molotov; and the new Chairman of the Council of Ministers was Nikolai Bulganin, formerly Minister of Defence. Thus Khruschev had to continue to share power, and neither the other leaders nor the party machine had any wish to give him the personal authority which Stalin had wielded.

Khruschev was a complex character, a convinced Communist and a tough-minded politician, who was innovative and reform-minded yet also adventurist and arrogant in the way he took decisions. In contrast to most Soviet leaders he was a very human figure viewed with some sympathy in the West, partly because in 1955–6 he supported a policy of 'peaceful co-existence'. Although a critic of the 'New Course' he effectively maintained it by improving pensions, expanding education, increasing holidays, introducing a minimum wage, improving agricultural incomes, and shortening the working week. The main difference from Malenkov was that Khruschev declared that heavy industry should still be given primacy in the share-out of resources. In 1957 as an egalitarian gesture he even banned the secret supplementary payments made to bureaucrats, introduced the first modest measure to restrict pollution in the USSR and finally addressed one of the great failings of Stalin's rule by stimulating housing construction, thus reducing overcrowding and communal living. Actually, Khruschev's changes still left privileged groups of party officials, government bureaucrats, factory managers and others appointed under the *nomenklatura* system, with higher salaries, better education, health and holidays, and access to high-quality foreign goods and *dachas* (country villas). The new apartments which housed ordinary workers were small, cheap and functional, built to drab standard design, usually on the outskirts of towns. In due course they became known as 'Khruschev slums'. Nevertheless, variations in personal wealth were never as great as in the West, employment and a decent income were now guaranteed to many people, and the Soviet Union was becoming a modern, consumer, urban society. In the 1960s most Soviet people lived in towns, as in Western society. (Only 15 per cent of Russians had lived in towns in 1917.) Diet, clothing and consumer goods were never as good as those in the West but Stalin's successors were able to use improved living standards to much the same effect as their capitalist counterparts, to ensure social peace and political stability. Compared to the past, Soviet people felt things were improving.

The reliance of the new Soviet leadership on the party machine and improved living standards to retain power was accompanied by attacks on hard-line Stalinism. In June 1955 it was announced that a new Party Congress was to be called and it was during the Congress, in February 1956, that Khruschev made his most celebrated attack on Stalin. In a speech which was supposedly secret but soon became public knowledge,  Khruschev attacked Stalin's personality cult, his elevation above political control, and his use of police methods and arbitrary arrests. It is important to emphasise that, yet again, Khruschev's speech was intended more as a guarantee of Communist party authority than as a step towards liberalisation. True, Khruschev allowed greater artistic freedom after 1956 and reduced the restrictions on travel abroad, but his main intention was to condemn Stalin's mistreatment of the Communist party during the purges, not the sufferings of the Soviet people in general. Khruschev, who continued to release and rehabilitate millions of Stalin's victims in the later 1950s, concentrated his criticisms on Stalin's use of terror against loyal Communists after 1934. But he pointedly did *not* question the USSR's one-party system, collectivisation of land or central economic planning, all of which he wished to keep in place.

Nonetheless, many members of government questioned the wisdom of Khruschev's exposure of Stalinist methods. After all, people like Malenkov and Molotov had been closely involved in carrying out Stalin's wishes. And however limited Khruschev's intentions were, the 'secret session' speech soon took on a mythical significance. Many Western Communists were shocked by the revelations about Stalin's terror, and hard-line Communist leaders in Eastern Europe and China believed that Khruschev had called their own political systems into question. Such criticisms from within the Communist bloc were intensified after November 1956  when the Red Army crushed an attempt by Hungarians to assert their independence. Yet Khruschev continued with his ambition of changing the Soviet Union. In February 1957, in an attempt to decentralise economic decision-making and so create a more efficient planning system, he actually proposed to abolish most of the central industrial ministries in Moscow and replace them with 105 regional planning councils under the supervision of a Supreme Economic Council. The new system was designed to reduce the bureaucracy, develop local initiative and make managers more responsible to popular needs. Since it gave more power to the regions (who already had wide authority over agriculture and services) it won support of regional party bosses and was approved in May. But it was a novel scheme, introduced without adequate testing, which created formidable new problems of cross-regional co-operation. It also alienated the bureaucrats, not least because they now had to leave Moscow and live in the regions. This was the immediate background to the 'anti-party plot' of June 1957.

The seriousness of the 'anti-party plot' only became clear to the outside world some time afterwards. What happened was that Stalinist conservatives and government representatives, alienated by Khruschev's secret session speech and economic reforms, tried to replace him as party leader. They almost succeeded. The 'anti-party group', led by Molotov (who had been replaced again as foreign minister in 1956) succeeded in voting Khruschev off the Presidium by eight votes to four. The latter, however, was not to be so easily replaced. He had cultivated the support of the army and the KGB, as well as party officials and all these groups now joined in his support. A meeting of the party's Central Committee was hastily called, the army helped Khruschev's supporters to attend it, and the meeting not only overturned the Presidium's decision but elected a new Presidium. This included Khruschev loyalists like Leonid Brezhnev. In contrast to Stalin's era members of the 'anti-party group' suffered humiliating demotions rather than execution. Molotov became Ambassador to Mongolia, whilst Malenkov was put in charge of a power station. But the crisis had left Khruschev in a very strong position, which he continued to reinforce with changes in government. In October 1957, for example, he removed Marshal Zhukov from the Presidium, which he had joined after helping to defeat the 'anti-party plot'. Zhukov was accused of 'Bonapartism' by creating a 'personality cult' in the army. In March 1958 Khruschev also secured the resignation of Bulganin and himself became Chairman of the Council of Ministers. He thus combined the leadership of the party and the Soviet government. His confidence was further boosted in October 1957 by the successful launch of 'Sputnik' the first satellite, and a great technological achievement.

In 1959–60 Khruschev was at the height of his power and genuinely believed that, by decentralising and reforming the Stalinist economic system, so that people were encouraged to work for themselves, Soviet Communism would be able to outstrip the capitalist West at all levels. Posing as a 'man of the people' he visited towns and farms to spread his ideas face-to-face. Further evidence of his faith in decentralisation had come in 1958 when he destroyed the USSR's machine tractor stations and distributed tractor-producing machinery to the farms. This, however, was yet another hasty action, taken without due preparation and it soon proved a major error. Despite the agricultural reforms since 1953, Soviet farmers remained poorly educated, with less incentives to work than factory employees and quite unable to order, run and maintain farm machinery, much of which soon fell into disrepair. Other setbacks followed for Khruschev's agricultural policies. His attempts to increase corn and livestock production, for example, increased costs, meant a reallocation of resources from other types of production and proved uneconomical in many areas. In the early 1960s meat production began to fall and 1962 proved a disastrous year for the corn harvest. Khruschev tried to return to the close direction of agricultural targets but a seven-year agricultural plan, begun in 1959, failed from the start to match its targets, and hopes of matching US output proved farcical. In 1961–2 Khruschev tried to increase production by penalising peasants who concentrated on farming their private plots, and by insisting that fallow land be utilised. But the attack on private plots simply cut production further, whilst the farming of fallow land led to its becoming exhausted. Even production in the Virgin Lands, such a success in the mid-1950s, began to fall off in the early 1960s as the soil became exhausted. A massive increase in fertiliser production proved impossible to achieve. People continued to be told that agricultural production was increasing but in 1963 the truth became known when a drought in the Virgin Lands forced the government to buy grain from abroad and there were meat and milk shortages.

It was a similar story with industrial production, where Khruschev's decentralisation of decision-making to regional councils caused great practical problems. Alterations to pay scales, alongside price rises in 1961, proved very unpopular with the workers. In 1961 a new Communist party, programme, which remained in effect for 20 years, promised the full achievement of Communism by 1980, including greater production of major industrial products than America. Measured against the growth rates of the first three post-war economic plans, of 1946, 1951 and 1956 this did not seem unreasonable. After all, in 1960 Soviet annual steel production was well above the target of 60 million tons set by Stalin in 1946. However, Soviet workers produced far less *per capita* than their Western counterparts. The quality of Soviet goods remained poor, attempts to improve technical education had limited effects, and Khruschev's promises about industrial growth soon proved illusory.

Khruschev's greatest mistake after 1957 was arguably not his economic and foreign policies, but his alienation of those elements who had supported him against the 'anti-party plot'. His confidence after 1957 and his development of a populist image had been accompanied by a flaunting of the party. Khruschev ignored his colleagues on the Presidium, appointed non-party figures to government bodies and finally began to carry out reforms which directly threatened the party's hold on power. At the Twenty-Second Party Congress in October 1961 Khruschev finally had Malenkov, Molotov and other 'anti-party' plotters expelled from the party but the mildness of their fate – compared to that of Stalin's opponents – probably meant that people did not fear Khruschev enough. The Congress saw more attacks on Stalin (whose body was moved from the mausoleum in Red Square) and it was followed by greater literary freedom including, in November 1962, the publication of Alexander Solzhenitsyn's *One Day in the Life of Ivan Denisovich*, about life in Stalin's labour camps. Again, it would probably be a mistake to read too much into Khruschev's 'liberalism'. He was ready to accept some public debate, but not the questioning of the Communist system itself, and he upset genuine liberals by cracking down on dissent again in 1963–4. But, as with the secret session speech, criticisms of Stalin could not but provoke some questioning of Communist ideology, and this offended many party members. In 1962 Khruschev took another step which could only alienate the party machine. In November he divided the party, at all but the highest levels, into urban and rural sections. This was yet another ill-considered scheme which halved the authority of existing party officials, created new rivalries in regional politics and caused hopeless confusion about local responsibilities. Those in charge of industrial-urban centres, for example, refused to help agricultural-rural areas at harvest time, which meant that some crops were left to rot. Khruschev directly challenged the security of party officials too by limiting the periods for which they could serve.

By 1964 Khruschev's competence was in doubt both at home, where he had launched a series of untested policies with particular ill-effects for agriculture, and abroad, where his bluff and brinkmanship had nearly provoked global war in the Cuban Missile Crisis of October 1962. The pursuit of détente with America in 1963 had certainly reduced international tensions but in the USSR even the Communist party felt threatened by Khruschev's personal power, his unpredictability, and his failure to consult the party. Khruschev had himself increased the power of the party in 1953–7 by limiting the power of the secret police, controlling the government bureaucracy and defeating the 'anti-party group', but he had now become a potential menace to his fellow leaders and in October 1964 he was overthrown. The coup which toppled him was organised by a former KGB chief, Alexander Shelepin, whilst Khruschev was on holiday on the Black Sea. Unlike 1957, the KGB, the Army and many local officials now opposed Khruschev, who was surprised by the coup. His opponents, with memories of 1957, sounded out members of the Central Committee before recalling Khruschev to Moscow and criticising his policies. On 14 October

179

he was forced to retire (on a pension) and a few of his close supporters were demoted. All-in-all it was a rapid, smooth operation which, whilst it took international opinion by surprise, was easily accepted by the Soviet people. The moderate way in which Khruschev was treated said much about the changes he had brought to Soviet politics since the terror and suspicion of Stalin's rule. But Khruschev had always remained an ardent Communist, he had preserved many elements of the Stalinist system and ultimately he was overthrown by the party machine whose importance to Soviet life had increased.

## Brezhnev and Stagnation, 1964–82

There was no obvious successor to Khruschev in October 1964, and for a time it seemed that there would be a return to the 'collective leadership' seen after Stalin's death. Once again power was divided at the centre between Leonid Brezhnev who became First Secretary of the Communist party and Andrei Kosygin, who was prime minister. Both were trusted, experienced ministers with characters very different to the brusque, adventurist Khruschev, and they immediately set out to please the elites in the party and government bureaucracy which Khruschev had alienated. Despite the emphasis on continuity and a smooth change of power, many of Khruschev's reforms were reversed. The division of the party into industrial and agricultural sections was ended in November 1964 and the inefficient system of regional economic councils was replaced by central ministries after September 1965. The restrictions on the duration of official tenures were removed at the Twenty-Third Party Congress in March–April 1966 and the Congress saw none of the attacks on Stalin which had marked Khruschev's leadership. The new leaders promised agricultural improvements and the extension of car ownership among the people. The Congress also restored the title 'General Secretary' to the party leader and the title 'Politburo' to the Presidium. Meanwhile, the leadership pleased the party members by taking a hard line against underground publications in the Soviet Union, which had grown after Khruschev's 1962 'liberalisation'. In September 1965 the writers Yuli Daniel and Andrei Sinyavsky were arrested and, after a trial in February 1966, were sent to labour camps for publishing anti-Soviet literature. Solzhenitsyn's works were no longer published. The KGB began a crackdown against dissidents which became particularly efficient after 1967 under the direction of Yuri Andropov. It was very different in scale to Stalin's purges, but thousands were imprisoned or condemned to internal exile.

The 1966 Party Congress showed the Politburo to be united, with Brezhnev and Kosygin firmly in control. But behind the scenes a power struggle was evidently taking place, which ultimately led to Brezhnev's clear predominance. Certainly Brezhnev and Kosygin seemed to work well together. The former controlled the party apparatus and relations with other Communist states, the latter controlled the economy and wider foreign policy issues. Together they also prevented any rivals becoming too strong. Thus Nikolai Podgorny, who seemed a threat at first, was put in the virtually powerless position of Soviet president in December 1965, whilst Alexander Shelepin, who had masterminded Khruschev's overthrow, was demoted to taking charge of trades unions in September 1967. There was still the possibility that Kosygin, through his control of the government bureaucracy, could establish primacy over Brezhnev. Brezhnev, however, was careful to move his own men, like Andropov, into leading party positions. Brezhnev also strengthened his grip on lower levels in the party, cultivated links with the KGB and Army, and made foreign minister Andrei Gromyko a close ally. At the Twenty-Fourth Party Congress in 1971 Brezhnev was clearly the dominant force, able to put forward the policy of détente with America, and in 1973 he was able to make Andropov (KGB) Gromyko (foreign ministry) and Marshal Grechko (the defence minister) into full Politburo members. Brezhnev's control over leading positions was so complete after this, that he was able to promote his supporters very rapidly. This explains the rise of Konstantin Chernenko (in 1976–8) and Mikhail Gorbachev (in 1978–80) to full Politburo status.

Brezhnev tended to promote men of his own generation to high office and even to remove younger men from the Politburo. (Gorbachev was an exception.) Brezhnev did not make anyone a clear successor, instead he increasingly concentrated authority in his own hands. Thus he introduced a new constitution in 1977 which, by asserting the predominance of the party over government and society, increased his own power. The constitution reinforced the role of the party as a 'guiding force' in the Soviet Union, safeguarding the sanctity of Marxist-Leninist doctrine. In practical terms this meant that the party leader was predominant over the prime minister, and that the Council of Ministers (in control of the bureaucracy) was responsible to the Supreme Soviet (the USSR's parliament) or, when the Soviet itself was not sitting, the Presidium of the Supreme Soviet. It was in order to strengthen his position under the new constitution that Brezhnev replaced Podgorny, in June 1977, as Chairman of the Presidium of the Supreme Soviet (or Soviet President), a position which was now more significant than in the past. Kosygin, with his role as Chairman of the Council of Ministers now reduced in significance, resigned and was succeeded by Nikolai Tikhonov. Brezhnev's dual position as party leader and President after 1977 was reminiscent of Khruschev's concentration of power after 1957, and was accompanied by similar evidence of a 'personality cult'. Already, in 1973, Brezhnev had been awarded the Lenin Peace Prize. In May 1976 he became Marshal of the Soviet Union. And in 1979 he was awarded the Lenin Prize for Literature as reward for his dull memoirs. Whereas Stalin's 'personality cult' had been associated with despotism and fear, Brezhnev's acceptance of honours seemed ridiculous, reflecting the fact that power now lay in the hands of a vain old man, whose rule had become identified with stagnation and corruption. In 1981–2, as Brezhnev became increasingly unwell, even members of his family were accused of corruption, and Andropov's KGB tolerated scurrilous attacks on the Soviet leader in the press.

Brezhnev's last years were troubled ones, marred by low growth rates, an absence of political idealism and renewed Cold War with the West. Yet in the first ten years following Khruschev's fall the Soviet Union had seemed very successful. Agriculture had recovered from the problems of the early 1960s, industry continued to expand and in the early 1970s even the United States recognised the USSR as an equal. How can this change in fortunes, from the early successes to the later difficulties, be explained? One answer is that the very continuity of policy under Brezhnev proved a problem in the long term. Brezhnev achieved stability and strength in the later 1960s at the price of stagnation in the later 1970s. He came to power at a time when the government bureaucracy and the Communist party were resisting Khruschev's reforms, when Khruschev had only partially achieved the 'de-Stalinisation' of society and when the modernisation of the Soviet economy was proving very difficult. Given Khruschev's fate in 1964, and his own original position as a 'first among equals', Brezhnev had to consult the Politburo, seek a consensus between the most powerful groups involved in policy-making, and keep the party and bureaucratic elites friendly. The changes brought about in 1964–6 reassured the party that its role in society was secure and reasserted the significance of the government bureaucracy. The Army and KGB were also strengthened. But all this helped to ensure a growing inertia in the system. Party and government officials, rather like Brezhnev himself, became more interested in preserving their positions and holding the levers of power, than pursuing dynamic reforms. For, as had become clear under Khruschev, attempts at reform might upset the political status quo, run the risk of failure and could provoke popular discontent. It was far easier to avoid experiment, prevent any further de-Stalinisation and try to build Communism gradually. Even when his political predominance seemed assured after 1975 Brezhnev showed that, in contrast to Khruschev, it was more important to please political elites than to tackle the USSR's weaknesses.

To explain how sources of strength could become liabilities it will be useful to look at the Army. Under Stalin patriotism and fear of war had been used to ensure loyalty to the regime. This was similar to many other countries of course, but the Soviet armed forces as well as guaranteeing national security and providing the country with pride and Superpower status, also had an important social role. The Soviet Army helped to hold the country together by drawing in conscripts from all regions, it provided conscripts with a technical education and it was a major element on the political scene. The Soviet armed forces were greatly expanded after 1964. Apart from bolstering support for Brezhnev, this brought numerous benefits. By 1969, at a time when the USA was tied down in Vietnam, the Soviets had substantial conventional forces and achieved nuclear parity with America; the USSR could now fight a conventional war, or hold Western Europe 'hostage' (with short-range nuclear weapons) or threaten America itself; the Soviet Navy was built up to threaten Western communications, and to extend Soviet influence world-wide. All of this helped Soviet diplomats to pursue détente with America as well as to support 'wars of national liberation' in Vietnam and, in the 1970s, Angola and Ethiopia. And the successful development of missiles, supersonic aircraft and the *Mir* space station emphasised Soviet ability to match Western technology. But there was also an enormous price to pay for military expansion. The military build-up took on its own momentum and became unrelated to the external threat in the 1970s. The insistence of Soviet generals that the armed forces must be expanded because an external threat *did* exist became self-fulfilling, since the Soviet arsenal terrified China, Western Europe and America, helping to undermine détente. The growing military influence on policy-making probably contributed to the decision in 1979 to intervene in Afghanistan, an event which finally killed off détente and led the Soviets to become involved in an 'unwinnable' guerrilla war, all too similar in many respects to American involvement in Vietnam. Soviet propaganda down-played the Red Army's direct involvement in the Afghan fighting, but the deaths and disaffection among conscripts easily became known at home. For their part the Americans, having recovered confidence, began an arms expansion in 1980 which threw down a major challenge in Moscow.

Military expansion had a particularly detrimental effect on the Soviet economy by distorting industrial production. Nearly half the output of machine industries, for example, became devoted to military needs. Given the amount of national wealth output, and the best scientific minds, which were directed their way, the armed forces did not prove a very efficient employer of resources. Nor were the technical advances, which the military undoubtedly made, shared well with the rest of Soviet industry. This would not have been so bad if the USSR's economic performance had made great strides outside the military field. But it did not. The Economy was a victim of Brezhnev's failure to reform, an area where greater efficiency was sacrificed in order to maintain Communist party control. In particular, to maintain its popularity, the party sought to guarantee full employment and low prices to people regardless of the effect on output and the quality of the goods. Factories, for example, were kept running even if there was no demand for their products. Agricultural prices were kept down to their 1961 levels even though this created a situation where the demand for food far outstripped supplies. The collective and state farms, feeling themselves inadequately rewarded, produced low quality food, but this did not prevent large queues being formed for what was available. Yet it became impossible to contemplate price increases since these could provoke discontent. Thus rents were held down at levels which could not even cover the costs of housing maintenance and consumer goods were heavily subsidised by the government as well. Soviet living standards did improve under Brezhnev, the output of consumer goods increased and by 1980 about a quarter of Soviet homes had a television, refrigerator and washing machine. But this was not even as good as some Eastern European countries, let alone

183

the West. The USSR had fallen short of Khruschev's hope of achieving full Communism by 1980. Housing, health-care and education were also under-funded.

Although official Soviet figures are difficult to interpret, and were sometimes deliberately falsified, the evidence of economic failure by 1980 was quite clear. Industrial output may have increased under Brezhnev and the USSR might produce more than the United States in certain sectors, including steel, timber and oil. (The USSR was the world's largest oil producer.) In modern industries like chemicals, electronics and machine tools however, the Soviets lagged far behind America, and Japan had overtaken the USSR as the world's second largest industrial power. In contrast to the West, the service sector in the Soviet economy had developed little. Even Soviet statistics showed that rates of growth had declined in every Five Year Plan since the war, and that the aims of all the plans after 1961 had been unfulfilled. Thus gross output was said to have increased by 85 per cent in 1951–5, and was still up by about 40 per cent in 1966–70, but it only increased by about 20 per cent in the plan of 1976–80. The growth of Soviet consumption was higher than the US between 1950 and 1980, but this was not surprising given the low point from which the Soviets began, and other capitalist countries – West Germany, France and Japan, for instance – have easily out-matched them. It has already been seen that the 'extensive' growth favoured by Stalin had been quite successful in the early stages of Soviet industrialisation and post-war reconstruction, but it was costly, wasteful and inefficient once a high degree of industrialisation was achieved.

In 1980 the state Planning Commission, GOSPLAN, was trying to co-ordinate the production of about four million different products in 50 000 factories. The challenge was an impossible one and the result was that, sometime after 1975, the USSR slipped into a position of zero growth (taking into consideration population changes and the impact of hidden inflation). The farms produced insufficient food, factory workers lacked incentives to work, absenteeism and alcoholism were rife (alcohol was one of the few growth industries), management and officials accepted bribes and lied about production targets, queues at official shops were larger than ever, and a black market had grown up. To make matters worse the Soviet population boom, which had fuelled Stalin's expansion, was now coming to an end (except in the Muslim areas of central Asia). Even natural resources were becoming exhausted. Signs around 1980 that oil supplies had reached their peak were particularly worrying because under Brezhnev much reliance was placed on oil. It was a cheap energy source, production of which had quadrupled in 1960–80. It was a major source of foreign earnings, yet it also helped the USSR continue to survive without  substantial foreign trade and to hold onto its control over Eastern Europe, which was provided with oil on generous terms. Oil supplies helped the USSR avoid the major crisis in 1973, provoked by OPEC price increases, which gravely harmed Western economic performance. Oil also accounted for most of the growth that did occur in the Soviet economy in the 1970s, helping to pay for agricultural investment, hydroelectricity schemes and educational improvements, as well as rearmament and the campaign in Afghanistan. A decline in oil production, therefore, could call the whole economic system into question.

Brezhnev's successors after 1982 would have to face up to the problems of an ageing population and stalling oil production, but after 1975 other difficulties were already clear enough and the response to them was inadequate. In fact the main attempt to create greater economic efficiency under Brezhnev had come ten years earlier, in the so-called 'Kosygin reforms' of September 1965. These changes, identified with the prime minister, basically kept the Stalinist economic system in place but sought to develop 'economic pragmatism' by reducing the amounts of detailed target-setting from GOSPLAN, amalgamating some enterprises and decentralising decisions to managers. Managers now had some direct contact with their suppliers, helping to reduce supply bottlenecks or shortages. Bonus systems were also changed to encourage a reduction in production costs. The reforms, however, were begun on a narrow front – in contrast to the sudden upheavals favoured by Khruschev – and only gradually extended. This allowed conservatives in the party and government to undermine them. GOSPLAN still directed the main inputs and outputs in the economy, local managers could not alter their overall production targets and there was no attempt to create a real market, where producers responded directly to popular demand for goods. Any move towards a market-based system would have led to inequalities of wealth, meant even less motivation in the state sector, encouraged the black market, reduced the Communist party's control in society, and ultimately have called Communist ideology itself into question. Other reforms were introduced in 1979 which allowed enterprises a greater say in setting production plans, but these still had to work within the overall context of the Five Year Plans.

Improvements in agriculture also proved inadequate. Social security payments were extended to collective farmers in November 1964, and regular wages were paid to farm workers instead of the cumbersome Stalinist system of rewards according to production levels. Farmers were no longer treated like lower-class citizens. Investment increased in agriculture, higher prices were paid by the government for produce and some of Khruschev's policies, including the decentralisation of tractor production, were abandoned. This gradually brought some beneficial results, as meat, milk and fertiliser production increased. And yet, as in the industrial sphere, by the end of the Brezhnev area Soviet agricultural growth had ceased. In some areas, like milk and fruit, output actually fell after 1975. Agricultural production and consumption were below even the East European average, food queues were lengthening, and in a speech of October 1981 Brezhnev acknowledged that agriculture was the USSR's most pressing economic problem. This was despite the fact that the country had the largest area of arable land in the world, and despite over a quarter of all investment being devoted to agriculture. Alongside unproductive defence spending, agricultural investment was absorbing a crippling amount of national wealth, and also made the country vulnerable to outside pressures since more agricultural purchases on the world market, especially of grain, were needed in the 1970s.

The reasons for this poor agricultural performance were many. Some things the government could not help, such as climatic changes that made harvests so unpredictable. A record harvest in 1978, for example, was followed by several bad years. Most problems, however, could be laid at the door of an inefficient, centrally-planned system which failed to link farm production to market demands. The government's refusal to increase food prices after 1961, despite increasing agricultural costs and higher individual incomes, meant that, whereas most people wanted to eat more meat, farmers found it cheaper to grow large amounts of potatoes and cabbage. Basically, peasants still felt distrusted by a government which sent them instructions from above, showing no understanding of local farming conditions. Young people tended to leave the land for the towns, farmers did the minimum amount of work to fulfil targets, absenteeism was rife, and factory workers had to be drafted in from the towns to collect harvests. Huge collective farms and state farms proved difficult to manage, machinery was of low quality and poorly maintained and rural transport was inadequate. Despite official discouragement peasants concentrated increasingly on growing high value products, such as meat and fruit, on their private plots for direct sale in the towns. By 1982 nearly a quarter of agricultural output came from these plots. In May 1982 the government launched a new 'Food Programme' designed to achieve greater self-sufficiency, especially in grain production, by 1990. There were to be new labour incentives, improvements in machinery and infrastructure and organisational changes at the top. Yet these simply tinkered with a system which had already proved unable to answer Soviet needs.

For all its growing economic problems, the Brezhnev era did not see any widespread political opposition. After the trial of Daniel and Sinyavsky in 1966, the KGB infiltrated and destroyed dissident groups quickly. Restrictions existed both on travel abroad and travel within the USSR, so that few Soviet people had any idea about alternatives to Communism and it was difficult to spread discontent. There were some defectors to the West including, embarrassingly, Stalin's daughter Svetlana. The Western press took a great interest in dissidents among the Soviet intelligentsia. Dissident activity was encouraged by détente in the 1970s and several groups were established to monitor Soviet human rights policy after the 1975 Helsinki Accords. The West also pressed for Jewish emigration from the USSR after 1971. An important element in the dissent was the underground movement in the regions, especially the Baltic states, the Ukraine and Armenia. Another problem was the fate of the Crimean Tartars and Volga Germans, moved from their homes *en masse* by Stalin. In 1967 these groups were legally rehabilitated by the leadership, but they were not allowed to return to their original homelands because of the upheaval this could cause, and so their resentment of Soviet rule continued.

Nonetheless, even taken together, these diverse opposition groups were a minority in Soviet society, and active opposition was generally sporadic: short-lived strikes organised by 'free trades unions'; a demonstration in Moscow against the invasion of Czechoslovakia in 1968 and another by Crimean Tartars in 1969; isolated bread riots in times of shortage; a bomb explosion in Moscow in 1977, evidently planted by an Armenian group. Dissident groups proved more long-lasting in the 1970s but they numbered only thousands in a population of 270 million, they were often educated intellectuals with little support from the wider population and the demise of détente after 1979 freed the KGB to deal with them harshly. The writer Solzhenitsyn had already been exiled abroad in February 1974. The scientist Andrei Sakharov was exiled internally, to Gorki, in January 1980. Lesser figures were put in psychiatric homes or labour camps, and in September 1982 Yuri Orlov's Helsinki Monitoring Group was forced to disband. The successful destruction of opposition highlighted the fact that, whatever its economic inefficiencies, the Soviet political system did possess some resilience. Its survival did not, by any means, rely only on the KGB apparatus. The Communist party, with its secure position and privileges, remained the vital cement which held society together. State control of the media, the massaging of statistics and avoidance of foreign contacts, meant that the scale of problems could be disguised from the people. Living standards, even if low by Western standards, had still improved under Brezhnev. A large nuclear arsenal, the space programme and sporting excellence buttressed national pride. Soviet people were shielded from the inflation and unemployment of the capitalist world in a society which, despite the privileges of the *nomenklatura*, was still quite egalitarian. In any case, in a society where dissent could cost you your job, your children's education and perhaps your freedom, most people proved too apathetic or fearful to indulge in opposition.

Brezhnev, after the upheavals of the Khruschev era, proved a cautious, conservative leader who maintained the Stalinist economic model and stabilised the position of the party and government bureaucracies. Only nine people were removed from the Politburo in Brezhnev's 18-year leadership, compared to 24 in Khruschev's nine-year predominance after 1954. Until 1975 at least the Brezhnev years had seen economic expansion, more consumer goods, an active foreign policy and the recognition of Soviet equality by a troubled United States. But this success was bought at the price of stagnation in what was already, at most, an inefficient socio-economic system. Defence spending was huge, agriculture was a disaster, technology was poor, economic targets were unfulfilled, an energy crisis was looming. In the late 1970s economic growth had come to an end, yet the Soviet people – who had come to expect rising standards – were still without adequate social welfare, housing or transport. Perhaps the most worrying of all was that the Soviet system seemed incapable of renewing itself. Genuine idealism about Marxist-Leninism was now a rarity. The Communist party, although it could not be described as a closed ruling class, had become dominated by educated male Russians from white-collar backgrounds, and its members were susceptible to the temptations of careerism, materialism and corruption. The party leadership on the other hand had become, like Brezhnev himself, ageing conservatives, the average age of the Politburo having risen in 1964–82 from 55 to 68. It would be ridiculous of course to blame all the problems on the Soviet President. After Khruschev's failed reforms, and given the power of the Communist party in October 1964, Brezhnev had arguably been forced to maintain the existing system as best he could. However, by putting the possession of power before reform, Brezhnev had condemned his heirs to a major crisis. When he died on 10 November 1982 it was not obvious who would succeed him or how they could deal with the daunting problems he left behind.

## The Crisis of Communism and Gorbachev's 'Perestroika', 1982–9

If Brezhnev had a preference about who should succeed him it was probably his old political ally, the conservative Konstantin Chernenko. He, however, was quickly out-manoeuvred in the struggle for power by Yuri Andropov. The former KGB chief had become the head of party ideology in May 1982, following the death of the dogmatic Mikhail Suslov. Andropov was not only calculating, ruthless and ambitious but also competent, incorruptible and in favour of modernisation. He had built up an alliance of supporters among those bureaucrats, KGB officers and party men who wished to crack down on corruption, re-invigorate the party and create a more efficient government – ideas which were particularly popular with younger leaders. The fact that he had left his KGB post in May helped both his challenge to Chernenko and his international standing, but stories in the West that he was an open-minded, liberal leader were mythical. Andropov *did* want reform, but he did *not* want liberalism. Instead he wished to make the Soviet system work more efficiently and end the stagnation of the Brezhnev years.

It has been seen that even Brezhnev's rule had been able to survive without either facing large-scale opposition or relying on Stalinist terror-tactics. The USSR, for all its faults, was a Superpower and a major industrial force with a large population, an enormous geographical area and considerable natural resources. By distancing itself from the world economy it had avoided the depressions suffered by the West in 1929, 1973 or 1979. It still seemed, therefore, to have a great deal of potential and there were various possible courses open to Soviet leaders if they chose to abandon Brezhnev's consensus-seeking. Then again, none of the possible choices was easy. The widespread adoption of market elements did not seem likely in 1982, since it would demand radical economic upheaval and would probably also necessitate a more sophisticated civil society with pluralist politics, something the Communist party would be loath to accept. The Soviets could have reneged on the debts they had built up with Western banks in 1970s and adopted an 'autarchic' approach, cutting themselves off again from the world economy. But this might also mean accepting some visible inflation and unemployment in the economy, it would upset other Eastern bloc countries who had come to rely on Western trade, and it was a dangerous course given that the USSR might exhaust some of its natural resources in the near future. A more likely development was that the Kremlin would reform the existing system, though even this left the question, what exactly should be done. Conservatives might favour a more centralised system, less emphasis on consumerism and a re-invigoration of Leninist idealism. But other reformers preferred to achieve efficiency by the Khruschev route of de-centralisation and even limited market elements, designed to answer consumer demands, and improve service and quality. Whatever reforms were adopted, they would have to secure change without alienating the power elites and the people, as Khruschev had done. The Communist party machine, for example, would not easily accept a reduction of its privileged position; the military would not easily accept a reduction in arms spending; and the people would not easily accept price increases or unemployment if market methods were adopted. This raised the whole, daunting issue of *whether* the system could be reformed. Could inefficient managers, appointed because of their loyalty to the party, become competent hard-working entrepreneurs? Could the Soviet workforce be fired by a new idealism and end its absenteeism and shoddy workmanship? Resolving the country's problems would not be easy – especially after Brezhnev had avoided telling the people that any serious problems existed.

The general lines of the debate on reform were only beginning and, although Andropov provided some basis for later change, he did not live long enough to make a real impact. He himself was to a large extent a victim of the Brezhnev era. At 68, the oldest man to become party leader, Andropov had only begun to replace Brezhnevites with younger men when he became ill in Summer 1983. Among those he supported were Yegor Ligachev, who supported his disciplinarian views, Viktor Chebrikov, who became KGB chief, Nikolai Ryzhkov, who became a party Secretary and Mikhail Gorbachev, who since 1978 had had the difficult role of supervising agriculture and who was the youngest Politburo member. By the time he died on 9 February 1984 Andropov had failed to secure Gorbachev's place as his successor and instead, five days later, the un-inspiring Chernenko inherited the position he had hoped for in November 1982. For Brezhnevites, who had felt threatened by Andropov's tentative changes, Chernenko seemed as reliable and safe as their old leader. Nevertheless, Chernenko appeared to recognise the need for reduced arms spending, more consumer products and better relations with the West. And he could only stave off greater changes. Even at Andropov's funeral he looked unwell and as leader he spent much of the time outside the public view. It appears that, in order to become leader, Chernenko recognised that Gorbachev would succeed him and it was the latter, with his young reformist allies, who established predominance in the party and government during 1984. His only strong, hard-line opponent was Grigori Romanov, the party's Secretary for Defence.

Chernenko finally died on 10 March 1985 and Romanov, hoping to buy time for his own bid for power, suggested that another ageing Brezhnevite, the Moscow party boss Viktor Grishin, should become party leader. But foreign minister Gromyko (himself 75) and KGB chief Chebrikov both supported Gorbachev's candidature, and the party's Central Committee agreed. At last, after more than two years of old and ailing leaders, the Communist party had a general Secretary who, although 54, was the youngest Politburo member, the youngest Eastern European leader and appreciably younger than America's President Reagan. In contrast to his predecessors Gorbachev had no memory of the purges and little of the war. He had only joined the party in October 1952, a few months before Stalin's death. Like many younger party members he was well educated, his outlook had been moulded by regional politics and he was interested in ideas for reform. He immediately began to portray himself as a dynamic leader, confirming that East–West arms talks were to be re-opened, and using Chernenko's funeral as an occasion to establish contacts with Western leaders. Yet, whatever the appearance of 'burying the past' with Chernenko, there were doubts about how far Gorbachev would, or could reform. Most outside observers had given up hope that the rigid Soviet system could really change. In part this was because Western observers saw little chance for far-reaching reform in a totalitarian regime. How could fundamental changes be made in a state where the people, party and government were supposedly one? Where were ideas for reform to be generated if there was no real civil society, no open debate, no legal opposition? What Gorbachev and his allies soon revealed was that, even under Brezhnev, atrophy was not complete. The political system had allowed them to come to the fore, and they were certainly ready to contemplate change.

In March 1985 Gorbachev faced a number of challenges. He had to consolidate his position by replacing leading Brezhnevites with his own nominees; he must decide what changes were needed, prepare the Soviet people for reform and then carry through the necessary measures; and all the time he had to cope with other day-to-day problems involved in running government, which could easily divert attention from long-term plans. From the first he showed a determination to 'lead from the front', but he often seemed uncertain about exactly what reforms he wanted. What he did call for was a change of attitudes, for honesty about the USSR's problems and discussion about how they could be overcome. Two of his principal concepts were 'glasnost' and 'perestroika'. 'Glasnost' meant 'openness', not in the sense of wanting free speech in the Western style, but rather in order to bring 'self criticism' to bear on Soviet society. Gorbachev hoped this would strengthen Communism by leading people to root out inefficiency and corruption. 'Perestroika' was a call to 're-structure' society, to bring such changes as greater discipline at work, improved management and the introduction of new technology. Again, this was probably *not* designed to change the fundamental nature of the USSR at first, but rather to re-kindle ideological commitment among the people and apply scientific methods to economic production. This was matched by 'new thinking' abroad where Gorbachev pursued détente with the West, retreated from involvement in Third World conflicts and re-established links to China.

Domestically, Gorbachev's policies began cautiously in 1985 with changes in the leadership. On 23 April Yegor Ligachev, Nikolai Ryzhkov and Viktor Chebrikov, all members of the 'Andropov coalition' of reformers, were made full Politburo members. Ligachev, now second to Gorbachev in the political hierarchy, also became the Communist ideology chief. Chebrikov's promotion reflected the continuing importance of the KGB and contrasted to the position of the Defence minister, Sergei Sokolov, who was only a non-voting member of the Politburo (a lesser position than a full member). This showed, at an early date, Gorbachev's desire to control the military and reduce defence spending. Other changes followed. In early July Gorbachev's rival Romanov was retired from his position, and Edvard Shevardnadze replaced Gromyko as foreign minister; on 27 September Ryzhkov replaced the ageing Tikhonov as prime minister; and in December another of Gorbachev's Brezhnevite opponents, Moscow party boss Grishin, was replaced by Boris Yeltsin. Romanov and Grishin had thus paid the price for their failure to defeat Gorbachev in March whilst Gromyko, who had supported Gorbachev's succession became Soviet President, but without real power. Shevardnadze, Yeltsin and Ryzhkov were all similar to Gorbachev in background – educated, experienced in industry, with regional political backgrounds. Gorbachev made other personnel changes throughout the party and government. The energetic new leader also developed a Western-style image, frequently appearing in public and being ready to answer questions. At first, however, his speeches were short on detail and treated by people as just 'another' propaganda campaign. The government tried to overcome such apathy by launching campaigns against alcoholism and corruption. Two leading officials were executed for accepting bribes and a former minister committed suicide after his trial for corruption. But this emphasis on discipline, alongside Gorbachev's support for puritanical leaders like Ligachev and Chebrikov, led to fears in the West that the USSR was becoming more, not less, illiberal.

1986 saw more certain signs of 'glasnost' with greater criticism, not only of individuals but also of institutions and policies, appearing in newspapers. Debate began on previously 'closed' issues – the role of women, the environment, crime. Political discussion was stimulated by the Twenty-seventh Communist Party Congress of February–March. A new party programme (ordered by Brezhnev in 1981 to replace Khruschev's ambitious 1961 programme) and a draft party statute were published before the Congress, to provide a basis for discussion. Neither document was particularly radical, but they continued to emphasise the need for greater efficiency and the fact that debate occurred at all was radical enough. The Congress saw over 40 per cent of members of the party's Central

Committee changed, but there was no dramatic speech like Khruschev's in 1956. Gorbachev *did* assert the need for major economic reform, but introduced no major economic changes. The Moscow economic ministries were re-organised in 1986–6 but policy under the new 1986–90 plan was still based on a heavily centralised system with incentives to workers to increase their output. The explosion at Chernobyl nuclear reactor near Kiev in April raised public awareness of environmental issues, and also provided the Soviet people with their first real 'media event'. But even after visiting the regions in Spring and Summer 1986, and talking to people about the economy at first hand, Gorbachev was slow to introduce reform. In November a new law extended the opportunities for private enterprise, but only in the service sector. Compared by many to Khruschev, another reformer with a populist style, Gorbachev perhaps wished to avoid his predecessor's mistake of introducing hasty, untested measures. But it also seems that the new leader took time to appreciate that, beneath all the false statistics, he had inherited an economic disaster from Brezhnev. In January 1987 Gorbachev frankly admitted to the Central Committee that economic problems were much worse than anyone feared. Another reason for delay was because it was important for Gorbachev to win genuine popular support for reform, not simply to use Stalinist-style coercion. Only by building up popular support and fostering honest debate about problems could he hope to overcome apathy and corruption within the government and party.

In 1987 the emphasis rested very much on political, rather than economic, reform. In December 1986 Andrei Sakharov and other dissidents had begun to be freed from internal exile and prison. Then, the following month, Gorbachev called a Central Committee meeting at which he insisted there was 'no alternative' to radical change. Now that he had manipulated his supporters into high office he seemed to aim at a major political transformation with the use of non-party experts in government, and the genuine protection of citizens' rights. How far this process would go remained unclear but June saw a few multi-candidate elections at local level, Gorbachev himself published a book on *Perestroika* and in August a group of independent political organisations met in Moscow. Gorbachev had thus moved from encouragement of discussion, through the toleration of diversity in a one-party state, to the apparent acceptance of political opposition. But these rapid political changes clearly provoked disagreements among the Andropov Coalition. As seen earlier, there was no clear consensus on how to reform after Brezhnev. By 1987 'Conservatives' like Ligachev and Chebrikov favoured disciplinarian reform without undermining the predominance of the Communist party. But others, especially Boris Yeltsin, believed that Soviet problems were too deep-seated for efficiency drives to suffice, argued that economic improvement relied on political reform, and hoped to move towards genuine mass involvement in politics and market-based economics. Arguments on these issues led in October to Yeltsin's dismissal from his post. But, in contrast to earlier expellees from the Politburo, he proved able to exploit his popularity and the new spirit of openness and remained politically active. His outspoken manner would continue to embarrass the General Secretary.

Following Yeltsin's dismissal, 1988 proved a difficult year for Gorbachev. This was not surprising since it began in January with, at last, a major package of economic reforms. 'Self-financing' was to be introduced in 1988–9, under which state enterprises were to draw up their own plans to meet customers' orders, and were to pay their way. Failure to be profitable could lead to merger or closure, so that 'open unemployment' was now a possibility. Efficiency was further encouraged by a process of dividing profits between bonus payments, welfare provisions, re-investment and payments to the state. To encourage workers' support and provide a democratic element, the reform also introduced elections for managerial positions, and it was accompanied by revelations about the real state of the economy under Brezhnev. These reforms, for which premier Ryzhkov and his government were particularly responsible, actually had severe limitations. They continued to operate under a centralised planning system and there was no reform of prices. Foreign trade was minimal. Nonetheless, the continuing drive for political democracy as well as economic efficiency provoked more trouble in the Politburo. Since November 1987 Gorbachev had encouraged criticism of Stalinism, but many Communists were worried by this. In March 1988, a widely-circulated article by the conservative Nina Andreyeeva, marked the beginning of a backlash against Gorbachev, whose policies now threatened various important groups, including the military (upset by arms cuts and, in April 1988, the decision to quit Afghanistan), factory managers (whose authority was undermined by the economic reforms), the KGB (faced by the need to monitor opposition groups) and the party bureaucracy (whose monopoly on power seemed threatened). Further offence was caused to conservatives when Gorbachev's political reforms threatened the unity of the multi-national Empire inherited from the Tsars. The USSR was made up of 15 republics of varying sizes. Regionalism, like so much else, had been forcibly repressed in the past but as early as December 1986 'glasnost' had been followed by riots in the republic of Kazakhstan, and after February 1988 there was a series of bloody clashes between Armenians and Azerbaijanis over territorial claims in the Caucasus.

In June–July 1988 a special party conference met to discuss reform, and saw open debates and disagreements for the first time at a Communist gathering since the 1920s. The special conference had been planned for 18 months and it decided on a range of reforms. In future there were to be contested elections of party representatives and members of the Soviets (the representative bodies at various levels of local and national government). The most important elections would be that of a Congress of People's Deputies to represent the whole country. This in turn would elect the Supreme Soviet (the USSR's parliament). There was also to be a clearer separation between the party and government, and there would be a limit of two five-year terms for holding major office. The last reform of course echoed one of Khruschev's changes. Discredited Brezhnevites remained quiet during the conference, but there were clear divisions between those loyal to Gorbachev, conservatives like Ligachev, and radicals like Boris Yeltsin. Gorbachev's criticisms of the command economy and of the way the 1917 Revolution had been warped by Stalin led to more resentment among conservatives, and in August – whilst the General Secretary was on holiday – Ligachev apparently tried to form a conservative alliance in the Politburo against Gorbachev. However, the latter's success in bringing his supporters into government paid off. Alexander Yakovlev, who had joined the Politburo the previous year, led the resistance to Ligachev and in September Gorbachev hit back by demoting both Ligachev (who now took charge of agricultural affairs) and Chebrikov (who was removed from the Politburo altogether in September 1989). The man who replaced Ligachev as ideology chief was another Gorbachev ally, Vadim Medvedev, and Gorbachev himself finally replaced the veteran Gromyko as President. This consolidation of power in the Politburo was followed in October by the re-organisation of the central party institutions, which reduced the number of full-time officials and gave Central Committee members a more active role in decisions. Thus Gorbachev had maintained the impetus for change and asserted the predominance of his own gradual style of reform over both Ligachev's conservative views and Yeltsin's radicalism.

Most impressive of all Gorbachev's changes was the election of the Congress of People's Deputies on 26 March. By Western standards this election fell short of real democracy. 2250 representatives were elected nation-wide, but 750 seats were reserved for groups like the Communist party, Komsomol and the trades unions. The Communist party dictated the choice of many candidates and in areas like Central Asia voters automatically chose Communist representatives. Compared to the past, however, it was still a revolutionary event. Many seats *were* contested, some Communist representatives were defeated, Yeltsin and the dissident Sakharov (who died later in the year) were elected. Although no formal opposition parties existed there were cultural, environmental and regional groups who supported independent candidates. The elections could thus be said to mark the end of one-party rule and showed that opposition was possible without violence. The elections were followed by intense debate when the Congress met. On 26 May the representatives elected a new 542-member Supreme Soviet, which would meet on a more regular basis than the Congress. Again conservative-minded Communists tried to restrict the democratic element in this process, and at first succeeded in keeping Yeltsin off the Supreme Soviet. But this provoked such intense criticism that one member who had been elected stepped down, allowing Yeltsin to take his place. Another important election was that of the Soviet Presidency, which Gorbachev won by a handsome margin. Furthermore, on 25 April a large number of older representatives were persuaded to 'resign' from the party's Central Committee. By now few leading figures, other than Gorbachev and his allies, survived in leading positions from the Chernenko period. Together with the end of involvement in Afghanistan in February 1989, and the successful completion of an Intermediate-range

Nuclear forces treaty with America, all this served to mark a major, rapid success for Gorbachev's 'new thinking'.

Nonetheless, the elections of 1989 only occurred amidst grave doubts about Gorbachev's ability to retain power and restructure the government and economy. Economic reforms, limited as they were, had apparently made matters worse. With state prices still unrelated to costs and with peasants anxious to concentrate on their private plots, the supply of meat and dairy products had fallen and queues had lengthened. Industry was little better: in 1988 soap, razor blades and refrigerators disappeared from the shops. Workers were unused to the idea of working for profit, managers lacked Western-style information technology and few Soviets had market skills. People were being asked to make greater sacrifices, to work harder, to throw off alcoholism, absenteeism, and the 'black market', and to produce better quality goods. But they did not see any immediate reward for this. Social welfare as still poor, salaries were low, housing overcrowded. Gorbachev often said change was 'irreversible' but his calls for 'perestroika' were marred by uncertainty about where exactly he was taking the country. Radicals claimed that his experiments were too tentative, that he was merely tinkering with the command economy and must move more rapidly to a market economy, destroying the power of the central economic ministers. But conservatives, like Ligachev, played on popular fears of unemployment, inflation and inequalities under a reformed system. March 1987 had seen the first Soviet bankruptcy; prices in the new co-operative shops and restaurants were far too high for most people to afford; and the advent of large wage differentials caused bitter resentment among Soviet workers raised on egalitarianism.

Gorbachev could point out the weaknesses of the old Brezhnevite system: the failure to build sufficient houses, roads, schools and hospitals; the huge state subsidies needed to hold prices down to unrealistic levels which meant that the USSR had an enormous budget deficit; the growing  debts to the West in the 1970s; the privileges of the *nomenklatura* elite; the reliance on oil output which since 1982 had ceased to increase much. But Gorbachev's criticisms undermined respect for Communist rule without creating a new idealistic fervour to take its place. 'Openness' about the failures of the past only led to more 'open' evidence of opposition to Communist rule. A series of strikes broke out in the mines in Summer 1989. There was a large pro-reform demonstration in Moscow in October. Inter-community unrest went on between Armenians and Azerbaijanis, and broke out in 1989 between Georgians and Abkhazians; whilst in Lithuania, Latvia and Estonia there were calls for independence; and there were also signs of nationalist discontent in Moldavia and the Ukraine.

It was clear at the end of 1989 that problems were likely to get even worse before they got better. On the economic side Ryzhkov and the government ministers could no longer avoid cuts in state subsidies to agriculture and industry, even if this meant higher prices, unemployment, and the re-deployment of workers. New reform proposals in December  were, however, gradualistic. On the political side the power of established elites in the armed forces, secret police and party bureaucracy were likely to be further undermined, but these institutions were growing restive and beginning – ironically – to use 'glasnost' for their own purposes, openly criticising the General Secretary. Gorbachev still controlled the main levers of power, could pose as a 'middle man' between Ligachev and Yeltsin, and had no obvious successor. He had had a major impact on the international scene and had brought astonishing changes to a system which, in 1982, had appeared moribund. Yet the controversy which surrounded his policies also called into question the whole Soviet system. Could the USSR be transformed into a market economy with democratic institutions, part of an independent world trading system? Or would Gorbachev be overthrown by the conservatives? Then again, might not the Union break up? Events in Eastern Europe at the end of 1989 could only itensify this debate.

# 8
# The Failure of Communism in Eastern Europe

## Communism and Stalinisation, 1945–53

Despite attempts to establish democracies in Eastern Europe\* after the First World War, most of the region was ruled by right-wing authoritarian regimes long before Hitler's conquests in the late 1930s. Following the turmoil of the inter-war years Eastern Europe then faced even greater suffering in the Second World War. The Germans and Italians exploited much of the area for labour, raw materials and agricultural produce, millions of lives were lost, the Jewish minority (particularly large in Poland) was subjected to Hitler's 'Final Solution' and borders were re-drawn to suit his 'New Order'. Hungary, Romania, Bulgaria and Finland actually became Germany's allies and all but Bulgaria joined in the invasion of Russia after 1941. Then the Red Army's advance towards Berlin in 1944–5 brought even more upheaval. Stalin had disbanded the Communist International, with its commitment to world revolution, to please the Western allies in 1943 and local Communists in Eastern Europe were generally few. Nonetheless, these facts did not prevent Soviet domination of Eastern Europe from replacing that of Nazis.

Not all areas of Eastern Europe fell under Soviet rule. The Western powers were generally powerless to resist the spread of Communism thanks to the power of the Red Army, but British troops landed in Greece in 1944 with Stalin's approval and Austria (like Germany, into which it had been absorbed in 1938) was placed under joint Allied occupation in 1945. Both these countries were able to establish independent, non-Communist governments. Further north, Finland, which had established its independence from Russia in 1917, had withdrawn from the war in 1944 without being subjected to Soviet occupation or a change of government. By agreeing to a non-aggression pact with Moscow in 1948, it too managed to preserve its freedom. In Yugoslavia and Albania,

\* I have used the familiar term 'Eastern Europe' to describe the lands between the Soviet Union and the Stettin–Trieste line, although 'central' or 'east-central' Europe makes better geographical sense.

on the other hand, *Communist* regimes were established at the end of the war, but these did not prove to be *Soviet* puppets. Instead, in these two countries local Communists were strong enough to install themselves in power, and did not fall under the Red Army's control. This chapter will pay some attention to Communism in Yugoslavia and Albania, but the main focus will be on countries which became fully Soviet satellites after 1945: Poland, Czechoslovakia, Hungary, East Germany, Romania and Bulgaria. All these countries were 'liberated', in whole or to a large extent, by the Red Army in 1944–5.

In the countries subjected to Soviet domination after 1945 indigenous Communism was weak and revolution was enforced 'from above' with Soviet assistance. The pattern was generally for the Soviets to support anti-fascist coalition, or 'front', governments which included Communists in important ministries. Communists built up their support and took key positions in local government, the army and police. The governments began to introduce Stalinist-type reforms in the economy: breaking up the old aristocratic estates and sharing them out between landless labourers and smallholders, nationalising important industrial and mining concerns (many of which had been taken over by Germany during the war) and beginning central planning. Gradually the established parties were destroyed, along with other traditional elements, such as the Romanian and Bulgarian monarchies. Non-Communist leaders were exiled, imprisoned or murdered, and rigged elections were held to try to legitimise Communist rule. Socialists were forced to unite with the Communists in single proletarian parties. In actual fact, since everyone knew the elections were rigged, the new regimes never did obtain real legitimacy in the eyes of the people. Instead, whatever the Marxist insistence on the 'inevitability' of Communism, the Eastern European governments were an alien political form, ultimately enforced by Soviet bayonets. Stalin may have used local Communists to establish control of Eastern Europe but they were dependent on him to remain in office.

Soviet domination was effectively the rule by February 1948 in Eastern Europe, the month when Czechoslovakia became a one-party state. The process of Communisation was helped by the weakness of the Eastern European states after the war. With communications disrupted, industrial output decimated, livestock slaughtered and harvests reduced they were easy victims for Stalin who was able to enforce a new territorial settlement on the area and to demand reparations from ex-enemy states. Direct Soviet rule was extended to eastern Poland, Bessarabia (from Romania), sub-Carpathian Ukraine (from Czechoslovakia) and parts of East Prussia (from Germany). Poland was literally shifted westwards as its losses to the USSR were compensated by gains from Germany. The establishment of totalitarian rule by 1948 did not mean an end to the revolutionary changes. Soviet policy instead entered a second phase (arguably beginning with the foundation of Cominform in September 1947) whereby Moscow's domination tightened still further, until in 1949–53 the local regimes could be described as 'Stalinist'. They were united not only against the

198

capitalist West but also against the independent policy of Yugoslavia's leader Tito who was expelled from Cominform in mid-1948. As in Russia, Stalin's use of terror tactics extended even to the Communist party. Those Communists who had shown 'nationalist' tendencies in the past, or who differed from their pro-Soviet colleagues, were now subjected to imprisonment and execution. Once again the West did little to prevent Soviet domination. Instead, Eastern Europeans became the principal victims of a system whereby peace was kept on the Continent because the West did *not* interfere in the Soviet sphere.

Eastern Europe had, by 1953, become a mirror image of the Soviet system, economically, politically and socially. The collectivisation of land began, agriculture was ruthlessly exploited, and heavy industrialisation was pursued under centralised Five Year Plans. There was genuine support for change from long-standing Communists, anti-fascists, trades unionists and those who gained from the reforms, especially party officials, bureaucrats and managers. Otherwise – as in the USSR – the use of police-state methods, the control of the Communist party over employment, and political apathy after years of upheaval, helped secure the Stalinists in power. Mass organisations, the press, freedom of movement, all were under the control of a centralised leadership. In 1945 much of eastern Europe was a peasant-aristocratic society, as unsuited to proletarian revolution as Russia in 1917. But the Communists rapidly created a Soviet-style social system. The old ruling classes were destroyed, along with middle-class groups, like artisans, businessmen and shopkeepers. The independent peasantry proved more resilient but collectivisation was eventually achieved, except in Poland, by about 1961. Professional groups, such as doctors, journalists and engineers were put into state employment, and ideals based on property and individualism gave way to nationalisation and egalitarianism. The urban working class, on the other hand, was greatly expanded as industrialisation gathered pace. About a quarter of the Hungarian work-force were manual labourers in 1945. By 1970 it was 50 per cent. But workers were subjected to heavy production demands, allowed few consumer goods and were unprotected by the official trades unions.

This process of Stalinisation was carried out with little regard to local problems. In particular it ignored the fact that Eastern European states, unlike the USSR, had limited raw materials. Nonetheless, the Stalinist economic model proved as effective in achieving rapid growth in Eastern Europe as it had been in the Soviet Union. Industrial output more than doubled in 1949–53 as the new governments mobilised previously untapped resources, drew on a plentiful supply of labour (including women workers) and made up for the losses of wartime. Only in 1952–3 did local Communist leaders become concerned about the growing evidence of raw material shortages, low agricultural output and shoddy workmanship. Even then they tended, like the Kremlin, to blame the problems on planning inadequacies rather than basic flaws in the system. Neither did they complain about the extent of Soviet domination. Instead, local leaders accepted Soviet influence over the armed forces and police, and allowed the USSR substantial economic benefits under the terms of the 'Council for Mutual Economic Aid' (COMECON) established in 1949. Thus the Soviet share of Czech trade mushroomed from one-twentieth in 1945 to more than one-third in 1955.

It has been said that Soviet domination was established according to a general pattern. In every country, however, there were different conditions at work and variations in the pace of Communist take-overs. Poland was the largest east European state, one of the first to be liberated and, given its strategic position between the USSR and Germany, the most vital for Stalin to control. A Polish resistance and government-in-exile existed during the war, Poland was strongly Catholic and the country had resisted Russian rule in the past. But Poland was weakened by six million wartime deaths and large territorial changes. The Soviets had already massacred Polish army officers at Katyn and elsewhere in 1939–40, after annexing parts of the country under the Hitler–Stalin pact. Then the Warsaw rising of August–October 1944, the attempt by the 'Polish Home Army' to establish an independent government, was crushed by the Germans as the Soviets looked on. Stalin ignored Poland's government-in-exile and instead gave his support to a group of Moscow-trained Communists, who joined with local Communists (like Wladyslaw Gomulka) to form a 'Committee of National Liberation' in August 1944. This group took over the administration of the country, passed a radical land reform in September and was recognised by Stalin in January 1945 as the 'provisional government' of Poland. A guerrilla war was maintained against the new regime until 1947, but the Western Allies agreed to recognise Stalin's puppet government in June 1945, after it was widened to include the liberal Stanislaw Mikolajcyk, a leader of the government-in-exile. Any idea that the Communists and Mikolajcyk could establish a democratic constitution proved illusory however. Non-Communist politicians were terrorised by the secret police, and elections were rigged in January 1947. In February, to disguise Poland's puppet status, a new government was formed under the premiership of a Socialist, Josef Cyrankiewicz, who proved a loyal dupe of the Communists. Real power was eventually concentrated in the hands of the Communist President, Boleslaw Bierut, and Mikolajcyk finally fled from Poland in October 1947.

Stalin himself had had grave doubts about how successful Communism could be in Poland, but by 1948 about a million Poles had joined the Communist party. The split with Tito that year was followed by the denunciation of Wladyslaw Gomulka, the Communist party Secretary who had earlier talked of a 'Polish road' to Communism. In September 1948 Bierut took over the party leadership from Gomulka and three months later the Socialists were forced to unite with the Communists in a 'Polish United Workers Party'. Central planning was extended in the economy and Bierut became a miniature Stalin, complete with his own personality cult. Following more rigged elections in July 1952, Bierut made himself prime minister as well as party leader. Among those imprisoned under his rule were Gomulka (in 1953) and the leading churchman Cardinal Wyszynski.

A similarly rapid thorough Sovietisation occurred in the Balkan countries of Romania and Bulgaria. Romania's dictator, Marshal Ion Antonescu, had led his country into war with the USSR in 1941, but this proved increasingly unpopular and in June 1944 the three main democratic groups (the Social Democrats, National Liberals and Peasant Party) joined the Communists in a 'National Democratic Front'. King Michael prudently helped to overthrow Antonescu in August, formed a coalition government with only one Communist minister and, in September 1944, changed sides in the war. But by then the Red Army had invaded Romania and helped the Communists obtain important positions in the press, police and local government. The Communists, despite a lack of genuine popularity, strengthened their position in the cabinet, encouraged land seizures by peasants and began to attack the other parties. So-called 'salami tactics' were used, whereby small democratic-looking parties were formed under Communist stooges to draw off support from the legitimate political groups. The Communists faced strong opposition from Iuliu Maniu, the Peasant Party leader, but in early 1945 the Soviets forced the appointment of a Communist-dominated Government. Rigged elections were held in November 1946, Maniu was imprisoned in August 1947, Michael was forced to abdicate in December 1947 and the Social Democrats were forced to unite with the Communists in a 'Romanian Workers Party' in February 1948. A thorough nationalisation law followed in June, state farms were established and the Securitate secret police expanded. Romania's Stalin was George Gheorghieu-Dej, General Secretary of the Party and also after June 1952, prime minister.

Like Romania, Bulgaria was effectively a Soviet puppet before the war ended. Bulgaria had genuine pro-Russian sympathies, having been freed from centuries of Turkish rule with Russian help in the 1870s. Bulgaria did not take part in Hitler's invasion of the USSR but was allied to Germany and in late 1944 faced a situation similar to Romania: the Communist and democratic parties were united in a 'Fatherland Front' (formed in 1942), who formed a coalition government in September; the country was invaded by the Red Army and changed sides in October; and there was a strong Agrarian Party which challenged the Communists. Anti-Communist forces in Bulgaria, however, were weakened by the fact that the King, Simeon II, was only a child. In 1945 liberal leaders were harassed, fraudulent 'democratic' parties were formed and an election gave the Fatherland Front 86 per cent of votes. In 1946 the monarchy was abolished and the Communist leader, George Dimitrov, became premier. The Agrarian Party leader, Nikolai Petkov, was executed in September 1947. Dimitrov, the former head of the Comintern and entirely loyal to Moscow, died in July 1949 but his brother-in-law Vulko Chervenkov was able to liquidate any rivals to become party leader and premier in 1950.

In Hungary the situation was more complex and the pace of the Communist take-over slower. From 1920 to 1944 the small land-locked country had been ruled by Admiral Horthy, 'Regent' for the deposed Habsburg monarchy, who ran a conservative regime, with a parliament dominated by the landlords. In 1941 Hungarian forces joined in Hitler's invasion of Russia but in September 1944, with the Red Army marching over his border, Horthy too tried to change sides. He failed and was overthrown by the Germans, leaving Hungary to be fought over by the *Wehrmacht* and the Red Army for several months, during which time the capital Budapest was devastated. In December 1944 a 'National Independence Front' was formed, including the Communists, who went on to take several key positions in a coalition government. Land reform was promised, but in 1945 Stalin did not seem as anxious to absorb Hungary as he did Poland, Romania and Bulgaria. Elections in November 1945 gave the Communists less than one-fifth of votes compared to the Smallholder Party's 57 per cent and the premier, from February 1946 to May 1947 was the Smallholder, Ferenc Nagy. The Smallholders, however, were actually a weak amalgam of conservative groups who were easily out-manoeuvred by the united and determined Communists under Matyas Rakosi. The Communists took control of the police and administration, forced other parties into a 'Left Bloc' and in Spring 1947 used mobs to demoralise the Nagy government. In August 1947 fraudulent elections were held which made the Communists the largest party, and other parties were then destroyed. Rakosi executed his rival Laszlo Rajk, after a show trial in October 1949, and combined the positions of party leader and premier in 1952.

Czechoslovakia presented particular difficulties to Stalin's expansionism because it was an Allied state, the victim of Munich in 1938 and an inter-war liberal democracy with a government-in-exile in London under Eduard Benes. Benes was ready to respect Soviet security interests in Eastern Europe, making a friendship treaty with Stalin in December 1943 and proving ready to work with the Czech Communist leader Klement Gottwald, so there seemed no need to destroy Czechoslovakia's independence to maintain its friendship. Resentment at Anglo–French betrayal in 1938, the fact that Czechoslovakia was an industrialised state with a large proletariat, and respect for the USSR's contribution to the war, all meant that there was a genuine support for Communism in Czechoslovakia. Communists received a third of government posts in 1945 including control over the police, armed forces and information services, and in 1946 they became the largest party in elections, with 35 per cent of the vote – without the need to 'rig' the result. Thus, Gottwald legitimately became premier. Support in the country for Communism simply made the ultimate destruction of Czech democracy easier. After September 1947 the Communists began to criticise their democratic allies and to call for radical nationalisation policies. Then, in February 1948, they carried out their swift, bloodless coup, using a 'workers militia' to intimidate opponents. The liberal foreign minister, Jan Masaryk, died soon afterwards, possibly murdered, but probably by suicide. The demoralised and helpless President Beneš died in September, leaving Gottwald secure as Czechoslovakia's dictator.

The last pro-Soviet regime to be founded was that in East Germany in October 1949, but this merely formalised Communist predominance which had been enforced in April 1946 when the Soviets forced Otto Grotewohl's Social Democrats to unite with the Communists in a 'Socialist Unity Party'. Events in eastern Germany had followed a course similar to that elsewhere: Moscow-trained Communists had taken a leading role in the administration; right-wing institutions were destroyed, and nationalisation begun in 1945; and the Liberal and Christian Democratic parties were allowed to survive after 1946 only because they were utterly powerless. Elections in Berlin (under four power control) in October 1946 highlighted the fact that real support for Communism at under 20 per cent, was limited. But East Germany was founded nonetheless as a People's Republic with Walter Ulbricht the predominant leader.

There were countries where Communists were strong enough to install themselves in power. In Albania in 1944 Enver Hoxha's Communist guerrillas were able to take over the country as German occupation forces withdrew. Hoxha's opponents were wiped out, the exiled King Zog was deposed, and rigged elections were held as early as December 1944. After 1945 Hoxha increasingly stood up to the Yugoslavs who seemed bent on dominating Albania. For this reason he sided with the Soviets in their arguments with Yugoslavia in 1948, executed the pro-Tito Koci Xoxe in 1949, and enforced a rigidly Stalinist system, all without a direct Soviet presence.

In Yugoslavia, as in Albania, local partisans under Josip Broz, known as Tito, were able to liberate the country from German rule largely unaided by the Red Army. Tito's followers ruthlessly wiped out the rival, pro-Royalist resistance and those who had collaborated with the Italians and Germans during the war. Yugoslavia was re-united as a federal state in which the rights of minorities, such as the Croats, Slovenes and Albanians, were to be better respected by the previously dominant Serbs. Representatives of the pre-war royalist government were brought into a coalition in March 1945 but all had been ousted within six months; and in November rigged elections were held, followed by the creation of a one-party state and the abolition of the monarchy. By then Yugoslavia looked, to Westerners, like any other Communist state, loyal to Stalin. Nationalisation and central economic planning were introduced, a police state was created under Alexander Rankovic and Tito sometimes seemed more anti-Western in his propaganda than the Kremlin itself. Yet Tito was never a Soviet puppet. He resented the Soviet recruitment of agents in Yugoslavia, their one-sided commercial arrangements and their attempts to dictate economic policy. Stalin, on the other hand, disliked Tito's independence in foreign policy, which included discussions of a 'Balkan Federation' with Bulgaria and Albania. The development of these arguments was disguised from the West until late June 1948 when Yugoslavia was expelled from the Cominform, after which Stalin began an economic blockade of the country. To help resist the Soviets, Tito proved willing to accept Western financial aid in 1949. In 1950–1 he also introduced some innovative economic reforms, including a reversal of collectivisation in agriculture and the establishment of 'workers councils' to give employees a share in the management of factories. But fundamentally, Yugoslavia remained a police-state. Meanwhile, however embarrassing Tito's split with the Eastern bloc was to Stalin, the episode allowed the Soviet dictator to enforce even tighter control over Eastern Europe. After June 1948 it was no longer enough to be a Communist to please the Kremlin: it was also necessary to be rigidly Stalinist. Throughout the Eastern bloc the crusade against 'Titoism' meant the final consolidation of Soviet rule and the surrender by local leaders of their own right to independence.

## 'DeStalinisation' and its Aftermath, 1953–64

Events following the death of Stalin in March 1953 revealed the problems of maintaining a united system of Communist states under Kremlin control. The new Soviet collective leadership was determined to maintain its grip on the satellite states, but the relaxation of Stalinist controls on society and the 'new look' in economics, caused unease among Eastern European leaders who had modelled their political and economic systems on Stalin's. Should East Europeans remain loyal to Stalinism or try to mirror the changes taking place in the USSR? To maintain Stalinism without support could prove difficult, given the reliance of local leaders on the Kremlin to remain in power. But to adopt reform could undermine the stability of local regimes. In general the years after 1953 did see some relaxation in police state methods, Stalinist ideology was fused with a new realism about local needs and there was some attempt to emulate Soviet policy changes, with greater agricultural investment and more light industrial production, for example, and also the release of political prisoners, like Gomulka in Poland. As in Moscow in 1953–4 there were also changes in the leadership of East European states, particularly the division of powers between the party leader and prime minister. Yet in most cases reform was cautious and the leadership changes simply disguised the continued predominance of one man. Thus, in March 1953 Czechoslovakia's Klement Gottwald died, and a new 'collective leadership' was formed, but party leader Antonin Novotny soon emerged as the leading figure, in similar style to Khruschev in the Soviet Union. Other East Europeans were slower to make changes: Albania's Enver Hoxha surrendered the premiership to Mehmet Shehu in 1954 but remained predominant; Gheorghieu-Dej gave up the Romanian party leadership in 1954 but took it up again in 1955 after Khruschev's triumph over Malenkov; Bulgaria's Vulko Chervenkov in February 1954 proved rather less adept, by remaining prime minister and handing the party leadership to Todor Zhivkov, who eventually ousted him; but in Poland, party leader Bierut sensibly gave the premiership to the ex-Socialist Josef Cyrankiewicz, who was prepared to be a loyal lieutenant.

Despite the retention of power by many hard-line Stalinists, there were signs of deeper problems in the Soviet bloc and the years 1953–6 were to prove a critical period. In Hungary, for example, a poor harvest, problems with central planning and evidence of popular discontent led Moscow to force a change of leadership in mid-1953. Matyas Rakosi, whilst remaining First Secretary of the party, was forced to hand the premiership to Imre Nagy, an earlier critic of centralised planning. As premier, Nagy slowed down on collectivisation, allowed the use of private workshops and increased agricultural investment. But such innovations antagonised the Stalinists and in March 1955 Rakosi (again emulating Khruschev's triumph over Malenkov) replaced Nagy once more. Meanwhile, far more serious problems had arisen in East Germany. Here too there were signs in early 1953 that the collectivisation of land and concentration on heavy industry were causing economic problems, and here too the Kremlin favoured reform. The East German leader, Ulbricht, nonetheless increased production targets in May 1953 and sparked off major discontent. On 16 June workers' demonstrations mushroomed into a general strike in East Berlin, the strike spread to other cities, and there were demands for economic changes. Before this could become a full political uprising the Red Army stepped in, quelled disorder on 17 June and imprisoned the strike leaders, about 40 of whom were executed. It was a short-lived episode, but it surprised the Soviet leaders, upset their détente policy with the West and was particularly worrying because it showed working-class discontent against Communism. It also showed that the Soviets needed to support strong local Communist leaders, so Ulbricht was allowed to remain in office, given Soviet financial assistance and allowed to tighten his political grip on the East German people.

Khruschev's triumph over Malenkov in Russia led to a renewed crisis in Eastern Europe. This was largely because of the character and policies of the new Soviet leader, who created grave uncertainty in the minds of East Europeans about what the Kremlin expected of them. As early as May 1955 the signs from Khruschev about his East European policy were confusing. On 14 May he created the Warsaw Pact with the satellites and Albania. This became a forum for discussion among his allies, it formalised the ties between their armed forces, replaced former bilateral treaties and marked a response to West German entry in NATO. The same month, however, Khruschev made a treaty with the Western powers which pulled his troops out of Austria on condition it remained a neutral country. This raised the possibility, especially in neighbouring Hungary, that other states could become politically independent of Moscow if they were neutralised. As a further demonstration of his flexibility, and of his desire for links to 'non-aligned' states Khruschev, also in May, visited Belgrade. Tito, against whom all the Eastern bloc had united after 1948 and who had given the East European Stalinists their *raison d'être*, suddenly became someone to be courted. Tito did not abandon his peculiar brand of Communism, nor did he join the Warsaw Pact. Yet it was partly to please him that, in April 1956, Khruschev dissolved the Cominform. His 'secret' speech to the Soviet Communist Congress of February 1956, with its criticisms of the Stalinist system, created more confusion. The Congress accepted that there could be 'different roads to Socialism', such as Yugoslavia's, and began the rehabilitation of Communist leaders in the USSR who had been executed under Stalin, but this also called into question the policies of those leaders who Stalin had installed in power in Eastern Europe.

Khruschev did not intend his policies to break up the Soviet satellite system. He aimed to preserve the 'people's democracies' whilst reducing the excesses of Stalinism and bringing some flexibility to his dealings with non-aligned states and the West. Nonetheless, his policies did cause uncertainty and raised the important question of precisely how far reform should go. Many East European leaders wanted the minimum of change; thus, in Czechoslovakia and Bulgaria the victims of Stalinisation after 1948 were sometimes rehabilitated, but new evidence of discontent was quickly stamped out; in East Germany, Romania and Albania there were no apologies for the past. The hard-liners won support from China, itself a powerful country which had established a Communist regime in 1949 without Soviet aid. The Chinese, under Mao Zedong, were doctrinaire hard-liners, critical of Tito's 'deviationism'. They criticised Khruschev's 'secret' speech for sowing dissension in Communist ranks. Elsewhere, however, there were those who wished to proceed with radical reforms. 'Revisionist' thinkers grew in number among the intelligentsia of Eastern Europe. Revisionists had various ideas but generally were critical of the Stalinist system and advocated political liberalisation, less bureaucracy, a decentralised economic system and greater attention to national needs. Many were attracted to Tito's economic reforms, especially the workers' councils.

Instead of radical reform 1956 ultimately witnessed a resurgence of Soviet control. Events centred on Poland and Hungary, where many hoped that Khruschev's ideas could lead to more liberal policies. In Poland political changes had begun with the death of Bierut, in February. He was succeeded by Edward Ochab, a reliable Communist but one ready to adopt some Khruschevite reforms. In April he announced an amnesty for political prisoners and encouraged the Polish parliament to engage in genuine debate about policy. Ochab had no intention of sharing power with other groups but his liberal tone soon sparked off a major crisis. Revisionists began to call for a free press and, as in East Berlin in 1953, workers showed their discontent over high production targets and poor wages, by forming representative organisations modelled on the Yugoslav 'workers' councils'. The parallels with East Berlin became even starker on 28 June 1956. Rumours that workers' representatives from Poznan had been arrested in Warsaw, led to strikes and a large demonstration in the city of Poznan which was immediately put down, not by the Red Army this time, but by Polish security forces. Fatal casualties were limited to about 50, but the Polish government's troubles were not over. Resisting the pressure from Stalinists for a repressive policy, during the summer the government promised improved living standards and new elections, and passed mild sentences on the leaders of the 'Poznan rising'. Nonetheless, whilst further demonstrations and violence were avoided, 'workers' councils' and other independent groups continued to meet, and it became clear that some radical act was needed to end the simmering discontent. In this situation many wanted power to be given to Wladyslaw Gomulka, the former party leader who had been denounced as a 'Titoist' under Bierut but fully rehabilitated by Ochab. Gomulka was detested by the Stalinists, but to the people he could be portrayed as a national hero. After talks between Khruschev and Polish leaders on 19–20 October it was agreed that Gomulka was the one man who could restore Communist authority, and he was then elected First Secretary. To help him, the Soviets agreed to remove the Russian Marshal Rokossovsky who had been made Poland's Minister of Defence. On 30 October the Soviets also acknowledged past 'mistakes' in economic policy in Eastern Europe. Gomulka went on to end the collectivisation of land, to decentralise economic decision-making, to provide limited freedom of speech and to release the Catholic Church leader Cardinal Wyszynski. He thus provided Poland with much greater independence of the USSR. However, he also preserved the one-party state, maintained the basic elements of state planning and made new arrangements for Soviet troops to remain on Polish soil. Thus, he basically satisfied the Soviets and other Communist leaders, whilst answering some demands of the Revisionists. In this task of restoring order he was aided by the bitter lesson of events in Hungary.

In Hungary independent political clubs had begun to form in 1955, there were calls from the disgraced ex-premier Imre Nagy for freer political debate and in June 1956 several thousand people attended a meeting in favour of press freedom. First Secretary Rakosi used the Poznan riots in Poland as an excuse to condemn Revisionism but his harsh line was currently out of favour with Khruschev and in July there were important political changes. Moderate Communists (including Janos Kadar, who had earlier been removed from the leadership) were promoted and Rakosi was replaced by another Stalinist, Ernoe Geroe. As in Poland these changes failed to halt discontent and in early October 300000 people joined a funeral procession, led by Nagy for Laszlo Rajk, the victim of Stalin's purges who had now been rehabilitated. Workers' councils were formed and many Communist party members joined in the demands for political freedom. The events of 19–20 October in Poland led to expectations that Hungary could follow a similar course, with Nagy as the Hungarian Gomulka. However, events after this ran out of control. On 23 October demonstrating students pulled down the Stalin monument in Budapest, amidst demands for free elections and the withdrawal of Soviet troops. At first the Communists took a moderate line. Nagy was hastily recalled to power as premier, then Kadar replaced Geroe as party leader whilst Soviet troops withdrew into the background. Soviet ministers who visited Budapest on 24 October evidently hoped the situation could be contained but over the following days Communist authority collapsed, to be replaced by workers' councils in the factories and 'revolutionary committees' at local level.

207

It was probably in a bid to re-assert his influence that Nagy promised, on 30 October, to restore a multi-party system and, on 1 November, undertook to leave the Warsaw Pact. For the Soviets, however, these concessions went far beyond anything Gomulka had promised in Poland, they threatened the Communist system and were unacceptable to China and other Eastern bloc leaders. On 3 November an alternative government to Nagy's was formed by Kadar, who had decided to remain loyal to Moscow. The next day the Red Army began forcibly to repress what was described as a 'counter-revolution'. Without Western aid and without military forces Hungarian resistance was useless. By 11 November the rising had collapsed. Three thousand people had been killed, about 2000 others were later executed and 20000 managed to flee abroad. The church leader, Cardinal Mindzenty, became a virtual prisoner in the US embassy, where he remained until 1971. Nagy himself was executed in 1958 and Kadar carried out a policy of repression as Moscow's loyal ally. Only after 1961 did he begin to moderate once more and, indeed, to develop into something of a Hungarian Gomulka, introducing reforms whilst preserving the one-party state.

The crushing of the Hungarian rising was a blow to East–West relations, to the confidence of Khruschev and to the unity of the Eastern bloc. In December 1956 Novotny and Ulbricht, the Czech and East German leaders called for unity under Soviet leadership, but most East European leaders viewed Khruschev with suspicion. They sought to tighten their grip on their own countries and, whilst ultimately relying on the Red Army to remain in power, showed sympathy for Mao Zedang, who condemned evidence of 'nationalist' threats to Communism, and wanted Eastern bloc leaders to be treated more as equals by the Soviets. Ulbrict, Novotny, Bulgaria's Zhivkov and Albania's Hoxha all maintained a strong police state, tightened their personal control over government and renewed the collectivisation of land. Romania's Georghieu-Dej particularly believed that he must build Communist power with less dependence on the volatile Kremlin. Whilst maintaining the police state and centralised economies, Dej posed as the defender of Romania's Latin culture, dealt harshly with the Hungarian, German and Jewish minorities, and even negotiated the withdrawal of the Red Army from Romania (which was not central to Warsaw Pact defences) in 1958. Gomulka and Khruschev were not pleased by this resurgence of Stalinism, but at a meeting in Moscow in November 1957 all the Communist states except Yugoslavia adopted a resolution which, whilst confirming Soviet supremacy in the bloc, promised greater equality among bloc members.

It became clear in 1957 that, although the Hungarian rising had shown the limits of Eastern European independence from Moscow, it had not recreated doctrinal unity under Soviet leadership. Khruschev's inability to shape the bloc as he wanted was revealed over the following years in a number of developments. Most dramatic was the Sino–Soviet 'split'. Given Chinese criticisms of Khruschev in 1956–7, China's independence from Soviet control and Mao Zedong's strong idealism, a growing rift between

Moscow and Beijing was not surprising. Mao's 'Great Leap Forward' after 1958 inspired other Eastern bloc leaders to intensify agricultural collectivisation, usually with disastrous results. Khruschev resented Mao's attempts to win the ideological leadership of the Communist bloc, and in 1960–1 the dispute between the two became acrimonious. Finally, in 1964, Mao condemned the USSR as an imperialist power. The Sino–Soviet split also led to a growing rift between Moscow and Albania. Albania, like other East European states, saw China as a protector, able to limit Soviet dominance. But unlike other East European leaders, who had relied on the Red Army to come to power, Enver Hoxha felt he could afford to side with Mao against Khruschev, especially since the latter remained friendly with Hoxha's old rival, Tito. In 1961, after openly criticising Khruschev, the Albanians accepted Chinese economic aid and technical advisers. At the Soviet party Congress in October 1961 Khruschev condemned Albanian policy and in December Moscow broke off relations with Albania, which then became a Stalinist regime cut off from the home of Stalin.

The late 1950s and early 1960s also saw growing differences in policy between those states who remained loyal to Moscow. In Poland, Gomulka continued to allow some free discussion even if his dictatorial personal style increasingly offended intellectuals, nationalists and Roman Catholics who had earlier welcomed his rise to power. The end of collectivisation brought some limited improvements in agricultural production, but Gomulka could not find a successful way to combine market elements with central economic planning and the economy became stagnant in the early 1960s. In Hungary after 1961, Kadar seeemed to emulate Gomulka by relaxing censorship, releasing political prisoners and removing Stalinists from high office. In 1963 Kadar also reformed the system of rewards to farmers and began to encourage artisans to trade again. As in Poland, these modest steps preserved the centralised economy intact, but they marked a real difference from, say, Bulgaria and East Germany where reforms were few. The building of the Berlin Wall in 1961 allowed the East German government to consolidate its hold on its people, hundreds of thousands of whom had fled to the West in the 1950s. The Ulbricht regime buttressed its position by improving the country's industrial output. Less successful in economic terms was the bloc's other major industrial producer, Czechoslovakia. Economic stagnation and popular disaffection here after 1960 finally led Antonin Novotny to tear down the Stalin monument in Prague, rehabilitate Stalin's victims and slacken Czech censorship.

The most remarkable developments in the Soviet sphere at this time were in Romania, where Gheorghieu-Dej continued to distance himself from Moscow and to build up a national power base. The Soviets could not easily challenge him because, in contrast to Poland and Hungary in 1956, Dej maintained totalitarian communism and did not threaten the Warsaw Pact. Romanian independence was particularly highlighted by debates in the Eastern bloc about strengthening COMECON, the organisation for economic co-operation founded in 1949. Under Stalin COMECON lacked much significance: each Eastern European state developed its own miniature version of Stalinist economics, with the creation of heavy industries, and commercial agreements were principally designed to satisfy Soviet needs. But in the mid-1950s Khruschev became more generous with Soviet financial aid, the foundation of the European Economic Community (EEC) presented an economic challenge to the East and by 1960 Khruschev believed that more radical action by COMECON was needed to boost flagging growth rates. At meetings in 1961–2 the Soviet leader advocated the 'international division of labour' in the Eastern bloc, and in 1963 there was even discussion of a supranational economic institution in the East, to match the EEC. By then Eastern European growth rates had fallen to half their level under Stalin and agricultural output was little better than before the Second World War. It was Dej who led the opposition to Khruschev's ideas, partly because they would reduce Romania's independence in economic affairs, and partly because Romania would almost certainly lose out in any Eastern 'common market'. Romania had been very successful at raising industrial production, in steel, chemicals and shipbuilding, in the late 1950s, but she had begun from a low level and (like Bulgaria) still had only about one-third of the industrial production per head of Czechoslovakia and East Germany. If COMECON states were now to specialise in certain areas of production Romania and Bulgaria (and probably Hungary and Poland) would be left as agricultural producers, subservient to the industrial power of Czechoslovakia, East Germany and the USSR. Technical problems with a 'common market', the Sino–Soviet split and the humiliating Cuban Missile Crisis also helped to weaken Khruschev in the face of Romanian opposition, and in July 1963 COMECON leaders abandoned the idea of multi-lateral co-operation beyond the establishment in 1964 of a clearing bank. Dej emphasised his independence at this time by retaining links to China and developing trade with the West. By 1964 it was clear that, whilst the Soviets could maintain a Communist system in Eastern Europe, they could not dictate a rigidly unified policy to it, nor prevent a remarkable degree of independence by Dej, nor even emulate the degree of co-operation between Western capitalist states in the EEC. Ironically, voluntary co-operation between sovereign states in Western Europe proved much more effective than Soviet attempts to enforce unity between their satellites. The splits with China and Albania were only the most dramatic examples of Communist disunity a decade after Stalin.

## Eastern Europe under the Brezhnev Doctrine, 1964–82

The fall of Khruschev in October 1964 came as another surprise to Eastern European leaders but since the new Soviet leaders put the emphasis on policy continuity, supported party dominance at home and were sympathetic to conservatives in the Eastern bloc, it was possible to minimise the significance of the change. Yet, as Brezhnev concentrated on resolving the USSR's problems, Eastern European states continued to drift apart. Local leaders sought to meet national needs, to satisfy both consumers and the 'new class' of Communist administrators and to legitimise their rule by a good economic performance and greater administrative efficiency.

By 1964, as in the USSR, it was clear to many in Eastern Europe that the Stalinist economic model had numerous failings, and that popular discontent could not forever be repressed by the secret police. Thus the 1960s and 1970s saw more and varied attempts to achieve greater efficiency, meet consumer demands, and improve social services whilst retaining the basics of central planning. Incentives, more decision-making by factory managers, elements of competition, an accent on quality – all these were attempted. However, since they merely tinkered with the system, they had limited success. The Eastern European states in the 1960s and 1970s shared similar problems to the Soviet Union of poor quality, incompetent and corrupt management, an irrational price structure and limited opportunities for foreign trade.* COMECON, especially under the 'Complex Programme' of 1970–1, developed joint projects, information exchanges and also an Investment Bank, but real integration was impossible, members tended to compete with each other rather than to co-operate, and joint projects were often costly, unnecessary and harmful to the environment. The entry into COMECON of Mongolia (1962), Cuba (1972) and Vietnam (1978) further reduced the organisation's cohesion. By the end of the Brezhnev era even the Soviets had ceased to gain from the COMECON system: increases in the oil price in the 1970s meant that the Soviets had to subsidise their allies by selling oil to them below the world price. Radical reformers argued that the only real way to improve matters was to move to a market-based system, but such a change would also demand inequalities of wealth, unemployment and – in order to motivate people – popular participation in decision-making. Faced with such a choice, many Communists preferred to rely on repression.

The difficult choices facing them explain why, in the period of détente in the 1970s, Eastern European leaders imported Western technology and took loans from Western banks. Ironically, Western aid was to be used to cure the deficiencies of Communism, at a time when the West seemed less threatening. Yet in the end the reliance on Western finance and technological inputs backfired. The centralised economic systems in the East were unable to adopt Western technology efficiently and attempts to pay for Western goods, by developing tourism (as in Bulgaria), establishing joint East–West projects, or simple resort to barter, failed to prevent a massive build-up of foreign debt. After 1979, in a situation of Western economic depression and renewed Cold War, the Eastern Europeans were forced to cut investment and consumption to try to repay their debts. By the end of the Brezhnev era they were facing still greater pressures to abandon Stalinist economics. The contradictions within the Communist system were by then intense. Warsaw Pact leaders tried to

* See Chapter 7, Section three.

portray themselves as legitimate, effective, national rulers, representing all the people, yet they shrank from free elections, concentrated real power in few hands, were unable to meet countries' material needs and ultimately relied on repression and Soviet support. Marxist-Leninism was still used to justify the system, but most people had become as materialist as their counterparts in the West, the working class were as likely to show discontent as anyone else, and party elites were frequently privileged, corrupt and cut off from the people, the Warsaw Pact claimed to defend national sovereignty, condemned Western imperialism, and kept Eastern Europe cut off from the other half of the Continent, yet sovereignty was denied to its peoples. The West was economically more successful and in the détente of the 1970s the 'imperialists' were treated as equals. Communism claimed to have a universal application and its values were indoctrinated through education, literature and propaganda, yet individualism, religion, and a desire to assert national identities could not be suppressed. In the 1960s even former Stalinists began to blame Stalin's 'mistakes' for current problems, yet they continued to advocate relatively minor reforms, to maintain centralised, bureaucratic regimes, and to oppose democratic aspirations.

Amidst the contradictions and failings Communists continued to hold onto power, bolstered by the security forces, control of public information, the fear, apathy and demoralisation of potential opposition groups, slow improvements in living standards, and the support of certain sections of the population, such as the bureaucracy and workers in inefficient industries (who would become unemployed in a market economy). Under Brezhnev the Communist system, as in the USSR, gradually stagnated, yet it survived. And basically the order which had developed under Khruschev was consolidated: local leaders were allowed to find their answers to problems and to diversify from Moscow and each other, but ultimately they had to remain loyal to the main tenets of Communism and the Warsaw Pact. The second half of this equation was made clear again in 1968 in Czechoslovakia, after which the unity of the pro-Soviet bloc was formally re-asserted in the 'Brezhnev Doctrine'. The Czechoslovakia crisis, with strong parallels to 1956, highlighted the problems that could arise in a Communist system when a change of party leader took place, when radical ideas for reform existed, when the working classes shared the discontent of the revisionist intelligentsia, and when there was uncertainty about Soviet intentions – in other words when confusion at the centre was challenged by strong protests from below. The Czech crisis coincided with discontent in many Western countries and was not the only example of unrest in the Communist world. In Yugoslavia in 1965–6 proposals to widen the market element in economic policy had already provoked a crisis in which Tito had ousted his old ally, the security chief Alexander Rankovic. In 1966–7 poor output and rising unemployment affected Yugoslavia and, in 1968, student demonstrators, inspired by events in Paris, took to the streets of Belgrade calling for greater democracy.

Whereas Yugoslavian demonstrations were treated mildly by Tito, events in Czechoslovakia led to violence and repression. In January 1968 the long-serving conservative Antonin Novotny, who tried to repress mounting discontent during 1967, was finally replaced as Czechoslovak party leader by a moderate, Alexander Dubcek. Dubcek hoped to make the Communist party more responsive to popular wishes whilst maintaining its authority but he had to steer a middle course between, on one side, radical students and intellectuals who exploited the relaxations of censorship to demand reform and, on the other, conservative Communists who feared a situation similar to Hungary in 1956. Reform groups began to form within the Communist party itself and during spring workers too began to call for changes. Many Czechs, like the playwright Vaclav Havel, hoped opposition parties might be formed and saw Dubcek as the only leader able to deliver this. Brezhnev, however, warned Dubcek to be cautious, and in early March 1968 the Warsaw Pact met in Sofia to discuss the Czech situation. Romania's desire to respect Czech independence meant that she was excluded from a subsequent Pact meeting on 23 March, in Dresden, where Dubcek was told not to go too far with liberalisation. A new Czech party programme, published in April, sought to maintain Communist political domination whilst extending parliamentary rights, promising an end to censorship and allowing free movements abroad. In May, however, there were signs of how difficult a 'middle course' was: the announcement that a special party conference was to be held in September led to renewed hopes of political reform; but the Soviets, East Germans, Poles, Hungarians and Bulgarians now formed the 'group of five' and issued more stern warnings about the need for caution. In June, as popular debate in Czechoslovakia became more widespread, there were hopes that the 'Prague Spring' could blossom into full democracy, and Dubcek tried to demonstrate his loyalty to Moscow by allowing Warsaw Pact military manoeuvres on Czech soil. But in mid-July the Czech leader refused to attend a meeting with the 'group of five' in Warsaw. He was then ordered by them to deal with his country's 'counter-revolutionary' movement.

Dubcek clearly had popular support in Czechoslovakia, the Communist party itself had ironically become a centre of calls for reform, and there were no riots to give the Soviets an excuse to intervene in the country, as there had been in Hungary in 1956. But the group of five evidently feared the results of the forthcoming Czech party conference and decided to intervene before it was held. On 21 August armed intervention by the five, under Soviet commanders, surprised Dubcek. Resistance, as in Hungary, was useless and despite some violence in Prague, bloodshed on the scale of 1956 was avoided. A general strike on 23 August soon petered out and on 26 August Czech leaders went to Moscow. There they agreed to scrap the special party conference, to end non-Communist organisations and restore censorship. The fact that the Communist party itself was a centre of reform made it a more complex task to reinforce totalitarian control than had been the case in Hungary and after the events of August thousands of people left the party. Sporadic protests were seen, notably when a student, Jan Palach, burned himself to death in Prague in January 1969. But Dubcek himself was finally removed as party leader in April 1969 and sent to be Ambassador in Turkey (a much milder fate than that of Imre Nagy). The new leader, Gustav Husak, was similar to Nagy's successor, Kadar: loyal to Moscow but a past opponent of Stalinism. Under Husak the Communist party was rebuilt, the reformers of 1968 were expelled from the party (and lost their jobs), and Czechoslovakia again became the reliable, conservative regime it had been under Novotny. Elections in November 1971 claimed a ridiculous 99 per cent vote for the official 'National Front'. Czechoslovakia developed Western trade links in the 1970s and remained one of the wealthier Eastern Bloc states, but opposition groups, like 'Charter 77', were ruthlessly suppressed.

The intervention in Czechoslovakia offended not only Western democrats, but also West European Communists (who developed 'Eurocommunism' in the 1970s), Albania (which finally quit the Warsaw Pact in 1968), China (which had its own armed clash with the Soviets in 1969) and Yugoslavia. But Tito became friendly with Moscow again in the early 1970s, Czechoslovakia did not prevent the development of détente with the West and Brezhnev made no apologies for Soviet action. Instead, in Poland in November 1968, he said that all Communist countries must act to preserve Communism wherever 'forces hostile to Socialism try to reverse the development of a Socialist country.' This was the 'Brezhnev Doctrine' and was maintained by the Soviet leader thereafter.

In 1982 Czechoslovakia and East Germany remained repressive, centralised regimes, close to Moscow, but Romania, Hungary and Poland had continued on their different courses. In Romania Gheorghieu-Dej had died in March 1965 to be succeeded by his protégé Nicolae Ceausescu, who maintained Dej's policies of internal repression alongside independence from Moscow. Ceausescu did much to end Soviet pressure for a reform of the Warsaw Pact in late 1965, just as Dej had sabotaged the reform of COMECON in 1961–3. Ceausescu then began to pose as an East European *Gaulliste*, emphasising that Moscow could no more dictate Eastern Bloc policies than Washington could dictate NATO decisions. In 1967 he upset the East Germans by entering diplomatic relations with West Germany, he was excluded from certain talks (and from a new series of bi-lateral treaties) between Warsaw Pact states, and of course he refused to intervene in Czechoslovakia in 1968. He maintained links to France – a fellow Latin country – and China, was visited by President Nixon in 1969, and was presented with various honorary awards by Western countries (including an honorary knighthood from Britain) because of his resistance to the Soviets. Yet at the same time Ceausescu suppressed all opposition, attacked religious and national minorities and concentrated enormous power in his own hands. By 1974 he was party leader, President and prime minister. His personal power and international links, along with Romania's insignificant geographical position, helped to ensure that his independence did not lead to Soviet intervention.

In Hungary the situation was radically different. After 1956 the country could not hope to emulate Romania's independence and dissidents were carefully watched, but gradually the Kadar regime built up its policy of economic reform and open discussion. In 1964 travel restrictions and censorship were eased, whilst in January 1968 a 'New Economic Mechanism' was introduced which decentralised economic decision-making, reformed the system of investment, prices and subsidies and introduced competitive elements in industry in order to improve quality. Events in Czechoslovakia in 1968 strengthened the hand of conservatives in Hungary who tried to limit the impact of reform but in the 1970s the country was in the forefront of Western commercial and financial contacts. In 1973 it acceded to the GATT agreement, in 1978 it was given 'most favoured nation' trading rights by America, and in 1982 it joined the World Bank and IMF. Aluminium and machine industries were expanded; consumer goods, public services and standards improved for much of the 1970s; and a productive 'underground' economy also grew up, which was tolerated by the government. But, though seen as a possible model for reform elsewhere, Hungary was vulnerable to raw material shortages, became very indebted to the West, preserved important elements of centralised control and faced economic stagnation again in the late 1970s. Other East European leaders viewed its reforms with suspicion.

Far more concern was generated by events in Poland between 1968 and 1982. In December 1970 low productivity and poor trade had led the Gomulka government to propose price increases, as a first step to much-needed economic reform. By then, however, Gomulka had disappointed the hopes of 1956 for a more liberal national leadership and, faced with higher prices, Polish workers went on the rampage in the Baltic Sea ports, ransacking Communist party buildings and forming independent 'councils'. The government, as in 1956, at first tried to repress the unrest, but the shooting of protesters in Gdynia on 17 December only led to more demonstrations and, faced with the danger of Soviet intervention, the Polish leaders decided to replace the discredited Gomulka. The new party leader, Edward Gierek, was a capable bureaucrat who withdrew the earlier price increases, brought younger, more pragmatic people into government and promised to consult the workers on future reforms. It was galling for Communists to see industrial workers in the forefront of discontent. It was also worrying to see them succeed in reversing reforms and, indeed, in toppling a leader. But the Soviets gave financial aid to Gierek and the new Polish government now tried, like others in Eastern Europe, to improve economic performance without upsetting the workers. The workers, after all, were supposedly the soul of the Communist system and their alienation was far more dangerous than that of middle-class groups.

In the 1970s, however, Gierek singularly failed to improve Poland's economy and living standards. An attempted 'boom' early in the decade merely ran up a huge Western debt. Striking workers again successfully forced the withdrawal of price increases in 1976. Bad harvests and the demoralisation of the peasantry meant that Poland, for all its arable land, was a food importer and, in 1979–80 there was a situation of negative growth. The election of a Polish Pope, John Paul II in 1978, added further to Gierek's discomfort. A Papal visit in 1979 fully revealed the power of the Roman Catholic Church in the country. In July 1980 Gierek, like Gomulka ten years before, was again forced to attempt price increases to rationalise the economy, and met the same result. Workers formed their own representative committees, went on strike and began to demand wage increases and also some political changes. On 14 August workers at the Lenin shipyard in Gdansk included in their strike demands the right to organise an independent trades union. Lech Walesa emerged as their leader, the strike spread and the government tried to end the discontent – now far worse than 1970 – with some dramatic concessions. Censorship wold be relaxed, incompetent managers removed, and independent trades unions could form. In September, as unrest continued, Gierek handed power to Stanislaw Kania and a 'Solidarity' trades union was formed in Gdansk. It soon gained ten million members and its existence was formally recognised by the government, after some delay, in November.

Official recognition of Solidarity brought a return to relative peace in Polish industry in December 1980. Nonetheless, an unprecedented situation had come about in a Communist country, whereby a powerful workers' organisation had been created which was beyond party control. Despite Polish hopes that Solidarity and the government could work together, the Kremlin and other Eastern European leaders were displeased and in December many observers expected armed intervention in Poland on the lines of 1956 or 1968. Such fears increased as Communist party authority continued to disintegrate and some in Solidarity called for self-management in industry and the liberalisation of political life. Instead however, as in 1956, Poland escaped intervention because a leader emerged who re-established authority from within, this time using, not the Communist party (whose reputation was in ruins), but the Army. General Wojtech Jaruzelski was appointed prime minister in February 1981 and in October he replaced Kania as party leader. Jaruzelski went on to surprise Solidarity on 13 December by declaring martial law, arresting 10 000 of the trades union's members and ruling through a 'Military Council for National Salvation'. Solidarity was forced underground and, although some unrest continued, the Polish people proved too exhausted and fearful to resist. When independent trades unions were banned once more a call from Solidarity for a protest national strike failed. By November 1982 the government felt strong enough to release Lech Walesa himself from imprisonment, and in December martial law was suspended. Thus, at the end of the Brezhnev era, the system of Soviet satellites remained intact and, even in Poland, local Communists proved able to maintain themselves in power without direct Soviet intervention. Yet the problems in the bloc were clearly immense.

## The Disintegration of the Soviet System, 1982–9

The Warsaw Pact states entered the post-Brezhnev era with low economic growth, little popular faith in Marxist-Leninism and increasing strains between the member states. In October 1983 the announcement of new Soviet intermediate-range missile deployments in East Germany and Czechoslovakia even led the normally loyal East Germans to complain. Under Eric Honecker since 1971 the East Germans had developed close economic ties with their Western neighbours and maintained the best economic performance in the Warsaw Pact. On 25 November Honecker publicly criticised the renewed arms race in Europe and called for political dialogue with the West. Only the Czechs showed much sympathy for Andrei Gromyko's tough 'Cold War' policies. In 1984 Honecker reluctantly accepted intermediate nuclear weapon deployment but his doubts about Soviet policy were a significant sign of strains within the Eastern alliance. The Soviet Union had itself done most to create the problems with Honecker. In the 1970s, unable to stimulate East European growth and unwilling to allow radical reforms, Moscow had encouraged links to the West; now the Kremlin was unable to resolve the satellites' financial and energy problems, but it nonetheless expected East Europeans to adopt an unfriendly policy towards capitalist states. Unsurprisingly many Eastern Europeans, like their counterparts in Western Europe, showed little enthusiasm for the renewed Cold War between Moscow and Washington.

When Mikhail Gorbachev became Soviet leader in 1985 he evidently hoped to retain control of Eastern Europe whilst improving relations with the West once more. Such a policy would please leaders like Honecker, Kadar in Hungary and Jaruzelski in Poland, whose countries craved for Western contacts. Gorbachev renewed the Warsaw Pact for 20 years in April 1985,* but also proved ready to recognise the equality of other leaders in the bloc, as seen in the new Soviet Communist programme published in 1986. In retrospect, however, there were indications that the satellite system might not long survive. East Europeans by 1985 were deep in debt to the West and a new wave of détente could draw them further away from Moscow – as some of Gorbachev's conservative critics warned. Yet this perhaps did not concern Gorbachev as much as it did previous Soviet leaders. For after all, if détente succeeded and the US and USSR no longer saw each other as enemies, it would not be necessary to preserve a defensive 'buffer zone' in Eastern Europe. Even without Gorbachev's 'new thinking', things had changed greatly since Stalin's day. Eastern Europe had arguably become a liability to the USSR, except as a barrier to Western attack. The Kremlin could not pay off the region's debts, was forced to subsidise Eastern Europe with oil and raw materials and carried the main burden of Warsaw Pact

---

* It had been renewed for ten years in 1975.

arms spending (15 per cent of its GNP in 1979 compared to 6 per cent for East Germany and less than 3 per cent for all the rest).

Nevertheless, whatever the problems in the Eastern bloc by 1985, there can be no doubt that Gorbachev's decisions in 1985–9 did most to end the Soviet system swiftly, just as Stalin's policies in 1945–53 had created the structure. One of the lessons of 1989, when the Communist states of Eastern Europe disintegrated, was that the system ultimately continued to rely on Red Army bayonets for its survival. However much leaders, like Ceausescu in Romania, had tried to build up local sources of power their rule could not survive once the Kremlin abandoned them. At that point Stalin's creation simply unravelled itself. Communism was revealed, even to its supporters, to be an alien, bankrupt ideology, maintained by leaders who lacked any real legitimacy. The 'Brezhnev Doctrine' was finally, formally renounced at a Warsaw Pact meeting in October 1989. Whether Gorbachev expected the rapid destruction of the satellite system which occurred in 1989 is questionable. There is evidence that, while allowing greater independence and favouring political and economic reforms, he hoped to bring about changes in line with his own policies of *glasnost* and *perestroika*,\* and to maintain influence in Eastern Europe. Once the change of regimes had occurred, however, and democratic elections were planned, he quickly accepted events and was able to argue that, even if it had failed in Eastern Europe, Communism could still survive in the USSR where it supposedly had legitimate national roots. Significantly, at the end of 1989, Communism only survived in Europe in those countries where domestic forces had brought it to power – in the Soviet Union, Yugoslavia and Albania.

In surveying the details of Communism's disintegration, it will again be best to look at each country in turn. Predictably, Hungary and Poland were in the forefront of change. More surprising perhaps, in contrast to the events of 1956, they were able to move towards democracy without violence. By 1982 there was already scope for private enterprise in Hungary in agriculture, and this was extended in 1982–4, evidently with the support of Soviet leader Yuri Andropov. Moves to create a 'regulated market', with its reduced central planning, the closure of unprofitable factories and the encouragement of small private businesses, met with less sympathy from Konstantin Chernenko in 1984–5 however, and a bad winter in early 1985 harmed the country's economic prospects. Hungary developed close relations with the West, improved agricultural output and founded a tourist industry, but it also remained deep in debt, was subjected to regular price increases and had poor public services. Many people survived only by taking second jobs in the 'underground' economy. To compensate for the squeeze on living standards the government tried political reforms, beginning in December 1983 with a law to introduce a choice of candidates in elections. All candidates had to swear loyalty to the existing political system but compared with past experience a

---

\* Discussed in Chapter 4, Section four.

major step had been taken and, in June 1985, a number of independents (but no leading dissidents) were elected to parliament. Gorbachev proved sympathetic to such reform and, in May 1987, Kadar said it was vital to involve the people in decision-making: it was finally acknowledged in Eastern Europe that the general population could only be galvanised to work if they had a real say in government.

The continued economic problems at this time showed that piecemeal changes to Communism were no longer sufficient. And in May 1988, at a special Communist conference, party members themselves – as in Czechoslovakia 20 years before – became forceful advocates of change. Disappointed with the leadership's most recent reform proposals, delegates called for an overhaul of the leadership. In this they were successful. A new party leader, Karoly Grosz, not only introduced younger technocrats into government, but listened to the demands for market economics and open political debate. The 75-year-old Kadar stunned by the criticism, was given the new, powerless position of party President and in January the government became the first in Eastern Europe to promise multi-party elections, with a law that legalised parties, trades unions and other organisations outside Communist control. With elections due in 1990, this helped to compensate for new price increases. Actually, new parties had already begun to form, starting in September 1988 with the progressive 'Democratic Forum'. Public demonstrations began again and, in a sign of new, ecological concerns, won the cancellation of a hydroelectric dam project on the Danube. In 1989 the government highlighted its readiness to break with the past by investigating the post-war show trials, denying that the events of 1956 were a 'counter-revolution' and, in June, re-burying Imre Nagy. 300000 attended the funeral which, ironically, came only a few weeks before the death of Janos Kadar. Reforms included the creation of a stock exchange and the right of foreigners to buy Hungarian companies. In July, for the first time since 1947, an opposition candidate won a by-election and in September an agreement was reached with opposition groups on how to hold elections in March 1990. To prepare for these elections, the Communist party loosened its ties to the government machine, changed its name in October to the Hungarian Socialist Party and, on 23 October, ceased to call the country a 'People's Republic'. In November, however, the people showed their continuing distrust for the Communists by voting against the government in a referendum on the new Presidency. In the referendum voters followed the advice of radical opposition groups and decided to delay Presidential elections until after the parliamentary elections.

Far from intervening in Hungary to prevent the rebirth of democracy, Gorbachev had begun in April 1989 to withdraw Soviet troops from the country. He was similarly tolerant of changes in Poland. Here, in 1984, General Jaruzelski had continued to ease the tough policies adopted in Poland in 1981, with a general amnesty for those imprisoned under martial law. Economic growth, however, remained negative and debt payments to Western banks were repeatedly re-scheduled. Consumer goods were few and food was of poor quality. In 1983 a visit by the Pope and the award of the Nobel Peace prize to Solidarity's Lech Walesa highlighted Communism's political unpopularity and there was outrage in October 1984 when secret policemen murdered a priest, Father Jerzy Popieluszko. Jaruzelski lacked support outside the security forces and the discredited Communist party, official trades unions won no respect and Solidarity continued its activities underground. Then again, the demoralisation of the Polish people was such that Walesa acknowledged in 1985 that widespread strike action had become impossible. In October 1985 the government even felt strong enough to promise a limited element of choice in future elections and in 1987 Jaruzelski, who had now become President, put forward a new package of reforms. In economics he wanted to decentralise decision-making, allow greater private enterprise, and allow the bankruptcy of unprofitable businesses. In politics he was ready to allow free association and hold multi-candidate elections, moves which might eventually result in a legal opposition.

By putting these proposed reforms to a referendum in November 1987 Jaruzelski over-estimated his new-found strength. Although most of those who voted were in favour of reform, they did not amount to half the *total* electorate, which the government had hoped for. This weakened Jaruzelski in 1988 when price increases sparked off a wave of strikes in April–May and again in August. The use of riot police against mineworkers failed to end the strikes and the government decided – as in 1980 – to talk to its opponents. A new prime minister, Mieczyslaw Rakowski, was appointed in September to take on the challenge of talks with Lech Walesa, but such conversations proved difficult to arrange. The government refused to recognise Solidarity's legal existence and many of Walesa's former supporters criticised him for talking to the Communists. But Walesa impressed the whole country in a television debate with a government representative on 30 November, and Jaruzelski himself then pressed the Communist party to accept Solidarity's existence. Round table talks finally began between the government, Walesa and the Roman Catholic Church in February 1989 and two months later it was agreed to re-legalise Solidarity, introduce economic reforms and, most dramatic of all, to allow greater democratic freedoms including freer elections to parliament. The elections went ahead in June and, despite the existence of 'reserved' and 'unopposed' seats (designed to protect the Communist position), they proved a major humiliation for the government. Solidarity won all but one of the seats where there was a choice of candidates and people exercised their right to cross out the names of 'unopposed' candidates, which meant that many Communists, including premier Rakowski, were defeated.

Events in Poland now began to move more rapidly than those in Hungary. Despite the lack of genuine free, multi-party elections Solidarity now possessed the power to defeat vital legislation in parliament. On 19 July, Jaruzelski, who had earlier seemed reluctant to stand, was re-elected President only on a narrow vote. In August he asked a Communist, Lieutenant-General Czeslaw Kiszczak, to form a government, but Kiszczak could not find sufficient support. Jaruzelski had reluctantly to accept a Solidarity-led coalition without Communist participation. Responsibility for forming such a government fell on 24 August to Tadeusz Mazowiecki, a friend of Walesa and founder of Solidarity's newspaper. Poland's problems were far from ended. A government was only formed on 12 September after some difficulties, and Mazowiecki took ill when he came to outline its programme to parliament. The new government hoped to privatise industry, move towards a market economy and make the Polish currency convertible in international markets but it faced formidable dangers of inflation and a large budget deficit. Yet, whatever the problems, a most dramatic change had taken place. For the first time the Warsaw Pact included a non-Communist government. Furthermore, Mikhail Gorbachev declared the change of government to be an 'internal affair'.

East Germany, Czechoslovakia and Romania predictably expressed concern at the events in Warsaw, little knowing that Communism's days were numbered in all three countries. In East Germany, Honecker had maintained his repressive regime after 1982 whilst attempting to modernise production, reduce inefficiency and tackle food shortages. With the strongest economy in the Eastern bloc he felt able to dismiss Gorbachev's reforms as 'inapplicable' to East German circumstances. In 1989, however, events in Hungary had a direct impact on East Germany and helped reveal that its people were tired of Communism. Economic success in Warsaw Pact terms did little to impress people who knew that living standards in West Germany were twice as high, and during the summer, when Honecker was ill, East Germans suddenly began to flee in large numbers to the West. Applications to leave had been rising for years. The Berlin Wall was still standing, but escape was possible through Hungary, which had re-opened its western borders in May. In August and September about 30000 East Germans crossed to the West in this way and others took refuge in West German embassies in Warsaw and Prague. This unedifying spectacle was similar to events before 1961 and the exodus included many young, skilled workers. Instead of emulating Khruschev's Berlin wall-building Gorbachev visited East Germany on 7 October and criticised Honecker's failure to understand popular opinion. Ironically, the meeting was in celebration of the regime's fortieth anniversary.

Faced by the sudden haemorrhage of its population, by mass demonstrations in major cities and by the formation of a 'New Forum' opposition group, and now without Soviet support, East German leaders shrank from the idea of repression and turned to reform. Honecker resigned as party leader on 18 October and was succeeded by Egon Krenz. Krenz had the reputation of being a hard-liner and survived in his new post only until 6 December, but he appointed the reformist Hans Modrow as prime minister, promised elections and finally, on 9 November, announced freedom to travel abroad. The last proved a most dramatic step. It led to breaches being made in the Berlin Wall on 9–10 November when about two million East Germans crossed into the West. With the greatest symbol of tyranny now broken most soon returned home. Communist authority had crumbled with astonishing speed in one of its most orthodox bastions. Within days Honecker was disgraced and corrupt officials sacked, non-Communist organisations were formed and, whatever Krenz's denials, German re-unification was 'on the agenda'.

It was a similar story in another orthodox Communist state, Czechoslovakia. Here too a long-standing leader, Gustav Husak, had continued to harass dissidents in the 1980s whilst achieving a better-than-average economic performance in the bloc. Husak claimed an interest in *perestroika* but did little to introduce reform. In 1987, whilst remaining President, he handed the party leadership to Milos Jakes, who had supported Soviet intervention in 1968. Demonstrations in January 1989 on the twentieth anniversary of Jan Palach's death were violently broken up by riot police. The Czechs did not face any great danger of their own people fleeing abroad, but the government was embarrassed when protests turned the official May Day rally into a demonstration in favour of human rights. Another big protest rally was held in late October. It appears in retrospect that the Soviet government favoured a change of leadership in Prague by now, and hoped that more demonstrations could bring this about. But attempts by Gorbachev to manipulate the public opposition to Communism were in vain. Mass demonstrations after 17 November and the formation of an opposition group, 'Civic Forum' on the 19th led to the resignation of the whole Politburo on 24 November. A new party leader, Karel Urbanek, who had not supported the Soviets in 1968, was appointed. People were astonished by the sudden success of their 'Velvet Revolution', but were not bought off by changes in the government. Instead a general strike was held on 24 November and the Communists were forced to give up their monopoly of power. Finally the reformers of 1968 were vindicated. In December, Alexander Dubcek became President of the Czechoslovak parliament and on 29 December Vaclav Havel, the Communists' most famous opponent, succeeded Husak as President. Elections were promised for 1990.

In the midst of these events a less dramatic, but equally sudden change of government had taken place in Bulgaria. Always loyal to Moscow, with no serious outbursts of opposition, events in Bulgaria were arguably in line with the peaceful move towards reform which Gorbachev himself wanted to see. Todor Zhivkov, Bulgaria's leader for three decades, talked of political and economic reform in the later 1980s but in July 1988 ousted reformers from the leadership and intensified his attempts to 'Bulgarianise' the Turkish minority. This Bulgarianisation programme led to a mass exodus of Turks – 80 000 left in June – which threatened the country's economic well-being. On 10 November, however, Petar Mladenov led a 'palace revolution' which toppled the 78-year-old Zhivkov. This coup had Gorbachev's support, and was remarkable for its ease. By promising reform and (as elsewhere in Eastern Europe) changing the Communists' name to the 'Socialist Party', as well as by exploiting Bulgaria's traditional toleration of its rulers, Mladenov was able to ensure a good vote for his party in elections in 1990, even though he soon resigned, implicated in the repression of the Zhivkov years.

In neighbouring Romania too, former Communists were to remain in office in 1990, but here there was no smooth change of power from the dictatorial Ceausescu. Instead, having built up – or so he believed – independent sources of power, Ceausecu felt he could retain office regardless of events elsewhere. Certainly the 'Securitate' secret police seemed to hold the country in an iron grip. Beneath the surface, nonetheless, there was considerable discontent. Consumer goods and many foodstuffs were in short supply. The Hungarian minority in Transylvania was oppressed, huge sums were wasted on the dictator's building schemes in the capital, and then Ceausescu began a policy known as 'systemisation', which involved the destruction of small villages and their replacement by large 'agro-industrial' centres. The Western powers were less tolerant of Ceausescu's human rights abuses in the Gorbachev era and even Warsaw Pact leaders were aghast at the Romanian leader's vanity and oppression. Ceausescu's end, when it came, was swift and violent. On 24 November 1989, apparently oblivious to events elsewhere in Europe, he was unanimously re-elected leader of the Communist party. On 15 December a deportation order on an Hungarian Protestant pastor, Father Laszlo Tokes, led to demonstrations in the city of Timisoara in Transylvania, but Ceausescu felt secure enough to go on a visit to Iran. On his return, however, his attempt to address a Bucharest crowd turned into a riot on 21 December and military leaders refused to open fire on the crowd. Only the Securitate showed any readiness to fight for the regime and Ceausescu was forced to try to flee. Later, as fighting broke out between the army and the Securitate, and as a 'National Salvation Front' was formed to replace his government, Ceausescu was captured. He and his wife, Elena, were executed on Christmas Day, but whether they were the victims of a popular rising or a palace coup was not clear. The new government included many old Communists, like the President, Ion Iliescu.

Even in Stalinist Albania there were signs of discontent in late 1989 although its leader Ramiz Alia managed to maintain the system created by Enver Hoxha (who had died in April 1985). In Yugoslavia too Communism had survived the death of its founder, Tito, in 1980, but the new collective leadership faced difficulties similar to those seen in the Soviet sphere of influence. Tito may have kept Yugoslavia united and independent but even he, in his later years, faced severe regional problems, inflation, a trade deficit and poor production levels. In 1989, like Gorbachev's USSR, the country experienced strong pressures for regional autonomy with violence from the Albanians of Kosovo province and a virtual declaration of independence from Slovenia. Then again Communism at least managed to survive the year in the two Communist states outside the Warsaw Pact.

To what extent the Kremlin tried to control events in Eastern Europe in 1989 is unclear, but a decision had clearly been made to let events run their course without intervention and once this became clear the whole

Communist system disintegrated. Only in Romania (where there were over 1000 deaths) was there any large-scale violence. The spell of fear, cast by Stalin, and renewed in 1956 and 1968, was broken and no-one could dictate the pace of change. By calling elections the new governments at least won for themselves the legitimacy which the People's Democracies always lacked. But there was no guarantee that political freedom would compensate people for the economic sacrifices which were now needed. All the new regimes lacked experience of democratic government and faced an economic crisis brought by indebtedness, raw material shortages and decades of inept planning. Czechoslovakia, for example, might be self-sufficient in agriculture but its farmers were demoralised by work on state farms, its soil was depleted by intensive cultivation and its livestock were poorly cared for in factory farms. East Germany might have been the Eastern bloc's strongest economy but compared to the West it was backward and faced large-scale unemployment once German re-unification came. Other problems included environmental pollution, uneven patterns of development across Eastern Europe and discontented national minorities. To some extent the new governments seemed like Spain, Portugal and Greece in the 1970s, hoping to end authoritarianism and inject themselves into the world economy. The scale of the problems they faced, however, was much greater. Southern Europeans in the 1970s at least had convertible currencies, a belief in private property, and well-developed service industries. The Eastern Europeans needed to create democratic institutions and a market-economy almost from scratch. They hoped to do so without recreating the large inequalities of wealth seen in the West. But the road they had taken could easily prove long and arduous. The Communist yoke had been thrown off but Eastern Europe still had to live with the legacy of Stalinism.

# Bibliography

This bibliography is intended to provide a brief pointer to some of the main works on Cold War Europe available in English, including those used in writing the present study. Inevitably the most serious historical work has been done on the earlier post-war years. For events in the late 1980s I have relied on newspapers or the invaluable *Keesing's Contemporary Archives: Record of World Events* (Longman, monthly). Unless otherwise stated the place of publication is London.

On Europe as a whole in the post-war world the best known account is Walter Laqueur's *Europe since Hitler* (2nd ed., Penguin, Harmondsworth, 1982). It looks at socio-economic, cultural and political developments and was originally published in 1970. G.A. Dorfman and P.J. Duignan, eds., *Politics and Western Europe* (University Press, Stanford, Cal. 1988) looks at nearly all the Western Europeans states in turn whilst D.W. Urwin, *Western Europe since 1945* (4th ed., Longman, 1989) has, like Laqueur, been updated since its first publication. It concerns itself with three themes: political and economic developments, European unity, and Western Europe's role in the world. The establishment, course and decline of the 'post-war settlement' in several European states (Britain, France, Germany, Italy, Sweden and the USSR) is the subject of M. Kesselman and J. Krieger's *European Politics in Transition* (D.C. Heath, Lexington, Massachusetts, 1987) and a valuable collection of essays on Western Europe in the 1980s is D.W. Urwin and W.E. Patterson, eds., *Politics in Western Europe Today* (Longman, 1989). The events of 1989, and their likely repercussions, are considered in R. Dahrendorf's stimulating *Reflections on the Revolution in Europe* (Chatto and Windus, 1990).

On the beginnings of the Cold War, H. Thomas, *Armed Truce* (Hamish Hamilton, 1986) is a conservative account, over-detailed on 1945–6, but a good antidote to D. Yergin, *Shattered Peace* (Deutsch, 1978), a left-wing interpretation of US policy in 1945–8. More basic is M. McCauley, *Origins of the Cold War* (Longman, 1983). The best coverage of US–European developments in the post-war decades is still provided by A. Grosser, *The Western Alliance* (Macmillan, 1980) whilst on US–Soviet relations see W. Lafeber, *America, Russia and the Cold War* (Wiley, New York, 1986) and J.L. Gaddis's thoughtful *The Long Peace, inquiries into the history of the Cold War* (Oxford University Press, 1987). More general on the history of the Cold War are S.R. Ashton, *In Search of Detente: the Politics of East–West Relations since 1945* (Macmillan, 1989), M. Dockrill, *The Cold War, 1945–63* (Routledge, 1988). On US policy in general see S.E. Ambrose's critical *Rise to Globalism* (Pelican, 5th ed., 1988) and J. Spanier's more favourable *American Foreign Policy since the Second World War* (Praeger, New York, 1985), whilst on the Soviets the best is J.L. Nogee and R.H. Donaldson, *Soviet Foreign Policey since the Second World War* (3rd ed., Pergamon, 1988), but see also R. Edmonds, *Soviet Foreign Policy: The Brezhnev Years* (Oxford University Press, 1985). M. Bowker and P. Williams, *Superpower Detente: a reappraisal* (Sage, 1988) provides an excellent account of the 1970s and the debate on the 'New Cold War' can be approached via N. Chomsky *et al, Superpowers in Collision* (Penguin, Harmondsworth, 1984) and F. Halliday, *The Making of the Second Cold War* (2nd ed., Verso, 1986). On Decolonisation see especially R.F. Holland, *European Decolonisation: an Introductory Survey, 1918–81* (Macmillan, 1985).

There is no good single history of the European Community but R. Pryce, ed., *The Dynamics of European Union* (Croom Helm, 1987) presents a series of essays on major developments in the Community's history, I. Barnes and J. Preston, *The European Community* (Longman, 1988) is a good overall review, and W. Nicoll and T.C. Salmon, *Understanding the European Communities* (Philip Alan, 1990) includes an historical overview. More detailed studies of the origins of the EC include: A.S. Milward's excellent *The Reconstruction of Western Europe, 1945–51* (Methuen, 1984), based on the archives; M.J. Hogan, *The Marshall Plan* (Cambridge University Press, 1987) on US efforts to shape post-war Europe; E. Fursdon's *The European Defence Community* (Macmillan, 1980); and, as a readable review of 1945–57, R. Mayne's *Postwar: the Dawn of Today's Europe* (Thames and Hudson, 1983). W. Lipgens, *A History of European Integration, vol. 1, 1945–7* (Oxford University Press, 1982) is unfortunately over-detailed. On the workings of the EC see especially S. Budd and A. Jones, *The European Community* (Kogan Page, 1989), J. Lodge, *The European Community and the Challenge of the Future* (Pinter, 1989) and N. Nugent, *The Government and Policies of the European Community* (Macmillan, 1989). A positive view of the changes due in 1992 can be found in P. Cecchini, *The European Challenge* (Wildwood House, Aldershot, 1988). On Britain's road to EC membership see J. Young, *Britain, France and the Unity of Europe, 1945–51* (Leicester University Press, 1984), M. Camps, *Britain and the European Community, 1955–63* (Oxford Univesity Press, 1964), and U. Kitzinger, *Diplomacy and Persuasion: how Britain joined the Common Market* (Thames and Hudson, 1973).

West Germany has recently been the subject of a large two-volume work in English by D.L. Bark and D.R. Gress, *A History of West Germany, Vol. 1, From Shadow to Substance, 1945–63* and *Vol. 2, Democracy and its*

*Discontents, 1963–88* (Blackwell, Oxford, 1989). This is good as a reference but right-wing in interpretation and needs to be treated cautiously. A shorter introduction, covering a range of issues, is H. A. Turner, *The Two Germanies since 1945* (Yale University Press, 1987) and for a study of the political framework see D. Childs, and J. Johnson, *West Germany* (St Martin's Press, New York, 1981), G. Smith, *Democracy in Western Germany* (3rd ed., Gower, Aldershot, 1986), D.P. Conradt, *The German Policy* (Longman, 1986) or R.M. Dalton, *Politics in West Germany* (Scott Foresman, Boston, 1989). Two historical surveys, which discuss both West and East German developments since 1945 are D. Childs, *Germany since 1918* (2nd ed., Batsford, 1980) and V.R. Bergahn, *Modern Germany: society, economy and politics in the twentieth century* (2nd ed., Cambridge University Press, 1987). K. Adenauer's *Memoirs* (Weidenfield and Nicolson, 1966) are unfortunately published in English only down to 1953 and T. Prittie, *Konrad Adenauer* (Tom Stacey, 1972) is now rather dated but J. Carr is good on *Helmut Schmidt* (Weidenfield and Nicolson, 1985). On international issues see E. Krippendorff and V. Rittberger, *The Foreign Policy of West Germany* (Sage, 1980). J. Ardagh, *Germany and the Germans* (Hamish Hamilton, 1987) looks at daily life and the arts, as well as politics and economics, and is rather livelier than C. Burdick, H-A. Jacobsen and W. Kudszus, eds., *Contemporary Germany: Politics and Culture* (Westview Press, 1984) which also tries to absorb a range of developments.

The most comprehensive treatment of post-war French history in English is M. Larkin, *France since the Popular Front* (Oxford University Press, 1988) but indispensable on *The Fourth Republic, 1944–58* is J.P. Rioux's book of that title (Cambridge University Press, 1987) and the best introduction to French politics under the Fifth Republic is V. Wright, *The Government and Politics of France* (3rd ed., Unwin Hyman, 1989). Other works which include general discussions of French politics and society are D.L. Hanley, A.P. Kerr and N.H. Waites, *Contemporary France* (2nd ed., Routledge and Kegan Paul, 1984) and J.E. Flower, ed., *France Today* (6th ed., Methuen, 1987). A recent historical study of the liberation period is H. Footitt and J. Simmonds, *France, 1943–5* (Leicester University Press, 1988) and on more recent events the most useful works are J. Ardagh, *France Today* (Secker and Warburg, 1987), S. Mazey and M. Newman, *Mitterand's France* (Croom Helm, 1987) and J. Tuppen, *France under Recession, 1981–6* (Macmillan, 1988). On 1968 the accounts are somewhat dated but see B.E. Brown, *Protest in Paris: Anatomy of a Revolt* (General Learning Press, Morristown, New Jersey, 1974). C. de Gaulle's *War Memoirs, Vol. III, Salvation, 1944–6* (Weidenfield and Nicolson, 1960) reveal his clear views on the world but *Memoirs of Hope* (Weidenfield and Nicolson, 1971) was unfinished at the time of his death and covers only 1958–62. For two good biographies see B. Ledwidge, *De Gaulle* (Weidenfield and Nicolson, 1982) and D. Cook, *Charles de Gaulle* (Putnam's, New York, 1983). Major decolonisation problems are discussed by J. Dalloz, *The Indochina War, 1945–54* (Gill and Macmillan, 1990) and A. Horne, *A Savage War of Peace* (Macmillan, 1977), whilst on foreign and defence issues see J. Young, *France, the Cold War and the Western Alliance, 1944–9* (Leicester University Press, 1990), E.A. Kolodziej, *French International Policy under De Gaulle and Pompidou* (Cornell University Press, Ithaca, 1971) and R. Aldrich and J. Connell, eds., *France in World Politics* (Routledge, 1989).

British contemporary history is best approached through A. Sked and C. Cook, *Postwar Britain* (2nd ed., Penguin, Harmondsworth, 1986) or P. Hennessy and A. Seldon, eds., *Ruling Performance: British Governments from Attlee to Thatcher* (Basil Blackwell, 1987), both of which cover the Thatcher years. D. Child's *Britain since 1945* (2nd ed., Methuen, 1986) and P.J. Madgwick, D. Steeds and L.J. Williams, *Britain since 1945* (Hutchinson, 1982) are also useful, and for a wider perspective see R. Blake, *The Decline of Power, 1915–64* (Granada, 1985). A more detailed history is being written by K. Middlemas, Called *Power, Competition and the State* it currently includes two volumes, *Britain in Search of Balance, 1940–61* (Macmillan, 1986) and *Threats to the Post-war Settlement in Britain, 1961–74* (1990). On the post-war Attlee government a number of detailed research works have now appeared, but the best is K.O. Morgan's *Labour in Power, 1945–51* (Oxford University Press, 1984), whilst A. Seldon's *Churchill's Indian Summer* (Hodder and Stoughton, 1981) makes substantial use of oral evidence in discussing the 1951–5 administration. Later governments are not so well covered, but see R. Lamb, *The failure of the Eden Government* (Sidgwick and Jackson, 1987), A. Horne's two-volume biography of *Harold Macmillan* (Macmillan, 1988 and 1989), C. Ponting, *Breach of Promise: Labour in Power, 1964–70* (Hamish Hamilton, 1989) and three books by M. Holmes on *Political Pressure and Economic Policy, 1970–4* (Butterworth, 1982), *The Labour Government, 1974–9* (Macmillan, 1985) and *The First Thatcher Government, 1979–83* (Wheatsheaf, Brighton, 1985). The standard book on the workings of government is R.M. Punnett, *British Government and Politics* (5th ed., Gower, Aldershot, 1987). On decolonisation issues see J. Darwin, *Britain and Decolonisation* (Macmillan, 1988).

An ideal introduction to Southern Europe is A. Williams, ed., *Southern Europe Transformed* (Harper and Row, 1984). On Italy, D. Sassoon, *Contemporary Italy: Politics, Economy and Society since 1945* (Longman, 1986) is a short, wide-ranging introduction and J. La Palombara, *Democracy Italian Style* (Yale University Press, 1987) a larger, detailed work on a complex political system. On Greece, C.M. Woodhouse, *Modern Greece: a short history* (4th ed., Faber and Faber, 1986) and R. Clogg, *A Short History of Modern Greece* (2nd ed., Cambridge University Press, 1986) compete as brief historical surveys, whilst Y.A. Kourvetasis and B.A. Dobratz, in *A Profile of Modern Greece* (Oxford University Press, 1987) surveys political, economic, social and international changes. There are a number of studies of the troubled 1940s including J.O. Iatrides, *Greece in the 1940's* (University Press of New England, Hanover, 1981) and L.S. Wittner, *American Intervention in Greece, 1943–9* (Colombia University

Press, New York, 1982), whilst on the era of the Colonels see C.M. Woodhouse, *The Rise and Fall of the Greek Colonels* (Granada, 1985). of the numerous books on political change in Portugal, R. Robinson, *Contemporary Portugal* (George, Allen and Unwin, 1979) includes background on Salazar, as does T. Gallagher, *Portugal: a twentieth century interpretation* (Manchester University Press, 1983). R. Harvey, *Portugal: Birth of a Democracy* (Macmillan, 1978) is a clear survey of events in the 1970s, but written a little too close to events, whilst H.G. Ferreira and M.W. Marshall, *Portugal's Revolution: ten years on* (Cambridge University Press, 1986) includes interviews with protagonists and a useful chronology of events. M. Kayman, *Revolution and Counter-Revolution in Portugal* (Merlin Press, 1987) is very critical of the post-1976 regime. Events in Spain in the 1970s have also drawn a lot of attention. E. Ramon Arango, *Spain: from Repression to Renewal* (Westview Press, 1985) is short, readable and provides the wider historical background but see also J. Maravall, *The Transition to Democracy in Spain* (Croom Helm, Beckenham, 1982), R. Gunther, G. Sani and G. Shabad, *Spain after Franco* (University of California Press, 1986) and P. Preston, *The Triumph of Democracy in Spain* (Methuen, 1986). On Spanish politics since 1982 see E. Moxan-Brown, *Political Change in Spain* (Routledge, 1989). And an exhaustive account of *The Franco Regime, 1936–75* (Wisconsin University Press, Madison, 1987) has been written by S.G. Payne.

The Soviet Union has received considerable attention from historians and political scientists. Some good introductions with a long term perspective, are L. Kochan and R. Abrahams, *The Making of Modern Russia* (Penguin, 1983) and D. Christian, *Power and Privilege: Russia and the Soviet Union in the Nineteenth and Twentieth Centuries* (Pitman, 1986), or, for a shorter time-span M. McCauley, *The Soviet Union since 1917* (Longman, 1981) and G. Hoskins, *A History of Soviet Russia* (Collins, 1985). However, probably most approachable and up-to-date is R. Sakwa, *Soviet Politics: an introduction* (Routledge, 1989) and vital on economics is A. Nove, *An Economic History of the USSR* (Penguin, Harmondsworth, 1982). A good recent study of *Stalin* – one of many – is by R.H. McNeal (Macmillan, 1988) and a short introduction to his political system is G. Gill's *Stalinism* (Macmillan, 1990), although for the post-war years another clear and sensible work is M. Lynch, *Stalin and Khruschev: The USSR, 1924–64* (Hodder and Stoughton, 1990). Additionally on Khruschev, R. and Z. Medvedev's *Khruschev: The Years in Power* (Oxford University Press, 1977), though written by two dissidents, presents a fair case. M. McCauley, ed., *The Soviet Union after Brezhnev* (Heinemann, 1983) is actually a good 'snapshot' of problems at the end of the Brezhnev era. Events under Gorbachev continue to move quickly but J. Sallnow, *Reform in the Soviet Union: Glasnost and the Future* (Pinter, 1989) provides short, simple coverage of domestic, international and nationalist problems, the essays in J. Bloomfield, ed., *The Soviet Revolution: Perestroika and the Remaking of Socialism* (Lawrence and Wishart, 1989) trace developments since 1982 sympathetically, whilst J. Cracraft, ed., *The Soviet Union Today:*

*an interpretative guide* (2nd ed., University Press, Chicago, 1988) is a handy reference work.

Recent events in Eastern Europe were, at the time of writing, less well-covered, but two excellent reference works are G. Schopflin, ed., *The Soviet Union and Eastern Europe* (Muller, Blond and Write, revised ed., 1986, in the *Handbooks to the Modern World* series), which includes historical reviews of key issues, and B. Jelavich's *History of the Balkans, Twentieth Century, Volume Two* (Cambridge University Press, 1983) which puts the post-war experience in a broader context. M. McCauley, ed., *Communist Power in Europe, 1944–9* (Macmillan, 1977) has a number of essays on the beginnings of Communist rule in Eastern Europe, as well as covering Finland, France and Italy, and F. Fejtö's *A History of the People's Democracies* (2nd ed., Penguin, 1974) remains an interesting, full and lengthy discussion of the twenty years after Stalin in Eastern Europe. On Yugoslavia see especially F. Singleton, *A Short History of the Yugoslav Peoples* (Cambridge University Press, 1985) and D. Wilson, *Tito's Yugoslavia* (Cambridge University Press, 1979). On individual countries under Soviet domination there are a number of interesting works, which often take a long-term historical perspective, including: O. Halecki, *A History of Poland* (Revised ed., Routledge and Kegan Paul, 1983); J. K. Hoensch, *A History of Modern Hungary* (Longman, 1988); D. Child's, *The GDR, Moscow's German Ally* (2nd ed., Allen and Unwin, 1988); H. Renner *A History of Czechoslovakia since 1945* (Routledge, 1989); and R. J. McIntyre, *Bulgaria: Politics, Economics and Society* (Pinter, 1988). (On East Germany see also some of the works under West Germany, above). The changes in regime in 1989 will doubtless allow fuller and more critical coverage of the Communist years to be written.

# Index

# Index

# Index